Smith Wigglesworth

UNDERSTANDING THE TRUE GRACE OF GOD

Teachings & Testimonies of God's Divine Grace at Work

Dr. Michael H. Yeager

This book is filled with Amazing Teachings, & Testimonies! From Smith Wigglesworth, and the Author Dr. Michael H Yeager,

ISBN: 9781098602826
Imprint: Independently published

DEDICATION

We dedicate this book to those who are longing to be filled with the spirit of **GRACE** in every area of their life. Those who have grasped the revelation that we were made for God's pleasure and purposes.

1 Corinthians 15:10 But by the grace of God I am what I am: and his grace which was bestowed upon me was not in vain; but I laboured more abundantly than they all: yet not I, but the grace of God which was with me.

Please Read This Introduction

Smith: I do not know of any greater words than those found in **Romans 4:16, "Therefore it is of faith that it might be by GRACE."**

GRACE is God's benediction coming right down to you, and when you open the door to Him, that is as an act of faith. Christ does all you want and will fulfill all your desires. **"It is of faith that it might be by GRACE."**

You open the way for God to work as you believe His Word, and God will come in and supply your every need every step of the way.

Doc Yeager: We need the grace of God that transforms people, and turns them into brand new people in Christ Jesus. It is not the people who are confessing their saved but living like the damned. It is not the people who are saying they love God, but give no evidence or proof of their Love for Jesus. Let us not love in word only, but in dead an action. Great grace was upon them all.

1 Corinthians 15:10 But by the grace of God I am what I am: and his grace which was bestowed upon me was not in vain; but I laboured more abundantly than they all: yet not I, but the grace of God which was with me.

CONTENTS

EXHORTATION

Smith Wigglesworth: This Is the Place Where God Will Show up!

You must come to a place of ashes, a place of helplessness, a place of wholehearted surrender where you do not refer to yourself. You have no justification of your own in regard to anything. You are prepared to be slandered, to be despised by everybody. But because of His personality in you, He reserves you for Himself because you are godly, and He sets you on high because you have known His name (Ps. 91:14). He causes you to be the fruit of His loins and to bring forth His glory so that you will no longer rest in yourself. Your confidence will be in God. Ah, it is lovely. "The Lord is the Spirit; and where the Spirit of the Lord is, there is liberty" (2 Cor. 3:17).

Born June 10th, 1859
Died March 4th, 1947

*Notice: There will be some repetition in this book. Please do not be offended by this fact.

CHAPTER ONE

Acts 4:33 And with great power gave the apostles witness of the resurrection of the Lord Jesus: and great GRACE was upon them all.

QUOTES ON: The GRACE of GOD

The **GRACE** of God is sufficient for the vilest. He can take the most wicked of men and make them monuments of his **GRACE**. He did this with Saul of Tarsus at the very time he was breathing out threatening's and slaughter against the disciples of the Lord. He did it with Berry the hangman. He will do it for hundreds more in response to our cries.

Smith: I do not know of any greater words than those found in Romans 4:16, "Therefore it is of faith that it might be by GRACE."

GRACE is God's benediction coming right down to you, and when you open the door to Him, that is as an act of faith.

Christ does all you want and will fulfill all your desires. "It is of faith that it might be by GRACE."

You open the way for God to work as you believe His Word, and God will come in and supply your every need every step of the way.

There is one thing I am very grateful to the Lord for, and that is that He has given me **GRACE** not to have a desire for money. The love of money is a great hindrance to many; and many a man is crippled in his ministry because he lets his heart run after financial matters.

Every day I live I am more and more convinced that very few who are saved by the GRACE of God have the divine revelation of how great is their authority over darkness, demons, death and every power of the enemy by the name of Jesus Christ.

"Hard things are always opportunities to gain more glory for the Lord as He manifests His power. Every trial is a blessing. … The hardest things are simply lifting places into the GRACE of God."

"We have a wonderful God, a God whose ways are past finding out, and whose GRACE and power are limitless."

"You open the way, by faith in Christ. Then God supplies your need, by GRACE."

“Put away all doubt. Open your heart to God’s GRACE, and God will come and place in you an active faith.”

“The Bible is the Word of God: supernatural in origin, eternal in duration, inexpressible in valor, infinite in scope, regenerative in power, infallible in authority, universal in interest, personal in application, inspired in totality. Read it through, write it down, pray it in, work it out, and then pass it on.

Truly it is the Word of God. It brings into man the personality of God; it changes the man until he becomes the epistle of God. It transforms his mind, changes his character, takes him on from GRACE to GRACE, and gives him an inheritance in the Spirit. God comes in, dwells in, walks in, talks through, and sups with him.”

When the Word and the Spirit come together, there will be the biggest move of the Holy Spirit that the world has ever seen.

"Far too many of us dwell on the lowlands of salvation. Can't you hear voices calling you to the uplands of divine GRACE? Mountain climbing is thrilling! Let's be off! Hebron's heights rise before us. Shall we explore our unclaimed inheritance in the heavenlies?"

“If you want to grow in God's GRACE; get hungry to be fed by it, thirsty to cry out for it & broken so you can't live without it.”

“The God of all GRACE, whose very essence is love, delights to liberally give us an inheritance of life, strength and power.”

"You open the way, by faith. Then God supplies your need, by GRACE."

"By the GRACE of God, I want to impart the Word and bring you to a place where you will dare to act on it!"

"We have a wonderful God, a God whose ways are past finding out, and whose GRACE and power are limitless."

"God is gracious and not willing that any should perish."

I always ask God for a leading of His **GRACE**. It takes **GRACE** to be in a meeting because it is so easy if you are not careful, to get into the natural thinking realm. A man who is a preacher, if he has lost the unction of the Spirit, will be restored if he will repent and get right with God, and get the unction back.

It never pays us to be less than always spiritual, and we must have a divine language and the language must be of God. Beloved, if you come into the will of God, with the **GRACE** of God, one thing will certainly take place in your life.

You will change from that old attitude of the world's philosophy where you were judging everybody, and where you were abrasive with everyone. And come into a place where you will have a heart that under no circumstances reviles again when you are reviled.

There is only one way to all the treasures of God, and that is

the way of faith. All things are possible, the fulfilling of all promises, to him that believeth. And it is all by GRACE. "By GRACE are ye saved through faith; and that not or yourselves: it is the gift of God."

Prayer changes hearts, but it never changes God. He is the same yesterday, and today, and forever and is full of love, full of compassion, full of mercy, full of **GRACE**, and ready to bestow his blessings upon us as we come in faith to Him.

Open your heart to God's GRACE. Then God will come in and place in you a position of Strong faith. He wants to remove every obstruction that is in the world before you. By His GRACE He will enable you to be so established in His truth, so strong in the Lord and in the power of His might, that whatever comes across your path to obstruct you, you can arise in divine power and rebuke and destroy it.

Ask God to give you the **GRACE** to use the faith you have. Peter had like precious faith. When you were saved it was by the like precious faith, wonderful faith.

Salvation is for all,
Healing is for all.
Baptism of the Holy Ghost is for all.
Reckon yourselves dead indeed unto sin, but alive unto God.
By His GRACE get the victory every time. It is possible to live holy.
He breaks the power of canceled sin,

He sets the prisoner free;
His blood can make the foulest clean,
His blood avails for me.

THE FALSE GRACE MESSAGE

Smith Taught about the False **GRACE** message that says you can live how you want as a believer and still be saved!

All the saints of God that get the real vision of this wonderful transformation are recognizing every day that the world is getting worse and worse and worse and ripening for judgment. And God is bringing us to a place where we which that are spiritual are having, a clear vision that we MUST at any cost PUT OFF the WORKS, of DARKNESSS. We must be getting ourselves ready for that glorious day when we see Christ.

These are the last days. What will be the strongest confirmation for me to bring to you the reality that we are living in the last days?

There are in the world TWO CLASSES of believers. There are believers who are disobedient, or I ought to say there are children who are saved by the power of God which are still choosing to live as DISOBEDIENT children. And then there are children who are just the same saved by the power of God but who all the time are longing to be MORE OBEDIENT.

In this fact, Satan has a great part to play. It is on this factor in these last years that some of us have been brought to great grief at the first opening of the door with brazen fact to sinful fleshly forces. And we heard the word come rushing, like the wind to a, "new theology" that is damnable, devilish, evil power that teaches you can be disobedient children, and still be right with God.

As soon as this was noised abroad everywhere, this "new theology," everybody began to say, "What is this new theology?"

It's an absolute live from the devil!

The spirit of this age is to get you to believe a lie. If you believe a lie, you cannot believe the truth When once you are seasoned with a lie against the Word of God, He sends you strong delusion that you shall believe a lie Who does? God is gracious over His Word His Word is from everlasting His Word is true.

When we see those things which are coming to pass, what do we know? We know the time is at hand. The fig tree is budding for these false prophets and these line spirits.

God wants to flow through you in marvelous power with divine utterance and GRACE, until your whole body is a flame of fire.

Everything that God does is too big to tell. His **GRACE** is too big. His love is too big. Why it takes all of heaven to even begin to reveal these truths. His salvation is too big to be told in which one cannot fully understand our grasp. It is so vast, mighty and wonderful, "in God;" but God gives us the power to understand it. Yes, of course, He does. Do you not know that ours is an abundant God? His love is far exceeding and abundant above all that we can ask or think. Hear!

And great GRACE was upon them all." Great GRACE is upon us when we magnify the Lord.

He has an abundance of **GRACE** for you and the gift of righteousness, and through His abundant **GRACE**, all things are possible.

I want to show you that you can be a living branch of the living Vine, Christ Jesus and that it is your privilege to be right here in this world what He is. John tells us, "As He is, so are we in this world." Not that we are anything in ourselves, but Christ within us is our all in all.

The Lord Jesus is always wanting to show forth his **GRACE** and love in order to draw us to Himself.

From GRACE to GRACE, spirit to spirit, until the whole church is one solid building in the Lord, a bride without spot or wrinkle, or any such thing. To this end as a choice vessel keep thine house in order, filled with oil, waiting for the consummation."

And truly the word of God changes a man until he becomes an epistle of God. It transforms his mind, changes his character, moves him on from **GRACE** to **GRACE**, and makes him an inheritor of the very nature of God. God comes in, dwells in, walks in, talks through, and sups with him who opens his being to the word of God and receives the Spirit who inspired it.

If you want to grow in GRACE and the knowledge of the GRACE of God, get hungry enough to be fed, be thirsty enough to cry, be broken enough you cannot have anything in the world without He comes Himself. I was reading last night in my Bible, it was so lovely, "And God shall wipe away all tears from their eyes..." (Revelation 21:4).

The people in the days of the apostles took joyfully the spoiling of their goods, [He 10.34] and I feel there is a measure of **GRACE** given to the man who says, "I will go all the way with Jesus."

What is that measure of **GRACE**? It is a girding with hopefulness in pressing forward to the goal that God would have us reach. But it is important that we forget not Paul's words, "Let no man take thy crown." [Rv 3.11] He saw there was a possibility lest any man who had been the means of sowing the good seed of the gospel should lose that for which God had apprehended him.

There is something very wonderful about being undefiled, there in the presence of my king to be undefiled, never to change, only to be more beautiful. Unless we know something about GRACE and the omnipotence of his love, we should never be able to grasp it. Love, fathomless as the sea. GRACE flowing for you and me.

Our God delights to be merciful, and His **GRACE** is vouchsafed daily to both sinner and saint. He shows mercy to all. If we would but realize it, we are only alive today through the **GRACE** of our God.

More and more I see that it is through the **GRACE** of God that I am preserved every day. It is when we realize the goodness of God that we are brought to repentance.

"GRACE and peace be multiplied unto you through the knowledge of God, and Jesus our Lord." We can have the multiplication of this GRACE and peace only as we live in the realm of faith. Abraham attained to the place where he became a friend of God, on no other line than that of believing God. He believed God, and God counted that to him for righteousness. Righteousness was imputed to him on no other ground than that he believed God. Can this be true of anybody else?

As we receive the Word of God, we come right into touch with a living force, a power which changes nature into **GRACE**, a power that makes dead things live, a power which is of God, which will be manifested in our flesh.

This power has come forth with its glory to transform us by divine act into sons of God, to make us like unto THE Son of God, by the Spirit of God who moves us on from **GRACE** to **GRACE** and from glory to glory as our faith rests in this living Word.

I find when God touches us it is a divine touch, life, power, and it thrills and quickens the body so that people know it is God and conviction comes, and they cry for mercy. Praise God for anything that brings people to the throne of GRACE.

God heals by the power of His Word. But the most important thing is, Are you saved, do you know the Lord, are you prepared to meet God? You may be an invalid as long as you live, but you may be saved by the power of God. You may have a strong, healthy body but may go straight to hell because you know nothing of the GRACE of God and salvation.

Without us, the Jews cannot be made perfect. So we are living in a great day; we are in the dispensation of the **GRACE** of God, with the fullness of the revelation of the inward power, personality, and presence of the Holy Ghost. And so we are in a greater day in every way than the Jews were. Not that the day isn't coming for the Jews; it is, but we are in a greater day than the Jews have had heretofore.

In Romans 4:16 we read, "It is of faith, that it might be by GRACE," meaning that we can open the door and God will come in. What will happen if we open the door by faith? God is

greater than our thoughts. He puts it to us, "Exceeding abundantly above all that we ask or think." When we ask a lot, God says "more."

Yes, if you lived in the law. But if you lived in the Spirit, then you would not go to law with your brother. It depends upon whether you live in law or live in **GRACE**. If you live in **GRACE**, you will never go into law.

I thank God that I was in business for twenty-five years and might have picked up a lot of money, but it is still left there because I would not go to law. I do not believe in it.

But I am not a law to you people. I tell you what law is and I tell you what **GRACE** is.

But we all, with open face beholding as in a glass the glory of the Lord, are changed into the same image from glory to glory, even as by the Spirit of the Lord. 2 Corinthians 3:18

So there are glories upon glories, and joys upon joys, exceeding joyous and abundance of joys, and a measureless measure of all the lot. Beloved, we get the word so wonderfully in our hearts that it changes us in everything. And we so feast on the Word of the Lord, so eat and digest the truth, so inwardly eat of Him, till we are changed every day from one state to another.

As we look into the perfect mirror of the face of the Lord we are changed from one state of **GRACE** to another, from glory to glory. You will never find anything else but the Word of God that takes you there. So you cannot afford to put aside that Word.

I beseech you, beloved, that you come short of none of these beatitudes w have been speaking of, in your life. These grand truths of the Word of God must be your testimony, must be your life, your pattern. You must be in it, in fact, you are of it. "Ye are...the epistle of Christ," God says to you by the Spirit. Then let us see that we put off everything that by the **GRACE** of God we may put on everything.

Where there is a standard which hasn't been reached in your life, God in His **GRACE**, by His mercy and your yieldedness, can fit you for that place that you can never be prepared for only by a broken heart and a contrite spirit, yielding to the will of God. If you come with a whole heart to the throne of **GRACE**, God will meet you and build you on His spiritual plane. Amen. Praise the Lord!

Receive Not God's GRACE in Vain

"We then, as workers together with him, beseech you also that ye receive not the **GRACE** of God in vain" (2 Corinthians 6:1). This is one of the mightiest words there is in the Scripture. People are getting blessed all the time, having a revelation, and they go from one point to another but do not establish themselves in that thing which God has brought to them.

If you do not let your heart be examined when the Lord comes with blessing or correction if you do not make it a stepping stone, if you do not make it a rising place, then you are receiving the **GRACE** of God in vain. People could be built far greater in the Lord and be more wonderfully established if they would move out sometimes and think over the **GRACE**s of the Lord.

GRACE is to be multiplied on conditions. How? In the first chapter of 2 Timothy, we have these words: "the unfeigned faith that is in thee."

Everyone in this place, the whole Church of God, has the same like precious faith within him. And if you allow this like precious faith to be foremost, utmost on everything, you will find that **GRACE** and peace are multiplied.

Just the same the Lord comes to us with His mercy, and if we do not see that the God of **GRACE** and mercy is opening to us the door of mercy and utterances, we are receiving it in vain.

I thank God for every meeting. I thank God for every blessing. I thank God every time a person says to me, "God bless you, Brother!" I say, "Thank you, Brother. The Lord bless you!" I see it is a very great place to have people desirous that we shall be blessed.

If we want strength in building in our spiritual character, we should never forget the blessings. When you are in prayer remember how near you are to the Lord. It is a time that God wants you to change strength there, and He wants you to remember He is with you.

When you open the sacred pages and the light comes right through, and you say, "Oh, isn't that wonderful!" thank God, for it is the **GRACE** of God that has opened your understanding.

When you come to a meeting like this, the revelation comes forth; you feel this is what you wanted, receive it as the **GRACE** of the Lord. God has brought you to a place where He might make you a greater blessing.

There was a young man at the meeting this particular night who had been saved the night before. He was all on fire to get others saved and purposed in his heart that every day of his life he would get someone saved. He saw this dejected hangman and began to speak to him about his soul. He brought him down to our mission and there he came under a wonderful and mighty conviction of sin. For two and a half hours he was literally sweating under conviction and you could see a vapor rising up from him in the cold air. At the end of two and a half hours he was graciously saved.

I said, "Lord, tell me what to do now." The Lord said, "Don't leave him, but go home with him." I went to his house. When he saw his wife he said, "God has saved me." The wife broke down and she too was graciously saved. I tell you there was a difference in that home. Even the cat knew the difference.

There were two sons in that house and one of them said to his mother, "Mother, what is happening here in our home? It has never like then this before. It is so peaceful. What is it?" She told him, "Father has been gloriously saved." Both sons were gloriously saved.

I took this man with me to many special services and the power of God was on him for many days. He would give his testimony and as he grew in **GRACE** he desired to preach the gospel. He became a powerful evangelist and hundreds and hundreds were brought to a saving knowledge of the Lord Jesus Christ through his ministry.

I will tell you what happened in Sydney, Australia. A man with a walking stick passed a friend and me. He had to get down and then twist over, and the tortures on his face made a deep impression on my soul. I asked myself, "Is it right to pass this man?" So I said to my friend, "There is a man in awful distress, and I cannot go any further. I must speak to him." I went over to this man and said to him, "You seem to be in great trouble." "Yes," he said, "I am in terrible shape and will be for the rest of my life." I said, "You see that hotel. Be in front of that door in five minutes and I will pray for you, and you shall be as straight as any man in in the world."

This is a declaration of active faith in Jesus Christ. I came back after paying a bill, and sure enough he was there waiting for me. I will never forget him wondering if he was going to be trapped, or what was up that a man should stop him in the street and tell him he should be made straight. I had said it, so it must be. If you say or declare anything you must stand with God to make it so. Never say anything for bravado, without you having the authority or the right to say it. Always be sure of your foundation, and that you are honoring God. If there is anything about what you're doing to make you somebody, it will bring you sorrow.

Your whole ministry will have to be on the line of humility, **GRACE** and blessing. We helped him up the two steps, passed him through to the elevator, and took him upstairs. It seemed difficult to get him from the elevator to my bedroom, as though Satan was making the last effort to take his life, but we got him there. Then in five minutes' time this man walked out of that bedroom as straight as any man has ever walked. He walked perfectly and declared he hadn't a pain in his body.

There is one thing I am very grateful to the Lord for, and that is that He has given me **GRACE** not to have a desire for money. The love of money is a great hindrance to many; and many a man is crippled in his ministry because he lets his heart run after financial matters. I was walking out one day when I met a godly man who lived opposite of my house and he said, "My wife and I have been talking together about selling our house and we feel constrained to sell it to you."

As we talked together he persuaded me to buy his place, and before we said good-by I told him that I would take it. We always make big mistakes when we are in a hurry. I told my wife what I had promised, and she said, "How will you manage it?" I told her that I had managed things so far, but I did not know how I was going to keep this commitment.

I somehow knew that I was out of God's divine order. But when a fellow gets out of divine order it seems that the last person he goes to is God himself. I was relying on an architect to help me, but that scheme fell through. I turned to my relations and I certainly had a mud on my face as one after another turned me down. I tried my friends and managed no better. My wife said to me, "Thou hast never been to God Yet." What could I do?

I have a certain place in our house where I go to pray. I have been there very often. As I went I said, "Lord, if you will get me out of this mess I got myself into, I will never trouble you on this line again." As I waited on the Lord He just gave me one word. It seemed a ridiculous thing, but it was the wisest counsel. There is divine wisdom in every word God speaks. I came down to my wife, saying, "What do you think? The Lord has told me to go to Brother Webster." I said, "It seems very ridiculous, for he is one of the poorest men I know." He was the poorest man I knew, but he was also the richest man I knew, for he knew God. My wife said, "Do What God says, and it will be right."

I went off at once to see him, and he said as he greeted me, "Smith, what brings you so early?" I answered, "The word of God." I said to him, "About three weeks ago I promised to buy a house of a man, and I am short 100 pounds ($500). I have tried to get this money, but somehow I seem to have missed God." "How is it," he asked, "that you have come to me only now?" I answered, "Because I went to the Lord about it only last night."

"Well," he said, "it is a strange thing; three weeks ago I had 100 pounds. For years I have been putting money into a co-operative system and three weeks ago I had to go and draw 100 pounds out. I hid it under the mattress. Come with me and you shall have it. Take it. I hope it will bring as great a blessing to you as it has been a trouble to me." I had my word from God, and all my troubles were ended. This has been multiplied in a hundred ways since that time. If I had been walking along filled with the Holy Ghost, I would not have bought that house and would not have had all that pressure. I believe the Lord wants to deliver us from things of earth. But I am ever grateful for that word from God.

I was traveling one day in a railway train in Sweden. At one station there boarded the train an old lady with her daughter. The old lady's expression was so troubled that I enquired what the matter with her was. I heard that she was going to the hospital to have her leg taken off. She began to weep as she told that the doctors had said there was no hope for her except through having her leg amputated. She was seventy years old.

I said to my interpreter, "Tell her that Jesus can heal her." The instant this was said to her, it was as though a veil was taken off her face, it became so light. We stopped at another station and the carriage filled up with people. There was a rush of men to board that train and the devil said, "You're done for now. There's no way you can pray with all of these people here" But I knew I had God working with me, for hard things are always opportunities to give the Lord more glory when He manifests His power. Every trial is a blessing.

There have been times when I have been pressed through circumstances and it seemed as if a dozen road engines were going over me, but I have found that the hardest things are just the right opportunities for the **GRACE** of God to work. We have such a lovely Jesus. He always proves Himself to be such a mighty Deliverer. He never fails to plan the best things for us.

The train began moving and I crouched down, and in the name of Jesus commanded the disease to leave. The old lady cried, "I'm healed. I know I'm healed." She stamped her leg and said, "I'm going to prove it." So when we stopped at another station she marched up and down, and shouted, "I'm not going to the hospital." Once again our wonderful Jesus had proven Himself a Healer of the broken-hearted, a Deliverer of one that was bound.

Faith in the living word

Every day I live I am more and more convinced that very few who are saved by the **GRACE** of God have the divine revelation of how great is their authority over darkness, demons, death and every power of the enemy by the name of Jesus Christ. It is a real joy when we realize our inheritance on this line.

I was speaking like this one day, and someone said, "I have never heard anything like this before. How many months did it take you to put together this sermon?" I said, "Brother, God impress upon my wife from time to time to get me to preach, and I promised her I would. I used to labor hard for a week to get a message together. I would simply give out my text and then sit down and say, 'I am done.'

O brother, I have given up getting the messages together anymore. They all come down from heaven, and the sermons that come down as He wants them. Then they go back to God, with much results in fruit, for the Word of God declares that His Word shall not return unto Him void. If you get anything from God, it will be fresh from heaven. But these messages were also transform you as you speak them.

Great GRACE Upon the Church

I have had some wonderful times in Belfast, Ireland, and in fact all over Ireland. I was in Belfast one day when a young man approached me and said: "Brother Wigglesworth, I am very much distressed," and he told me why. They had an old lady in their assembly who used to pray heaven down upon them. She had an accident. Her thigh was broken and they took her away to the infirmary. They put her in a plaster of Paris cast and she was in that condition for five months.

Then they broke the cast and lifted her on to her feet and asked her to walk. She fell again and broke her leg in another place. To their dismay they discovered that the first break had never knitted together. They brought her home and laid her on the couch and the young man asked me to go and pray for her. When I got into the house I asked: "Do you believe that God can heal you?" She said "Yes. When I heard you had come to the city I thought, 'This is my chance to be healed.'

"An old man, her husband, was sitting in a chair, had been sitting there for four years; helpless. And he said : "I do not believe. I will not believe. She was the only help I had. She has been taken away with a broken leg, and they have brought her back with her leg broken twice. How can I believe God?"

I turned to her and said: "Now is this correct? Yes," she said, "it is the truth." The right leg was broken in two parts. Physicians can join up bones beautifully, and make them fit together, but if God doesn't come in with His healing power, there is no physician who can heal them. As soon as the oil was placed upon her head and hands laid on, instantly down the right limb there was a stream of life, and she knew it. She said: "I am healed." I said: "If you are healed, you do not need anybody to help you." So I left the room. Immediately after I left she took hold of the mantle shelf above her head and pulled herself up and walked all around the room. She was perfectly healed.

The old man said: "Make me walk." I said: "You old sinner, repent." Then he began: "You know, Lord, I didn't mean it." I really believe he was in earnest, and to show you the mercy and compassion of God, the moment I laid hands upon him, the power of God went thru him and he rose up after four years being in that chair and walked around the room. That day both he and his wife were made whole.

I received a telegram once urging me to visit a case about 200 miles from my home. As I went to this place I met the father and mother and found them broken hearted. They lead me up a staircase to a room and I saw a young woman on the floor and five people were holding her down. She was a frail young woman but the demonic power in her was greater than all those young men. As I went into the room the evil powers looked out of her eyes and they used her lips saying, "We are many, you can't cast us out."

I said, "Jesus can." He is more than enough in every situation. He is waiting for an opportunity to bless, heal and deliver. He is ready to save and to deliver souls. When we receive Jesus it becomes a reality in us that, "Greater is He that is in you than he that is in the world." He is greater than all the powers of darkness. No man can meet the devil in his own strength, but any man filled with the knowledge of Jesus, filled with His presence, filled with His power, filled with faith is more than a match for the powers of darkness. God has called us to be more than conquerors through Him that loved us.

The living Word is able to destroy satanic forces. There is power in the name of Jesus. I would that every window in the street had the name of Jesus written large upon it. His name, through faith in His name. Brought deliverance to this poor, bound soul, and thirty-seven demons came out giving their names as they came forth.

The dear woman was completely delivered and they were able to give her back her child. That night there was heaven in that home and the father and mother, son and his wife were all united in glorifying Christ for His infinite **GRACE**. The next morning we had a gracious time in the breaking of bread. All things are wonderful with our wonderful Jesus. If you would dare rest your all upon Him, things would take place and He would change your whole circumstance. In a moment, through the name of Jesus, a new life can be realized.

The False GRACE message that says you can live how you want as a believer and still be saved!

All the saints of God that get the real vision of this wonderful transformation are recognizing every day that the world is getting worse and worse and worse and ripening for judgment. And God is bringing us to a place where we which that are spiritual are having, a clear vision that we MUST at any cost PUT OFF the WORKS, of DARKNESSS. We must be getting ourselves ready for that glorious day when we see Christ.

These are the last days. What will be the strongest confirmation for me to bring to you the reality that we are living in the last days?

There are in the world TWO CLASSES of believers. There are believers which are disobedient, or I ought to say there are children which are saved by the power of God which are still choosing to live as DISOBEDIENT children. And then there are children which are just the same saved by the power of God but who all the time are longing to be MORE OBEDIENT.

In this fact Satan has a great part to play. It is on this factor in these last years that some of us have been brought to great grief at the first opening of the door with brazen fact to fleshly sinful forces. And we heard the word come rushing, like the wind to a, "new theology" that is damnable, devilish, evil power that teaches you can be disobedient children, and still be right with God.

As soon as this was noised abroad everywhere, this "new theology," everybody began to say, "What is this new theology?" It's an absolute live from the devil!

The spirit of this age is to get you to believe a lie. If you believe a lie, you cannot believe the truth When once you are seasoned with a lie against the Word of God, He sends you strong delusion that you shall believe a lie Who does? God is gracious over His Word His Word is from everlasting His Word is true.

When we see those things which are coming to pass, what do we know? We know the time is at hand. The fig tree is budding for these false prophets and these line spirits.

"We then that are strong ought to bear the infirmities of the weak." (Romans 15:1).

If you want a church full of life you must have one in which the Spirit of God is manifested. And in order to keep fire ignited from that blessed incarnation of the Spirit, you must be as simple as babies; you must be as harmless as doves and as wise as serpents (Matthew 10:16).

I always ask God for a leading of His **GRACE**. It takes **GRACE** to be in a meeting because it is so easy if you are not careful, to get into the natural thinking realm. A man who is a preacher, if he has lost the unction of the Spirit, will be restored if he will repent and get right with God, and get the unction back.

It never pays us to be less than always spiritual, and we must have a divine language and the language must be of God. Beloved, if you come into the will of God, with the **GRACE** of God, one thing will certainly take place in your life. You will change from that old attitude of the world's philosophy where you were judging everybody, and where you were abrasive with everyone. And come into a place where you will have a heart that under no circumstances reviles again when you are reviled.

I know Godly people who think before they speak or respond. Here is a great word: **"For your obedience is come abroad unto all men. I am glad therefore on your behalf: but yet I would have you wise unto that which is good, and simple concerning evil" (Romans 16:19).**

You have come to the place where there is No inward corruption or defilement, that is full of distrusts. But you have attained a holy, divine likeness of Jesus that dares believe that God Almighty will surely watch over all. Hallelujah!

"There shall no evil befall thee, neither shall any plague come nigh thy dwelling. For He shall give his angels charge over thee, to keep thee in all thy ways" (Psalm 91:10,11).

The child of God who is founded in the bosom of the Father has the sweetest touch of heaven, and the honey of the Word is always manifested in him.

If the saints only knew how precious they are in the sight of God they would scarcely be able to sleep for thinking of His watchful, loving care. Oh, He Jesus is so precious! He is our wonderful and lovely Savior! He is divine in all of His attitude toward us, and makes our hearts to burn. There is nothing like it. "Oh," they said on the road to Emmaus, "did not our heart burn within us, as He walked with us and talked with us?" (Luke 24:32). Oh beloved, it must be so today.

WHAT IF WE BELIEVED?

In a place in England I was dealing on the lines of faith and what would take place if we believe God. Many things happened. But when the meeting was over, it appeared one man who worked in a coal mine had heard me. He was in terrible pain with a stiff knee. He said to his wife, "I cannot help but think every that the sermon from Wigglesworth's was to stir us to act upon the Word. I cannot get away from this feeling. All the men in the mine know how I walk with a stiff knee, and you know how you have wrapped it with yards of flannel. Well, I am going to act upon Gods Word.

You have to be the congregation." He got his wife in front of him. "I am going to act and do just as Wigglesworth did." He got hold of his leg unmercifully, saying, "Come out, you devils, come out! In the name of Jesus. Now, Jesus, help me. Come out, you devils, come out."

Then he said, "Wife they are gone! Wife, they are gone. This is too good. I am going to act now." So he went to his place of worship and all the collier boys were there. It was a prayer meeting. As he told them this story these men became delighted. They said, "Jack, come over here and help me." And Jack went. As soon as he was through in one home he was invited to another, loosing these people of the pains they had gotten in the colliery.

Ah, brothers and sisters, we have no idea what God has for us if we will only begin! But oh, the **GRACE** we need! We will at times make mistakes. If you are being motivated by pride, if you do it for yourself, and if you want to be someone, you will be an utter failure. We shall only be able to succeed if our heart is right and as we do it four and in the name of Jesus. Oh, the love that God's Son can put into us if we are only humble enough, meek, weak enough, and helpless enough to know that except Christ Jesus does it, it will not be done!

"What things so ever ye desire when ye pray, believe that ye receive and ye shall have them."

Live in the Spirit, walk in the Spirit, walk in communion with the Holy Spirit, talk with God. All leadings of the divine Spirit are for you. I pray that if there are any who have turned to their own way and have made God second, they will come to repentance in every area of their life. Separate yourself from every earthly touch, and desires. And God will bring you to the end of yourself. You can Begin with God this very moment.

One day as I was waiting for a car I stepped into a shoemaker's shop. I had not been there long when I saw a man with a green shade over his eyes, crying pitifully and in great agony. It was heartrending and the shoemaker told me that the inflammation was destroying his eyes. I jumped up and went to the man and said, "You devil, come out of this man in the name of Jesus."

Instantly the man said, "It is all gone, I can see now." That is the only scriptural way, to begin to work at once, and preach afterwards. You will find as the days go by that miracles and healings will be manifested as act upon the quickening of Gods Spirit! Because the Master was touched with the feeling of the infirmities of the multitudes they instantly gathered around him to hear what He had to say concerning the word of God.

However, I would rather see one man saved than ten thousand people healed. If you ask me why, I would call to your attention the word which says, "There was a [rich man and he] fared sumptuously every day." [Lk 16.19] Now we don't hear of this man having any diseases but it says, **"In hell he lift up his eyes." [Lk 16.23]** We also read that there was a poor man full of sores [Lk 16.20] and **"he lifted up his eyes in heaven,"** so we see that a man can die practically in good health but be lost, and a man can die in disease and be saved; so it is more important to be saved than anything else.

But Jesus was sent to bear the infirmities and the afflictions of the people and to destroy the works of the devil. He said that the thief (which is the devil) cometh to steal and to kill and to destroy, but **"I am come that [ye] might have life, and have it more abundantly." [Jn 10.10]**

I maintain that God wishes all his people to have this (ZOE) life more abundant; that if we understood sin as we ought to understand it and realized that there is no sickness without disobedience, ignorance of Gods will, or lack of Faith! You will say that this is rather strong, but we have the remedy in the word of God! Jesus paid the full price and the full redemption for every need, and where sin abounded, **GRACE** can come in and much more abound, [Ro 5.20] and dispel all the sickness.

From the author Dr. Michael H Yeager's

*God's **GRACE** will be displayed in your flesh. I believe it is what we call the quickening of the spirit. Most people are calling it the anointing. I believe it is the divine ability of God that causes you to do things that are beyond the human ability of natural man. It is the very life of God. Jesus said I am come that you might have life and have it more abundantly. The Bible says that the law came by Moses, but **GRACE** and truth came by Jesus Christ. Now, what's **GRACE** and truth? He said, the works that I do shall you also do and greater works than these shall you do because I go onto my Father. It is God's ability being manifested in your mortal flesh. I'm telling you right now, you don't know me from the past, but I was absolutely incapable of doing anything successfully before I got saved.

I had many Physical problems. I had lung problems, hearing problems, speech impediment, born tongue-tied. I mean they had me in special Ed back in them days. They called me mentally retarded. They couldn't understand what I said. I couldn't understand what they were saying because I was born with immovable bones in my ears. Yet when the **GRACE** of God came upon me, He gave me back my hearing. He gave me back my lungs. He gave me back the ability to speak.

The **GRACE** of God came upon me and delivered me from the drugs, the alcohol, the pornography, the lying, the stealing, the cussing, and the immorality. The **GRACE** of God was exceedingly great in me. It says in the book of Acts; great **GRACE** came upon them all. We need great **GRACE**. When people come in addicted to drugs. Alcohol, terrible habits, they walk out, delivered. They come in obsessed and possessed, but they leave free by the Grace of God.

We need the **GRACE** of God that transforms people and turns them into brand new people in Christ Jesus. Not people who are confessing they're saved but living like the damned. Not people who are saying they love God, but give no evidence or proof. Let us not love in word only but in dead an action. Great **GRACE** was upon them all.

Now, believe it or not, the way that the **GRACE** of God comes is by FAITH in Christ and the Knowledge of Christ!

2 Peter 1:2Grace and peace be multiplied unto you through the knowledge of God, and of Jesus our Lord,

Hebrews 13:8, "Jesus Christ the same yesterday, and today, and forever."

Why God heals me Every Time

While reading my Bible as a brand-new believer, (1975) I discovered that Jesus Christ went about healing **ALL** who were sick and oppressed of the devil. I began to search the Scriptures on this subject, and as I studied I discovered many Scriptures that support this:

Surely he hath borne our griefs, and carried our sorrows: yet we did esteem him stricken, smitten of God, and afflicted. But he was wounded for our transgressions, he was bruised for our iniquities: the chastisement of our peace was upon him; and with his stripes we are healed (Isaiah 53:4-5).

Who his own self bare our sins in his own body on the tree, that we, being dead to sins, should live unto righteousness: by whose stripes ye were healed.*1 Peter 2:24*

When the even was come, they brought unto him many that were possessed with devils: and he cast out the spirits with his word, and healed all that were sick: That it might be fulfilled which was spoken by Esaias the prophet, saying, Himself took our infirmities, and bare our sicknesses. *Matthew 8:16-17*

As I read and meditated upon these Scriptures, something wonderful happened within my heart. Great, overwhelming sorrow took a hold of me as I saw the pain and the agony that Jesus went through for my healing. In my heart and in my mind, I saw that Jesus had taken my sicknesses and my diseases. I then experienced a great love for the son of God, and recognize the price he paid for my healing. And then it happened!

It was like an open vision **(God's GRACE)** in which I saw my precious **Lord and Savior** tied to the whipping post. I saw the Roman soldiers striking the back of Jesus with the cat of nine tails. In this vision, I saw the flesh and the blood of my precious Savior sprinkling everything within a 10-foot radius, with each terrible strike of the soldier's whip causing his blood to splatter. As I saw this open vision, I wept because I knew it was for me this was done. To this day, even as I retell this story great love and sorrow fills my heart, yet I have great joy because I know that by the

stripes of Jesus I am healed.

In this moment of this vision something exploded within my heart, an amazing faith possessed me with the knowledge that I no longer have to be sick. In the name of Jesus for over 40 years I have refused to allow what my precious Lord went through to be for nothing. I have refused to allow sickness and disease to dwell in my body, which is the temple of the Holy Ghost.

Jesus has taken my sicknesses and my diseases. No if, Ans, or butts, no matter what it looks like or how I feel, I know within my heart Jesus Christ has set me free from sicknesses and diseases. At the moment of this revelation great anger, yes great anger, rose up in my heart against the enemy of my Lord. The demonic world has no right to afflict me or any other believer, because Jesus took our sicknesses and bore our diseases.

Now I had been born with terrible physical infirmities, but now I found myself speaking aloud with authority to my ears, commanding them to be open and to be normal in the name of Jesus Christ of Nazareth. Then I spoke to my lungs, and commanded them to be healed in the name of Jesus Christ of Nazareth. Next I commanded my sinuses to be delivered, so I could smell normal scents in the name of Jesus Christ of Nazareth.

The minute I spoke the Word of God to my physical man, my ears popped completely open. Up to this moment I had a significant hearing loss, but now as I was listening to Christian music playing softly (at least I thought it was) the music became so loud that I had to turn it down. My lungs were clear, and I haven't experienced any lung congestion since in 40 years.

I used to be so allergic to dust that my mother had to work extra hard to keep our house dust-free. I would literally end up in an oxygen tent in the hospital. From that moment to now dust, allergies, mold, or any such thing have never come back to torment me or cause me problems. Instantly my sense of smell returned! I had broken my nose about four times due to fights, accidents, and rough activities. I could barely smell anything.

Suddenly, I could smell a terrible odor. I tried to find out where it was coming from and then I looked at my feet and wondered if it could be them. I put my foot on a night stand and bent over toward it. I took a big sniff and nearly fell over. Man, did my feet stink! I went straight over to the bathroom and washed them in the sink.

For over 40 years I have aggressively, violently, persistently, taken a hold of my healing. I refuse to let the devil rob me of what Jesus so painfully purchased. It is mine, and the devil cannot have it. The thought has never even enter my mind to go see a doctor when physical sickness attack my body, for I already have a doctor, his name is Jesus Christ of Nazareth. He is the great physician, and he has already healed me with his stripes. Yes, there has been times when the manifestation of my healing seemed like it would never come, there has been many times when it looked like in the natural I was going to die, but I know, that I know, that I know by the stripes of Jesus I am healed. Jesus Christ is the final authority in my life when it comes to the divine will of the Father. His life, and his word is the absolute voice of God pertaining to every situation. Without this revelation and foundation, the enemy will be able to easily lead you astray, and destroy you.

The very 1st thing we must do is to let go of all our traditions, philosophies, doctrines, and experiences that contradict what is revealed to us through Jesus Christ. We must go back to Matthew, Mark, Luke, and John rediscovering who Jesus Christ is. Whatever Jesus said and did is what we agree with wholeheartedly. Any voice or teaching that contradicts Christ, and his redemptive work I immediately reject.

John 10:3 To him the porter openeth; and the sheep hear his voice: and he calleth his own sheep by name, and leadeth them out. :4 And when he putteth forth his own sheep, he goeth before them, and the sheep follow him: for they know his voice. ...:27 My sheep hear my voice, and I know them, and they follow me:

Isaiah 42:16 And I will bring the blind by a way that they knew not; I will lead them in paths that they have not known: I will make darkness light before them, and crooked things straight. These things will I do unto them, and not forsake them.

How I Was HEALED of a Broken Back

In the winter of 1977, I was working at the Bellevillc Feed and Grain Mill. My job was to pick up the corn, wheat, and oats from the farmers, and bring it to the mill. There it would be mixed and combined with other products for the farmers' livestock. One cold, snowy day, the owner of the feed mill told me to deliver a load of cattle feed to an Amish farm. It was an extremely bad winter that year, with lots of snow. I was driving an International 1600 Lodestar. I backed up as far as I could to this Amish man's barn without getting stuck.

The Amish never had their lanes plowed in those days, and they most likely still do not. I was approximately seventy-five feet away from his barn, which meant that I had to carry the bags at least seventy-five feet. I think there were about eighty bags of feed, with each bag weighing approximately one hundred pounds. During those years, I only weighed about 130 pounds.

I would carry one bag on each of my shoulders, stumbling and pushing my way through the heavy, deep snow to get up the steep incline into the barn. Then I would stack the bags in a dry location. As usual, nobody came out to help me. Many a time when delivering things to the farms, the Amish would watch me work without lending a helping hand. About the third trip, something frightening happened to me carrying two one-hundred-pound bags upon my shoulders. I felt the bones in my back snap. Something drastic just happened. I fell to the ground at that very moment almost completely crippled. I could barely move.

I had been spending a lot of my time meditating in the Word of God. Every morning, I would get up about 5:00 a.m. to study. I had one of those little bread baskets with memorization scriptures in it. I believe you can still buy them to this day at a Christian bookstore. Every morning I would memorize from three to five of them. It would not take me very long, so all day long I would be meditating on these verses. So what I do next will determine my future. Okay I hear the voice of my body, I hear the voice of my mind, I hear the voice of my emotions, and they all say to me: you are in big trouble! I choose to listen to the voice of my Jesus.

He says this to me: by my stripes you our healed now! The voice of Jesus is more real to me then my body. So, this is how I responded. The very minute I fell, immediately I cried out to Jesus, asking him to forgive me for my pride, and for being so stupid in carrying two hundred pounds on my small frame. After I asked Jesus to forgive me, I commanded my back to be healed in the name of Jesus Christ of Nazareth. Since I believed I was healed, I knew that I had to act now upon my faith. Please understand that I was full of tremendous pain, but I had declared that **"I was healed by the stripes of Jesus"**. The Word of God came out of my mouth as I tried to get up and then fell back down.

Even though the pain was more intense than I can express, I kept getting back up, then I would fall back down again. I fell more times than I can remember. After some time, I could take a couple of steps, then I would fall again. This entire time I was saying, "In the name of Jesus, in the name of Jesus, in the name of Jesus." I finally could get to the truck.

I said to myself if I believe I'm healed then I will unload this truck in the name of Jesus. Of course, I did not have a cell phone to call for help and the Amish did not own any phones on their property. Now, even if they would have had a phone, I would not have called for help. I had already called upon my help, and His name was Jesus Christ. I knew in my heart that by the stripes of Jesus I was healed. I then pulled a feed bag off the back of the truck, with it falling on top of me. I would drag it a couple of feet, and then fall.

Tears were running down my face as I spoke the Word of

God over and over. By the time, I was done with all the bags, the sun had already gone down. I painstakingly pulled myself up into that big old 1600 Lodestar. It took everything within me to shift gears, pushing in the clutch, and driving it. I finally got back to the feed mill late in the evening. Everybody had left for home a long time ago with the building being locked up. I struggled out of the Lodestar and stumbled and staggered over to my Ford pickup. I got into my pickup, and made it back to the converted chicken house. I went back to my cold, unheated, plywood floor room. It took everything in me to get my clothes off. It was a very rough and long night.

The next morning when I woke up, I was so stiff that I could not bend in the least. I was like a board. Of course, I was not going to miss work, because by the stripes of Jesus I was healed. To get out of bed, I had to literally roll off the bed, hitting the floor. Once I had hit the floor, it took everything for me to push myself back up into a sitting position. The tears were rolling down my face as I put my clothes and shoes on, which was a miracle. I did get to work on time, though every step was excruciatingly painful. Remember, I was only twenty-one at the time, but I knew what faith was and what it wasn't. I knew that I was healed no matter how it looked, that by the stripes of Jesus Christ I was healed.

When I got to work, I did not tell my boss that I had been seriously hurt the day before. I walked into the office trying to keep the pain off my face. For some reason, he did not ask me what time I made it back to work. I did not tell him to change the time clock for me to be paid for all the hours I was out on the job. They had me checked out at the normal quitting time. (The love of money is what causes a lot of people not to get healed.) My boss gave me an order for feed that needed to be delivered to a local farmer. If you have ever been to a feed and grain mill, you know that there is a large shoot where the feed comes out. After it has been mixed, you must take your feed bag, and hold it up until it's filled. It creates tremendous strain on your arms and your back, even if you're healthy. As I was filling the bag, it almost felt like I was going to pass out, because I was in tremendous pain.

Now, I'm simply saying, "In the name of Jesus, in the name of Jesus, in the name of Jesus" under my breath. The second bag was even more difficult than the first bag, but I kept on saying, "In the name of Jesus." I began on the third bag and as I was speaking Jesus' name, the power of God hit my back and I was completely and totally healed from the top of my head, to the tip of my toes. I was healed as I went on my way. My place of employment never did know what had happened to me.

CHAPTER TWO

Smith: Full of GRACE

We read in the Word that by faith Abel offered unto God a more excellent sacrifice than Cain; by faith Enoch was translated that he should not see death; by faith Noah prepared an ark to the saving of his house; by faith Abraham, when he was called to go out into a place which he should after receive for an inheritance, obeyed. There is only one way to all the treasures of God, and that is the way of faith. All things are possible, the fulfilling of all promises, to him that believeth. And it is all by **GRACE**. "By **GRACE** are ye saved through faith; and that not or yourselves: it is the gift of God."

There will be failure in our lives if we do not build on the foundation, the Rock Christ Jesus. He is the only way, the truth, and the life. The Word He gives us is life-giving. As we receive the Word of life, it quickens, it opens, it fills us, it moves us, it motivates us, it changes us; and it brings us into a place where we dare to say Amen to all that God has said. Beloved, there is a lot in an "Amen."

You never get any place until you have the Amen, let it be so on the inside of you. That was the difference between Zacharias and Mary. When the word came to Zacharias he was filled with unbelief until the angel said, "Thou shalt be dumb because thou believest not my words." Mary said, "Be it unto me according to thy word." And the Lord was pleased that she believed that there would be a performance of the word given by the angel. When we believe what God has said, there shall be a performance.

Read the 12th chapter of Acts, and you will find that there were people waiting all night and praying that Peter might come out of prison. But there seemed to be one missing ingredient despite all their praying, and that was faith. Rhoda had more faith than all the rest of these praying saints. When the knock came at the door, she ran to it for she was expecting an answer to her prayers; and the moment she heard Peter's voice, she ran back and announced to them that Peter was standing at the door. That God had gloriously answered their prayers. And all the people said, "You are mad. It isn't so." That was not faith. When she insisted that he was there, they said, "Well, perhaps God has sent his angel." But Rhoda insisted, "It is Peter." And Peter continued knocking. And they went out and found it so. What Rhoda had believed for had become a glorious fact.

Beloved, we may do much praying and groaning, but we do not receive from God because we do not believe. And yet sometimes it takes God a long time to bring us through the groaning and the crying before we can believe.

I know this, that no man by his praying can change God for you cannot change Him. Prayer does not change God, but it changes us. Finney said, "Can a man who is full of sin and all kinds of ruin in his life, change God when he starts to pray?" No, it is impossible. But when a man labors in prayer, he groans and travails because his tremendous sin is weighing him down, and he becomes broken in the presence of God; and when properly melted he comes into perfect harmony with the divine plan of God, and then God can work in that clay. Up to this moment He could not change us. Prayer changes hearts, but it never changes God. He is the same yesterday, and today, and forever and is full of love, full of compassion, full of mercy, full of **GRACE**, and ready to bestow his blessings upon us as we come in faith to Him.

Believe that when you come into the presence of God you can have all you came for. You can take it away, and you can use it, for all the power of God is at your disposal in response to your faith in Christ. The price for all was paid by the blood of Jesus Christ at Calvary. Oh, He is the living God, the One who has power to change us! "It is He that hath made us, and not we ourselves." And He purposes to transform us so that the greatness of His power may work through us. Oh, beloved! God delights in us, and when a man's ways please the Lord, then He makes all things to move according to His own blessed purpose.

We read in Hebrews 11.5, "By faith Enoch was translated that he should not see death.... Before his translation he had this testimony, that he pleased God." I believe it is in the mind of God to prepare us for translation. But remember this, translation comes only in the round of holy obedience and a walk according to the good pleasure of God. We are called to walk together with God by the Spirit. It is delightful to know that we can talk with God and hold communion with Him.

Through this wonderful Baptism in the Spirit which the Lord gives us, He enables us to talk to Himself in a language that the Spirit has given, a language which no man understands but which He understands, a language of love. Oh, how wonderful it is to speak to Him in the Spirit, to let the Spirit lift, and lift and lift us until He takes us into the very presence of God! I pray that God by His Spirit may move all of us so that we walk with God, even as Enoch walked with Him.

But beloved, it is a walk by faith and not by sight, a walk of believing the Word of God. I believe there are two kinds of faith. All people are born with a natural faith, but God calls us to a supernatural faith which is a gift from Himself. In the 26th chapter of Acts Paul tells us of his call, how God spoke to him and told him to go to the Gentiles, "to open their eyes, and to turn them from darkness to light, and from the power of Satan unto God, that they may receive forgiveness of sins, and inheritance among them which are sanctified by faith that is in Me."

The faith which was in Christ was by the Holy Spirit to be given to those who believed. Henceforth, as Paul yielded his life to God, he could say, **"I am crucified with Christ: nevertheless I live; yet not I, but Christ liveth in me: and the life which I now live in the flesh I live by the faith of the Son of God, who loved me, and gave Himself for me".** The faith of the Son of God communicated by the Holy Spirit to the one who puts his trust in God and in His Son.

I want to show you the difference between our faith and the faith of Jesus. Our faith is limited and comes to an end. Most people have experienced coming to the place where they have said, "Lord, I can go no further. I have gone so far, and I cannot go on." But God can help us and take us beyond this. I remember one night, being in the north of England and going around to see some sick people, I was taken into a house where there was a young woman lying on her bed, a very helpless case. Her reason was gone and many things were manifested that were absolutely Satanic, and I knew it.

She was a beautiful young woman. Her husband was quite a young man. He came in with a baby in his arms, leaned over and kissed his wife. The moment he did so she threw herself over on the other side of the bed, just as a lunatic would do, with no consciousness of the presence of her husband, or baby. It was heart-breaking. The husband took the baby and pressed the baby's lips to the mother. Again there was a wild frenzy. I said, to the sister who was attending her, "Have you anybody to help?" She answered, "We have done everything we could." I said, "Have you no spiritual help?" Her husband stormed and said, "Spiritual help? Do you think we believe in God after we have had seven weeks of no sleep and this maniac condition? If you think we believe in God, you are mistaken. You have come to the wrong house."

There was a young woman about eighteen who grinned at me as she passed out of the door, as much as to say, "You cannot do anything." But this brought me to a place of compassion for this poor young woman. And then with what faith I had I began to penetrate the heavens by prayer. I was soon in heaven by the Spirit! I tell you I never have seen a man get anything from God who prayed on the fleshly level. If you get anything from God you will have to pray right into heaven, for all you want is there. If you are living an earthly life, all taken up with sensual things, and expect things from heaven, they will never come. God wants us to be a heavenly people, seated with Him in the heavenlies, and laying hold of all the things in heaven that are at our disposal.

I saw there, in the presence of that demented girl, limitations to my faith; but as I prayed there came another faith into my heart that could not be denied, a faith that grasped the promises, a faith that believed God's Word. I came from the presence of the glory back to earth. I was not the same man. I confronted the same conditions I had seen before, but in the name of Jesus. With a faith that could shake hell and move anything else, I said to the demon power that was making this young woman a maniac, "Come out of her, in the name of Jesus!" She rolled over and fell asleep, and awoke fourteen hours later perfectly sane and perfectly whole.

Enoch walked with God.

During those many years of his life he was penetrating the heavens, laying hold of and believing God, living with such co-operation and such a touch of God upon his life that heaven came to him on earth. He became so heavenly in his heart and mind that it was not possible for him to stay on earth any longer. Oh, hallelujah!

I believe God wants to bring all of us into this place with His will, so that we shall penetrate into the heavenlies and become so empowered that we shall see signs and wonders and divers gifts of the Holy Spirit in our midst on a daily basis. These are wonderful days and these are days of the outpouring of the Holy Spirit. You ask me, "When would you have liked to have lived on the earth?" My answer is, "NOW. It is wonderful to know that I can be filled with the Holy Spirit. That I can be a temple in which God dwells, and that through this temple there shall be a manifestation of Gods power that will bring glory to His name."

Enoch walked with God. I want to live in constant communion with God. I am so grateful that from my youth up, God has given me a hunger for the Bible. I find the Bible food for my soul. It is strength to the believer. It develops the character of God in us. And as we receive with meekness the Word of God, we are being changed by the Spirit from glory to glory. And by this Book comes faith, for faith cometh by hearing, and hearing by the Word of God. And we know that "without faith it is impossible to please Him."

I believe that all our failures come because of an imperfect understanding of God's Word and will. I see that it is impossible to please God on any other order then by faith, and everything that is not of faith is sin. You say, "How can I obtain this faith?" You see the secret in Hebrews 12.2, "Looking unto Jesus the author and finisher of our faith." He is the author of faith. Oh, the might of our Christ who created the universe and upholds it all by the might of His power!

God has chosen Him and ordained Him and clothed Him, and He who made this vast universe will make us a new creation. He spoke the word and the stars came into being. Can He not speak the word that will produce a mighty faith in us? Ah, this One who is the author and finisher of our faith comes and dwells within us, quickens us by His Spirit, and molds us by His will. He comes to live His life of faith within us and to be to us all that we need. And He who has begun a good work within us will complete it and perfect it; for He not only is the author but the finisher and perfecter of our faith.

"The Word of God is living and powerful, and sharper than any two-edged sword, piercing even to the dividing asunder of soul and spirit, and of the joints and marrow, and is a discerner of the thoughts and intents of the heart." How the Word of God severs the soul and the spirit. The soul which is corrupted by carnality, and filled with selfishness and evil! Thank God, the Lord can sever from us all that is earthly and sensual, and make us a spiritual people. He can bring all our selfishness to the place of death, and bring the life of Jesus into our being to take the place of that earthly and sensual thing that is destroyed by the living Word and Spirit. The living Word pierces right to the very marrow.

When I was in Australia, so many people came to me with double curvature of the spine; but the word of the Lord went right down to the very marrow of their spines, and instantly they were healed and made straight, as I laid hands on them in the name of Jesus. The divine Son of God, the living Word, through His power, and Spirit moved upon those curvatures of the spine and straightened them out. Oh, thank God for the mighty power of the Word!

The Word of God comes in to separate us from everything that is not of God. It destroys. It also gives life. He must bring to death all that is carnal in us. It was after the death of Christ that God raised Him up on high, and as we are dead with Him we experience the revelation that we are raised up and made to sit in heavenly places in the new life that the Spirit gives.

God has come to lead us out of ourselves into Himself, and to take us from the ordinary into the extraordinary, from the human into the divine, and make us after the image of His Son. Oh, what a Savior! What an ideal Savior! It is written, “Now are we the sons of God, and it doth not yet appear what we shall be: but we know that, when He shall appear, we shall be like Him; for we shall see Him as He is.” But even now, the Lord wants to transform us from glory to glory, by the Spirit of the living God. Have faith in God, have faith in the Son, have faith in the Holy Spirit; and the Triune God will work in you, working in you to will and to do all the good pleasure of His will.

Smith - "Perfect love will never want the preeminence in everything, it will never want to take the place of another, it will always be willing to take the back seat."

Look to God for special GRACE

Nothing is more lovely than prayer, but a prayer meeting is killed if you will go on and on in your own soul when the Spirit of God is finished with you. You say as you come from some meetings, "That was a lovely message if the preacher only had stopped half an hour before he did." Learn to cease immediately the unction of the Spirit lifts. The Holy Ghost is jealous. Your body is the temple, the office of the Holy Ghost, but He does not fill the temple for human glorification, but only for the glory of God. You have no license to continue beyond a "Thus saith the Lord."

There is another side to this. God would have the gathering as free as possible, and you must not put your hand upon the working of the Spirit or it will surely turn sourer. You must be prepared to allow a certain amount of extravagance in young and newly baptized souls. You must remember that when you were brought into this life of the Spirit you had as many extravagances as anybody, but you have now become somewhat more mature. It is a pity that some do get to sober, for they are not where they were in the early days. We have to look to God for wisdom that we do not interfere or dampen the Spirit or quench the power of God when it is manifested in our meetings. If you want to have an assembly full of life you must have an assembly full of manifestation. Nobody will come if there is no manifestation. We need to look to God for special **GRACE** that we do not move back to looking at things from a natural viewpoint.

The preacher, after he loses his unction, should inwardly repent and get right with God and get the unction back. We are no good without the unction of the Spirit of God. If you are filled with the **GRACE** of God you will not be judging everybody in the assembly, and you will not be easily frightened at what is happening. You will have a heart to believe all things, and to believe that though there may be some extravagances, the Spirit of God will take control of things and will see that the Lord Jesus Christ Himself is exalted, glorified, and revealed to hungry hearts that desire to know Him. The Lord would have us wise unto that which is good and simple concerning evil, free from distrust, entering into a divine likeness to Jesus that dares believe that God Almighty will surely watch over all. Hallelujah!

The Holy Ghost is the One who magnifies the Lord Jesus Christ, the One who gives illumination of Him. If you are filled with the Holy Ghost, it is impossible to keep your tongue still. Talk about a dumb baptized soul! It is not to be found in the Scriptures or outside of the Scriptures. We are filled with the Spirit in order that we may magnify the Lord, and there should be no meeting in which the saints do not glorify, magnify, praise, and worship the Lord in Spirit and in truth.

I would like to give one word of caution, for failure often comes through our not recognizing the fact that we are always in the body. We will need our bodies as long as we live. But our body is to be used and controlled by the Spirit of God. We are to present our bodies, holy and acceptable unto God, which is our reasonable service. Every member of our body must be so sanctified that it works in harmony with the Spirit of God. Our very eyes must be sanctified. God hates the winking of the eye. From the day that I read in the Proverbs what God had to say about the winking of the eye (Prov. 6:13 and 10:10) I have never winked. I desire that my eyes may be so sanctified that they can always be used for the Lord. The Spirit of God will bring within us a compassion for souls that will be seen in our very eyes.

God has never changed the order of things, first there comes the natural, and then the spiritual. For instance, when it is on your heart to pray, you begin in the natural and your second word will probably be under the power of the Spirit. You begin and God will end. It is the same in giving forth utterances under the Spirit's power. You feel the moving of the Spirit within and you begin to speak and the Spirit of God will give forth utterance. Thousands have missed wonderful blessings because they have not had faith to move out and begin in the natural, in faith that the Lord would take them into the realm of the supernatural. When you receive the Holy Ghost you receive God's Gift, in whom are all the gifts of the Spirit.

Paul counsels Timothy to stir up the gift that was within. You have power to stir up God's Spirit within you. The way you stir up the gift within you is by beginning in faith, and then He gives forth what is needed for the occasion. You will never begin if you think you have to be full of God. When we yield to timidity and fear we simply yield to Satan. Satan. Whispers, "It is all self." He is a liar. I have learned this, if the Spirit of God is stirring me up, I have no hesitation in beginning to speak in tongues, and the Spirit of God gives me utterance and gives me the interpretation. I find that every time I yield to the Lord on this order I get a divine touch, I get a leading thought from the Spirit of God and the meeting is moved into the realm of faith.

You attend a meeting in faith, believing that the Lord is going to meet you there. But perhaps the evangelist is not in harmony with God. The people in the meeting are not getting what God wants. The Lord knows it. He knows His people are hungry. What happens? He will take perhaps the smallest vessels and put His power upon them. As they yield to the Spirit they break forth in a tongue. Another yields to the Spirit and there comes forth the interpretation. The Lord's church has to be fed, and the Lord will take this means of speaking to His people. Pentecostal people cannot be satisfied with the natural message. They are in touch with heavenly things and cannot be satisfied with anything less. They feel when there is something lacking in a meeting, and they look to God and He supplies that which is lacking.

When a man is filled with the Spirit he really has very little understanding of what he has. We are so limited in our understanding of what we have received. The only way we can know the power that has been given to us is through the ministration and manifestation of the Spirit of God. Do you think that Peter and John knew what they had when they went up to the temple to pray? They were limited in thought, and limited in their expression. The nearer we get to God the more conscious we are of the poverty of our human soul and we cry with Isaiah, "I am undone, I am unclean." But the Lord will bring the precious blood and the flaming coals for cleansing and refining and send us out to labor for Him empowered by His Spirit.

God has sent forth this outpouring that we may all be brought into a revelation of our son ship - that we are sons of God, men of power, that we are to be like the Lord Jesus Christ, that we are to have the powers of son ship, the power to lay hold of that which is weak and to quicken it. The Baptism of the Spirit is to make us sons of God with power. We shall be conscious of our human limits, but we shall not limit the Holy One who has come to dwell within. We must believe that since the Holy Ghost has come upon us we are indeed sons of God with power. Never say that you can't. All things are possible to them that believe. Launch out into the deep and believe that God has His all for you, and that you can do all things through Him who strengthens you.

Peter and John knew that they had been in the upper room, they had felt the glory. That they had been given divine utterances. They had seen conviction on the people. They knew that they had come into a wonderful thing. They know that what they had would be ever increasing and that it would be ever needful to cry, "Enlarge the vessel that the Holy Ghost may have more room within." They knew that all the old things were moved away and they had entered into increasing and ever increasing knowledge of God, and that it was their Master's wish that they should be filled with the Spirit of God and with power every day and every hour. The secret of power is the unveiling of Christ, the all-powerful One within, the revelation of God who comes to abide within us.

As they looked upon the crippled man at the Beautiful Gate they were filled with compassion. They were prompted by the Spirit to stop and speak with him. They said to the lame man, "Look on us." It was God's plan that the man should open his eyes with expectation. Peter said, "Of silver and gold we have none. But we have something and we will give it to you. We don't know what it is, but we give it to you. It is all in the name of Jesus." And then began the ministry of God.

You begin in faith and then you see what will happen. It is hidden from us at the beginning, but as we have faith in God He will come forth. The coming forth of the power is not of us but of God. There is no limit to what He will do. It is all in a nutshell as you believe

God. And so Peter said, "Such as I have I give to thee: in the name of Jesus Christ of Nazareth rise up and walk." And the man who had been in that way for forty years stood up, and began to leap, and entered into the temple walking and leaping and praising God.

"For to one is given by the Spirit the word of wisdom." I want you to keep in mind the importance of never expecting the gifts of the Spirit apart from the power of the Spirit. In coveting the best gifts, covet to be so full of God and His glory that the gifts in manifestation will always glorify Him. We do not know all and we cannot know all that can be brought forth in the manifestation of the word of wisdom. One word of wisdom from God, one flash of light on the Word of God, is sufficient to save us from a thousand pitfalls. People have built without a word from God, they have bought things without a word from God, and they have been ensnared. They have lacked that word of wisdom which will bring them into God's plan for their lives. I have been in many places where I have needed a word from God and this has been my place of refuge.

I will give you one instance. There is one thing I am very grateful to the Lord for, and that is that He has given me **GRACE** not to have a desire for money. The love of money is a great hindrance to many; and many a man is crippled in his ministry because he lets his heart run after financial matters. I was walking out one day when I met a godly man who lived opposite me and he said, "My wife and I have been talking together about selling our house and we feel constrained to sell it to you." As we talked together he persuaded me to buy his place, and before we said good-by I told him that I would take it.

We always make big mistakes when we are in a hurry. I told my wife what I had promised, and she said, "How will you manage it?" I told her that I had managed things so far, but I did not know how I was going to get through this. I somehow knew that I was out of divine order. But when a fellow gets out of divine order it seems that the last person he goes to is God. I ended up relying on an architect to help me, but that scheme fell through. I turned to my relations and I ended up with mud on my face as one after another turned me down. I tried my friends and managed no better. My wife said to me, "Thou hast never been to God Yet." What could I do?

I have a certain place in our house where I go to pray. I have been there very often. As I went I said, "Lord, if You will get me out of this mess, I will never trouble You on this line again." As I waited on the Lord He just gave me one word. It seemed a ridiculous thing, but it was the wisest counsel. There is divine wisdom in every word He speaks. I came down to my wife, saying, "What do you think? The Lord has told me to go to Brother Webster." I said, "It seems very ridiculous, for he is one of the poorest men I know." He was the poorest man I knew, but he was also the richest man I knew, for he knew God. My wife said, "Do What God says, and it will be right."

I went off at once to see him, and he said as he greeted me, "Smith, what brings you so early?" I answered, "The word of God." I said to him, "About three weeks ago I promised to buy a house of a man, and I am short 100 pounds ($500). I have tried to get this money, but somehow I seem to have missed God." "How is it," he asked, "that you have come to me only now?" I answered, "Because I went to the Lord about it only last night." "Well," he said, "it is a strange thing; three weeks ago I had 100 pounds. For years I have been putting money into a co-operative system and three weeks ago I had to go and draw 100 pounds out. I hid it under the mattress. Come with me and you shall have it. Take it. I hope it will bring as great a blessing to you as it has been a trouble to me." I had a word from God, and all my troubles were ended.

This has been multiplied in a hundred ways since that time. If I had been filled with the Holy Ghost, I would not have bought that house and would not have had all that pressure. I believe the Lord wants to loose us from things of earth. But I am ever grateful for that word from God. There have been times in my life when I have been in great crises and under great weight of intercession. I have gone to the meeting without the knowledge of what I would say, but somehow or other God would give by the Spirit some word of wisdom, just what some souls in that meeting needed. As we look to God His mind will be made known, and His revelation and His word of wisdom will be forth coming.

"If thou shalt confess with thy mouth JESUS AS LORD, and shalt believe in thine heart that God hath raised him from the dead, thou shalt be saved" (Romans 10:9).

"For TO THIS END Christ died and lived again, THAT HE MIGHT BE LORD of both the dead and the living" (Romans 14:9).

Smith - "I know that God's word is sufficient. One word from Him can change a nation. His word is from everlasting to everlasting. It is through the entrance of this everlasting Word, this incorruptible seed, that we are born again, and come into this wonderful salvation. Man cannot live by bread alone, but must live by every word that proceeded out of the mouth of God. This is the food of faith. "Faith cometh by hearing, and hearing by the Word of God."

Dare To Believe, Then Command

1919

"Truly, truly, I say unto you; He that believes on Me, the works that I do shall he do also: and greater works than these shall he do; because I go unto My Father. And whatsoever ye shall ask in My name, that will I do, that the Father may be glorified in the Son. If ye shall ask any thing in My name, I will do it." John 14:12-14.

Jesus is speaking here, and mat the Spirit of God can take these words of His and make them real to us. **"He that believeth on Me… greater works than these shall he do."** What a word! Is it true? If you want the truth, where will you get it? "Thy word is truth," Christ said to the Father. When you take up God's Word you get the truth. God is not the author of confusion or error, but He sends forth His light and truth to lead us into His holy habitation, where we receive a revelation of the truth like as unto the noon day in all its clearness.

The Word of God works effectually in us as we believe it. It changes us and brings us into new fellowship with the Father, with the Son, and with the Holy Spirit, into a holy communion, into an unwavering faith, into a mighty assurance, and it will make us partakers of the very nature and likeness of God as we receive His great and exceeding precious promises and believe them. Faith comes by hearing, and hearing by the Word of God. Faith is the substance of His operative power.

We read that Christ opened the understanding of His disciples, and He will open up our understanding and our hearts. He will show us wonderful things that we should never know but for the mighty revelation and enlightenment of the Spirit that He gives to us.

I do not know of any greater words than those found in Romans 4:16, "Therefore it is of faith that it might be by **GRACE**." **GRACE** is God's benediction coming right down to you, and when you open the door to Him, that is as an act of faith, He does all you want and will fulfill all your desires. "It is of faith that it might be by **GRACE**." You open the way for God to work as you believe His Word, and God will come in and supply your every need every step of the way.

Our Lord Jesus said to His disciples and He says to us in this passage in the 14th of John, "You have seen Me work and you know how I work. You shall do the very same things that I am doing, and greater things shall you do, because I am going to the Father, and as you make petition in My name I will work. I will do what you ask, and by this the Father shall be glorified."

Did anyone ever work as He did? I do not mean His carpentering. I refer to His work in the hearts of the people. He drew them to Him Self. They came with their needs, with their sicknesses, with their oppression, and He relieved them all. This royal Visitor, who came from the Father to express His love, talked to men, spent time with them in their homes, found out their every need. He went about doing good and healing all who were oppressed of the devil, and

He said to them and He says to us, “You see what I have been doing, healing the sick, relieving the oppressed, casting out demons. The works that I do shall ye do also.” Dare you believe? Will you take up the work that He left and carry it on?

“He that believeth on Me!” What is this? What does it mean? How can just believing bring these things to pass? What virtue is there in it? There is virtue in these words because He declares them. If we will receive this word and declare it, the greater works shall be accomplished. This is a positive declaration of His, “He that believeth on Me, greater works than these shall he do,” but unbelief has hindered our progress in the realm of the spiritual.

Put away all unbelief. Open your heart to God’s **GRACE**. Then God will come in and place in you a position of Strong faith. He wants to remove every obstruction that is in the world before you. By His **GRACE** He will enable you to be so established in His truth, so strong in the Lord and in the power of His might, that whatever comes across your path to obstruct you, you can arise in divine power and rebuke and destroy it.

It is a matter of definite and clear understanding between us and God. To recognize that Christ has a life power to put into us, which changes everything, to the extent that we will dare to believe. He that believes that Jesus is the Christ overcomes the world. Because we believe that Jesus is the Christ, the essence of divine life is in us by faith and causes a perfect separation between us and the world. We have no room for sin. It is a joyful thing for us to be doing that which is right. He will cause that abundance of **GRACE** to so flow into our hearts that sin shall not have dominion over us. Sin shall not have dominion; nor sickness, nor affliction. **“He that believeth”,** he that dares to believe, he that dares to trust, will see victory over every oppression of the enemy.

A very needy person came to me in a meeting once, all withered and wasted. He had no hope. There was nothing but death in his eyes. He was so helpless that he had to have someone on each side to bear him up. He came to me and said in a whisper, “Can you help me?” Will Jesus answer? “He that believeth on Me, the works that I do shall he do also; and greater works than these.... Behold, I give you power… over all the power of the enemy."

These are the words of our Lord Jesus. It is not our word but the word of the Lord, and as this word is in us He can cause it to be like a burning passion in us. We make the Word of God as we believe it our own. We receive the Word and we have the very life of Christ in us. We become supernatural by the power of God. We find this power working through every part of our being by Faith in Christ.

Now Christ gives us more than just faith. He gives us something to make faith effectual. Whatsoever you desire, if you believe in your heart you shall have. Christ said, "Have faith in God. For verily I say unto you, That whosoever shall say unto this mountain, Be thou removed, and be thou cast into the sea; and shall not doubt in his heart, but shall believe that those things which he saith shall come to pass; he shall have whatsoever he saith. Therefore I say unto you, what things so ever ye desire, when ye pray, believe that ye receive them, and ye shall have them." Mark 11:22-24. Whatsoever he saith! Dare to say in faith and it shall be done. These things have been promised by Christ and He cannot lie.

This afflicted man stood before me helpless and withered. Cancer had filled his stomach. The physicians had operated upon him to take away the cancer from the stomach, but complications had arisen with the result that no food could enter the man's stomach. He could not swallow anything. So in order to keep him alive they made a hole in his stomach and put in a tube about nine inches long with a cup at the top, and he was fed with liquid through this tube. For three months he had been just kept alive but had become like a skeleton.

What was I to say to him? "If you would believe, you would see the glory of God."

Here was the word of Christ, "He that believes on me, the works that I do shall he do also, and greater works than these shall he do; because I go unto My Father." The Word of God is truth. Christ is with the Father and grants us our requests, and makes these things manifest, if we believe. What should I do in the presence of a case like this? "Believe the Word." So I believed the Word which says, "He shall have whatsoever he saith." Mark 11:23. I said, "Go home, and have a good supper." He said, "I cannot swallow." "Go home, and have a good supper," I repeated. "On the authority of the Word of God I say it. Christ says that he that believes that these things which he says shall come to pass, he shall have whatsoever he says. So I say, Go home in the name of Jesus, and have a good supper."

He went home. Supper was prepared. Many times he had had food in his mouth but had always been forced to spit it out again. But I dared to believe that he would be able to swallow that night. So that man filled his mouth full as he had done before, and because someone dared to believe God's Word and said to him, "You shall have a good supper in the name of Jesus," when he chewed his food it went down in the normal way into his stomach, and he ate until he was quite satisfied.

He and his family went to bed filled with joy. The next morning when they arose they were filled with the same joy. Life had begun again. Naturally he looked down to see the hole that had been made in his stomach by the physicians. But God knew that he did not want two holes, and so when God opened the normal passage He closed the other hole in his stomach. This is the kind of God we have, a God who knows, a God who acts, and brings things to pass when we believe. Dare to believe, and then dare to speak, and you shall have whatsoever you say if you doubt not.

A woman came to me one night and inquired, "Can I hear again? Is it possible for me to hear again? I have had several operations and the drums of my ears have been taken away." I said, "If God has not forgotten how to make drums for ears you can hear again." Do you think God has forgotten? What does God forget? He forgets our sins, when we are forgiven, but He has not forgotten how to make drums for ears. God gave her a new set of ear drums!

Not long ago the power of God was very much in a meeting that I was holding. I was telling the people that they could be healed without my going to them. If they would rise up I would pray and the Lord would heal them. There was a man who put up his hand. I said, "Can that man rise?" The folks near him said he could not, and lifted him up.

The Lord healed him. The ribs that were broken were knit together again and were healed instantly. There was such faith in the place that a little girl cried out, "Please, gentleman, come to me." You could not see her, she was so small. The mother said, "My little girl wants you to come." So I went down there to this child, who although fourteen years of age was very small. She said with tears streaming down her face, "Will you pray for me?" I said, "Dare you believe?" She said, "O yes." I prayed and placed my hands on her head in the name of Jesus. She was instantly healed!

"This is God."

The ministry of Christ did not end at the cross, but the Acts and the epistles give us accounts of what he continued to do and teach through those whom he indwelt. And our blessed Lord Jesus is still alive, and continues his ministry through those who are filled with his Spirit. He is still healing the brokenhearted and delivering the captives through those on whom he places his Spirit.

I was traveling one day in a railway train in Sweden. At one station there boarded the train an old lady with her daughter. The old lady's expression was so troubled that I inquired what the matter with her was. I heard that she was going to the hospital to have her leg taken off. She began to weep as she told that the doctors had said there was no hope for her except through having her leg amputated. She was 70 years old. I said to my interpreter, "Tell her that Jesus can heal her."

We stopped at another station and the carriage filled up with people. There was a rush of men to board that train and the devil said, "You're done." But I knew I had the best proposition, for hard things are always opportunities to get to the Lord more glory when he manifests his power. Every trial is a blessing. There have been times when I have been pressed through circumstances and it seemed as if a dozen road engines were going over me, but I have found that the hardest things are just lifting places into the **GRACE** of God. We have such a lovely Jesus. He always proves himself to be such a mighty deliverer. He never fails to plan the best things for us.

The train began moving and I crouched down, and in the name of Jesus commanded the disease to leave. The old lady cried, "I'm healed. I know I'm healed." She stamped her leg and said, "I'm going to prove it." So when we stopped at another station she marched up and down and shouted, "I'm not going to the hospital." Once again our wonderful Jesus had proven himself a healer of the brokenhearted, a deliverer of one that was bound.

At one time I was so bound that no human power could help me. My wife was looking for me to pass away. There was no help. At that time I had just had a faint glimpse of Jesus as the healer. For six months I had been suffering from appendicitis, occasionally getting temporary relief. I went to the mission of which I was pastor, but I was brought to the floor in awful agony, and they brought me home to my bed.

All night I was praying, pleading for deliverance, but none came. My wife was sure it was my home call and sent for a physician. He said that there was no possible chance for me because my body was too weak. Having had the appendicitis for six months, my whole system was drained, and because of that, he thought that it was too late for an operation. He left my wife in a state of broken heartedness.

After he left, there came to our door a young man and an old lady. I knew that she was a woman of real prayer. They came upstairs to my room. This young man jumped on the bed and commanded the evil spirit to come out of me. He shouted, "Come out, you devil; I command you to come out in the name of Jesus!" There was no chance for an argument, or for me to tell him that I would never believe that there was a devil inside of me. The thing had to go in the name of Jesus, and it went, and I was instantly healed.

I arose and dressed and went downstairs. I was still in the plumbing business, and I asked my wife, "Is there any work in? I am all right now, and I am going to work." I found there was a certain job to be done and I picked up my tools and went off to do it.

Just after I left, the doctor came in, put his plug hat down in the hall, and walked up to the bedroom. But the invalid was not there. "Where is Mr. Wigglesworth? he asked. "Oh, doctor, he's gone out to work," said my wife. "You'll never see him alive again," said the doctor; "they'll bring him back a corpse." Well, I'm the corpse.

Since that time the Lord has given me the privilege of praying for people with appendicitis in many parts of the world; and I have seen a great many people up and dressed within a quarter of an hour from the time I prayed for them. We have a living Christ who is willing to meet people on every line.

About eight years ago I met Brother [D.W.] Kerr and he gave me a letter of introduction to a brother in Zion City named Cook. I took his letter to Brother Cook, and he said, "God has sent you here." He gave me the addresses of six people and asked me to go and pray for them, and meet him again at 12 o'clock. I got back at about 12:30 and he told me about a young man who was to be married the following Monday.

His sweetheart was in Zion City dying of appendicitis. I went to the house and found that the physician had just been there and had pronounced that there was no hope. The mother was nearly distracted and was pulling her hair, and saying, "Is there no deliverance?" I said to her, "Woman, believe God and your daughter will be healed and be up and dressed in 15 minutes." But the mother went on screaming.

They took me into the bedroom, and I prayed for the girl and commanded the evil spirit to depart in the name of Jesus. She cried, "I am healed." I said to her, "Do you want me to believe that you are healed? If you are healed, get up." She said, "You get out of the room and I'll get up." In less than 10 minutes the doctor came in. He wanted to know what had happened. She said, "A man came in and prayed for me, and I'm healed." The doctor pressed his finger right in the place that had been so sore, and the girl neither moaned nor cried. He said, "This is God."

It made no difference whether he acknowledged it or not; I knew that God had worked. Our God is real in saving and healing power today. Our Jesus is just the same, yesterday, and today, and forever. [He 13.8] He saves and heals today just as of old, and he wants to be your savior and your healer.

Oh, if you would only believe God! What would happen? The greatest things. Some have never tasted the **GRACE** of God, have never had the peace of God. Unbelief robs them of these blessings. It is possible to hear and yet not conceive the truth. It is possible to read the word and not share in the life it brings. It is necessary for us to have the Holy Ghost to unfold the word and bring to us the life that is Christ. We can never fully understand the wonders of this redemption until we are full of the Holy Ghost.

I was once at an afternoon meeting. The Lord had been graciously with us and many had been healed by the power of God. Most of the people had gone home and I was left alone, when I saw a young man who was evidently hanging back to have a word. I asked, "What do you want?" He said, "I wonder if I could ask you to pray for me." I said, "What's the trouble?" He said, "Can't you smell?"

The young fellow had gone into sin and was suffering the consequences. He said, "I have been turned out of two hospitals. I am broken out all over. I have abscesses all over me." And I could see that he had a bad breaking out at the nose. He said, "I heard you preach, and could not understand about this healing business, and was wondering if there was any hope for me."

I said to him, "Do you know Jesus?" He did not know the first thing about salvation, but I said to him, "Stand still." I placed my hands on his head and then on his loins and cursed that terrible disease in the name of Jesus. He cried out, "I know I'm healed. I can feel a warmth and a glow all over me." I said, "Who did it?" He said, "Your prayers." I said, "No, it was Jesus!" He said, "Was it he? Oh, Jesus! Jesus! Jesus, save me." And that young man went away healed and saved. Oh, what a merciful God we have! What a wonderful Jesus is ours!

Are you oppressed? Cry out to God. It is always good for people to cry out. You may have to cry out. The Holy Ghost and the word of God will bring to light every hidden, unclean thing that must be revealed. There is always a place of deliverance when you let God search out that which is spoiling and marring your life.

That evil spirit that was in the man in the synagogue cried out, "Let us alone!" [Lk 4.34] It was a singular thing that the evil spirit had never cried out like that until Jesus walked into the place where he was. Jesus rebuked the thing, saying, "Hold thy peace and come out of him," and the man was delivered. [Lk 4.35]

He is just the same Jesus, exposing the powers of evil, delivering the captives and letting the oppressed go free, purifying them and cleansing their hearts. Those evil spirits that inhabited the man who had the legion did not want to be sent to the pit to be tormented before their time, and so they cried out to be sent into the swine. [Lk 8.31-32] Hell is such an awful place that even the demons hate the thought of going there. How much more should men seek to be saved from the pit?

God is compassionate and says, "Seek ye the Lord while he may be found." [Is 55.6] And He has further stated, "Whosoever shall call on the name of the Lord shall be saved." [Ac 2.21] Seek him now, call on his name right now; and there is forgiveness, healing, redemption, deliverance, and everything you need for you right here and now, and that which will satisfy you throughout eternity.

Exceedingly above all you can ask or think

January-March 1918.

Read Ephesians 3 carefully. This is a lovely chapter on Paul's mission to the gentiles. God has grafted us Gentiles in. In other ages, it was not made known that the Gentiles should be fellow-heirs, of which he was made a minister by the effectual working of his power. [Ep 3.5-7] This power in Paul wrought a very effectual work; it worked in him to such effect that he said he was the least of all saints; [Ep 3.8] that to him was given this **GRACE** of mystery and revelation. It came forth as a living reality of a living substance indwelling him. "To the intent that now unto the principalities and powers in the heavenly places might be known through the church the manifold wisdom of God." [Ep 3.10]

Faith and love

And on the morrow, when they came from Bethany, he was hungry: And seeing a fig tree afar off having leaves, he came if haply he might find anything thereon: and when he came to it, he found nothing but leaves; for the time of figs was not yet. And Jesus answered and said unto it, No man eat the fruit of thee hereafter forever. And his disciples heard it.

And in the morning, as they passed by, they saw the fig tree dried up from the roots. And Peter calling to remembrance saith unto him, Master, behold, the fig tree which thou cursed is withered away. And Jesus answering saith unto them, Have faith in God. For verily I say unto you, That whosoever shall say unto this mountain, Be thou removed, and be thou cast into the sea; and shall not doubt in his heart, but shall believe that those things which he saith shall come to pass; he shall have whatsoever he saith. Therefore I say unto you, What things soever ye desire when ye pray, believe that ye receive them, and ye shall have them. Mark 11:12-14, 20-24

The Lord wants me to speak to you about the subject of faith. May God bring us into this place of the rest of faith. There is a big difference between saying that you have faith and having it. God wants to impart to us a faith that can laugh at impossibilities and rest in peace. There is no other faith which appropriates that which God has for us. The greatest sin in all the world is "unbelief." It will cut off from you everything that God has for you. It will hinder your progress, and darken the prospects of your life. It will shut heaven off and open hell up; but if you believe God your faith will shut off hell and open heaven. Faith is the substance of things hoped for and the evidence of things not seen.

God's work is a perfect plan. There is no such thing as reading the Word of God and remaining ordinary after you read it. It is the power of God; the Christ of God; the revelation of God; It is God! God manifested in the flesh. The Word which was made flesh and was breathed through this flesh was the Word of God. This is the power and personality of God. This is God incarnated! It is impossible for you to have a refusal from God if you believe Him. O the times that I have proved this in my life that God is a rewarder of them that diligently seek Him. It is impossible to have faith without peace.

There are nine gifts of the Spirit and nine fruits. The third gift is the gift of faith, and the third fruit is peace, and it is impossible to have faith without peace, and I want to say that it is not howling and screaming and rolling on the floor; it is not making a lot of to-dos; it is simply God manifested in the flesh through a faith which rests upon the omnipotent Word of God. O this blessed incarnation of the Spirit through the Word of God. What does faith really mean?

One thing God has shown me through the Baptism of the Holy Ghost. It is 2 Cor. 13: 3-5. I want you to understand there is a personal manifestation of power by the Holy Ghost which absolutely changes us into the likeness of God. "The **GRACE** of our Lord Jesus Christ and the love of God and the Communion of the Holy Ghost be with you."

O that Communion of the Holy Ghost! I feel to-night, as I speak to you: O that men that are saved would yield themselves for the cleansing power of the blood till they could be filled with the power of the Holy Ghost; and then, by the communication of the Holy Spirit, He would speak to you and would converse with you. He would direct you and give you the word of wisdom, and the time would come that you would know that you were in a new realm, where God is working, and it is not you.

There is One greater than all; His Name is Jesus! O the powers of the enemy! And Jesus wants us to know that by the power of the Spirit that you can be filled with the presence of God, arid God wants you to know that His Name never fails. God said, concerning Him: “He (Jesus) was manifested to destroy the works of the devil.” O, I do thank God for the extremity of humanity, which is God’s opportunity, and if you have come to a place where you know there is no help in yourself, then He is able, O, it is true! When we come to a place where we have no other leader or companion but Him when He is the whole purpose of our life, the joy of our souls, then may we truly say:

Jesus shall lead me night and day
Jesus shall lead me all the way
He is the truest friend to me

From the author Dr. Michael H Yeager's

*Many times when the Bible talks about the **GRACE** of God, it is referring to **signs, wonders, and miracles**. The **GRACE** of God is manifested in signs and wonders and miracles. If what we have been believing is true, it ought to make us more like Jesus. It should set us free from materialism and worldly pleasures. Now, we do not take a vow of poverty, but the things of this world do not excite us.

We will not care about gold and silver, diamonds and fancy cars, fancy houses. The scripture tells us that one soul is worth more than all of the wealth of this world. That's is the place the early church lived in. The early church even got rid of stuff that was interfering with their walk and commitment to Jesus Christ.

Here is an example, I've been eating German chocolate cake ever since I was a little kid. I like German chocolate cake. Now, if you gave me a cake that looks like German chocolate, cake but it was not one, I would be able to tell with the first mouthful. I can tell real quick from experience is not a German chocolate cake. It should be the same way when it comes to knowing what the real grace of God is.

Read the book of Acts if you want to see what the Real Gospel produces. It produces people who loved one another. They will know you are my disciples because of your love for one another. It produces people who will take all the natural they have in order to help feed others and ministered to others, and to have unity. A harmony produced by Divine Love. They have power with God! People come in sick, and they go out Healed. People come in one way, and they come out another way. That's the real church.

I feel like we've been robbed. Don't you ever feel like you've been robbed? Have you ever bought a product and spent a lot of money? You got it. You found out it was a dog. I mean like fireworks you buy for the fourth of July. You light them, and none of them go off. You go, man, I got robbed.

I don't know about you, but I want to see some fireworks. I want to see God do wonderful things. You do not have to be content where you are at spiritually. If you're content where you're at spiritually, you are Luke warm.

We need a revelation of who Jesus is. We need a revelation of the will of God, the word of God. The spirit of God needs to give us revelation. Jesus said to Peter: Blessed are thou Simon Barjona for flesh and blood has not revealed this to you, but my Father, which is in heaven. The revelation of who Jesus is, that he was the Christ. Once we get a revelation of who Jesus is, nothing else will matter. In Jesus, we live and move and have are being. If we are risen with him, then seek those things which are above. When you got a revelation of who Christ is, you will be seeking things above and not on things on the earth. For you are dead and your life is hidden with Christ in God. When Christ, who is our life, I said He is our life. He is our life.

Say that to yourself over and over. **He is my life. He is my life**. Come on. **He is my life**. When Christ who is our life shall appear, you shall appear with him in glory! The sufferings of this present time are not worthy of being compared with the glory that shall we be revealed in them that love him.

Do you know why I read my Bible? Do you know why I pray? Do you know why I Go after God? Do you know why? Because I love God and because I also have a fear of the Lord in my Heart. Be not deceived. God is not mocked. Whatever a man sows he will reap.

My Wife's Bags Packed to Leave Me!

My wife and I were going through some major issues in our marriage. We had been married for 21 years up to this point, back in the year 2000. A tragic accident had taken place in 1998 with our little girl Naomi becoming seriously hurt. For 2 1/2 years, we both worked day and night keeping her fed, exercised, and taken care of. Then, one night, I put her to bed and she was gone the next morning. She was four and a half years old when she passed on. That same year at Christmas, my mom passed away with whom I was very close. In additional to all the stress at home, our church was experiencing multiple problems at the same time as well, which served to compound our ongoing marriage problems which we had already been experiencing for several years.

One day as I was in prayer in the churches sanctuary, I heard the Lord say to me, **"Leave your wife alone!"** It was not Him suggesting or asking, but demanding. Then he spoke to me, "Her bags are packed, and she is ready to leave you." What I heard from the Lord was so real to me that I began to weep uncontrollably for two reasons: first because I know the voice of God and what I heard was true, and second because I love my wife so much. God had given us to each other. We had been through so much together. I had the privilege of delivering three of our own children. On two of these occasions, the midwife was not there because she had been called away. We had seen God perform so many miracles in our lives and many others. (Read our book: Living in the Realm of the Miraculous)

I did not want to lose my wife. She was my beloved babe, the apple of my eye, the wife of my youth and the mother of my children. She had been my partner through thick and thin. I cried out to God, "Lord, what should I do?" And then he said to me, just love her! That's what your job is: to love her as Christ loves the church and gave himself for her.

And then unexpectedly he asked me a very strange question, "Do you wear your wife's bra or girdle"? I said what Lord? Surely, he did not say what I thought he just said to me. Once again, I heard, "Do you wear your wife's bra or girdle"? I said, **NO LORD**! Then I heard him say to me, "If you do not wear your wife's undergarments then why do you keep trying to use her scriptures?" I said, what do you mean, Lord? And he spoke to my heart saying, **"Ephesians 5:22, 23, and 24 is not yours.** Where it says, wives submit yourselves unto your own husbands.......... Those are not your scriptures, so why do you keep using them? Your Scriptures are **Ephesians 5:25 to 33 Husbands love your wives even as Christ also loved the church and gave Himself for it."**

At that very moment it was like a sledgehammer hit me between the eyes. I clearly saw what I had been trying to do all these years. I had literally put myself in the place of God and was trying to change my wife. My job was not to make her submit to me! My job was to love her even as Christ loves the church! I went back to my house with tears rolling down my face asking my wife to please forgive me, explaining that it was not my job to make her submit and that her submission was completely between her and God. My job is to love her...... end of story!

I just asked her the other day if what I heard the Lord say was correct, did she really have her bags packed, and was she ready to leave me? She replied yes, not only did I have my bags packed but I had called my mom telling her to please be ready to come and pick me up at any moment. I told my mom that I was going to try to stick it out as long as possible, but there was only so much I could handle. Thank God for his mercy, kindness, goodness, and love, and that He still speaks today, and tries to turn us away from destruction of our own making. We must maintain a meek and teachable, humble spirit. We must be quick to repent and turn away from our evil deeds.

Psalm 25:9 The meek will he guide in judgment: and the meek will he teach his way.

Job 17:9 The righteous also shall hold on his way, and he that hath clean hands shall be stronger and stronger.

Matthew 11:29 Take my yoke upon you, and learn of me; for I am meek and lowly in heart: and ye shall find rest unto your souls.

We need to submit to God, resist the devil, and he will flee from us. Every time you disobey your conscience you are hardening your heart. Jesus said that they have ears, but they hear not, eyes, but they see not. He could have simply said: they choose not to hear, and they choose not to listen. When we harden our hearts, we are headed for death and destruction. Right now, we need to boldly proclaim in the name of Jesus: I will no longer harden my heart to the voice of God or my conscience. The devil gets people to lie about you, to gossip about you, to attack you, to get you to harden your heart through bitterness. He is hoping that you will become extremely offended, bitter and hateful towards people and then towards God.

Hebrews 12:15 looking diligently lest any man fail of the grace of God; lest any root of bitterness springing up trouble you, and thereby many be defiled;

Jesus was absolutely - innocent and blameless, that's why he was called the lamb without spot or blemish. Jesus had a conscience that was clear before God and man. The Scripture says that Christ was like a **tender root** growing out of the dry ground.

His conscience and his heart was tender and sensitive to the voice of his Father. In order to commit sin, we must harden our hearts to the voice of our conscience. The more that we do this, the less we will hear, comprehend, or respond to the voice of God.

Christ said that the prince of this world was going to come to destroy him, but that the enemy would find no sin in his heart. The enemy of our soul wants to get us to be bitter, to be resentful, to be angry, to get you to harden your heart, to not keep a tender conscience, but to become hardhearted. To be meek is to be teachable, sensitive, and responsive to your conscience.

My 2nd son dying from rabies

When my son Daniel was 16 years old in 2000, he brought home a baby raccoon. He wanted to keep this raccoon as a pet. Immediately, people began to inform me that this was illegal. I further learned that to have a raccoon in Pennsylvania; one had to purchase one from someone who was licensed by the state to sell them. The reason for this was because of the high rate of rabies carried among them. But stubbornness arose up in my heart against what they were telling me, and I hardened my heart and did not listen to my conscience.

You see, I had a raccoon when I was a child. Her mother had been killed on the highway and left behind a litter of her little ones. I had taken one of the little ones and bottle-fed it, naming her Candy. I have a lot of fond memories of this raccoon, so when my son wanted this raccoon, against better judgment, the warnings of my conscience and against the law of the land, I said okay.

I did not realize that baby raccoons could have the rabies virus lying dormant in them for three months before it would manifest. I knew in my heart that I was wrong to permit him to keep this raccoon. But, like so many when we are out of the will of

God, we justify ourselves. We are completely blind and ignorant of the price that we must pay because of our rebellion and disobedience.

Daniel named his little raccoon Rascal. And he was a rascal because he was constantly getting into everything. Several months went by, and one night my son Daniel told me that he had a frightening dream. I should have known right then that we needed to get rid of this raccoon. He said in his dream, Rascal grew up and became big like a bear and then attacked and devoured him.

Some time went by, and my son Daniel began to get sick, running a high fever. One morning, he came down telling me that something was majorly wrong with Rascal. He said that he was wobbling all over the place and was bumping into stuff. Immediately, the alarm bells went off. I asked him where his raccoon was. He informed me that Rascal was in his bedroom. Immediately I went upstairs to his room, opening his bedroom door. And their Rascal was acting extremely strange. He was bumping into everything and had saliva coming from his mouth.

Immediately, my heart was filled with great dread. I had grown up around wildlife and farm animals. I had run into animals with rabies before. No ifs, an, or buts, this raccoon had rabies. I immediately went to Danny asking him if the raccoon had bitten him or if he had gotten any of Rascal's saliva in his wounds? He showed me his hands where he had cuts on them, informing me that he had been letting rascal lick these wounds. He had even allowed rascal to lick his mouth.

Daniel did not look well and was running a high-grade fever. He also informed me that he felt dizzy. I knew in my heart that we were in terrible trouble. I immediately called up the local forest ranger. They put me on the line with one of their personnel that had a lot of expertise in this area. When I informed him of what was going on, he asked me if I knew it was illegal to take in a wild raccoon. I told him I did know but that I had chosen to ignore the law.

He said that he would come immediately over to our house to examine this raccoon and if necessary to take it with him. I had placed Rascal in a cage making sure that I did not touch him. When the forest ranger arrived, I had the cage sitting in the driveway. He examined the raccoon without touching it. You could tell that he was quite concerned about the condition of this raccoon.

He looked at me with deep regret informing me that in his opinion with 30 years' wildlife service experience, this raccoon had rabies. He asked me if there was anyone who had been in contact with this raccoon with any symptoms of sickness. I informed him that for the last couple of days my son Daniel had not been feeling well. In fact, he was quite sick. When I told him the symptoms that Daniel was experiencing, it was apparent the ranger was shaken and quite upset.

He told me that anybody who had been in contact with this raccoon would have to receive shots. He went on to explain that from the description of what my son Daniel was going through and considering the length of his illness, it was too late for him! He told me that he felt from his experience that there was no hope for my son. He fully believed that my son would die from rabies. He loaded the raccoon up in the back of his truck, leaving me standing in my driveway weeping. He said that he would get back to me as soon as they had the test results and that I should get ready for state officials to descend upon myself, my family, and our church.

I cannot express to you the hopelessness and despair that had struck my heart at that moment. Just earlier in the spring, our little girl Naomi had passed on to be with the Lord at 4 ½ years old. And now my second son Daniel was dying from rabies. Both situations could have been prevented.

Immediately, I gathered together my wife, my first son Michael, my third son Steven, and my daughter Stephanie. We all gathered around Daniel's bed and began to cry out to God. We wept, cried, and prayed crying out to God. I was repenting and asking God for mercy. Daniel, as he was lying on the bed running a high fever and almost delirious, informed me that he was barely able to hang on to consciousness. He knew in his heart, he said, that he was dying!

After everyone disbursed from his bed with great overwhelming sorrow, I went into our family room where we had a wood stove. I opened the wood stove which still had a lot of cold ashes from the winter. Handful after handful of ashes I scooped out of the stove, pouring it over my head and saturating my body, with tears of repentance and sorrow running down my face.

And then I lay in the ashes. The ashes got into my eyes, mouth, and nose and my lungs, making me quite sick. But I did not care, all that mattered was that God would have mercy on us and spare my son and all our loved ones from the rabies virus. As I lay on the floor in the ashes, crying out to God with all I had within me, one could hear the house was filled with weeping, crying, and praying family members.

All night long I wept and prayed, asking God to please have mercy on my stupidity. To remove the rabies virus not only from my son but from everyone else that had been in contact with this raccoon. I also asked God to remove the virus from Rascal as a sign that he had heard my prayers. I continued in this state of great agony for over 16 hours praying until early in the morning, when suddenly the light of heaven shined upon my soul. Great peace that passes understanding overwhelmed me. I got up with victory in my heart and soul.

I went upstairs to check on my son Daniel. When I walked into his bedroom, the presence of God was tangible. The fever had broken and he was resting peacefully. Our whole house was filled with the tangible presence of God. From that minute forward, he was completely healed. A couple of days later, I was contacted by the state informing me that, to their amazement, they could find nothing wrong with the raccoon. God had supernaturally removed the rabies virus not only from my son and those in contact with Rascal, but from the raccoon itself. Thank God that the Lord's mercy endures forever!

When the Dell Lake Damn Broke

If I had not heard the **still small voice** of God, my family and I would have been swept away when the dam broke at Dell Lake in Wisconsin! On June 8, 2008, my family and I were in Wisconsin at Dell Lake ministering in special meetings for an Indian tribe called the Ho-Chunk Nation. We were there at their invitation. They had provided the facility and all the advertisements. Their reservation was located about five miles away from the lake where we were camping. We had had some wonderful services. It was the second night of these meetings. At the end of the service, unexpectedly, I heard the still small voice of God say: pack up your camper and leave tonight!

It had been a long da, and my flesh sure did not want to leave, but I know the still small voice of God. I told the sponsors of the meetings that I was sorry, but we had to go back to Pennsylvania, tonight. I could tell they were extremely disappointed. They tried to convince me to stay because God was moving in such a wonderful way, but I know the voice of God.

My family members were also disappointed. They asked me why we were leaving. They reminded me that I have never canceled or shortened my commitments. I told them I understood this. But we had to leave tonight. I did not know why, but I had heard the still small voice of the Lord in my heart telling me we must pack up and leave tonight.

We arrived back at the Dell Lake campgrounds. It was beginning to rain extremely hard. My family asked if we could wait until the next morning because it was late, dark and raining heavily. I said no, we had to go now! I backed my truck up to the fifth wheel trailer. I saw the spirit of God come upon my second son Daniel in a powerful way. It had to be God because he does not like to get wet or to work hard. I mean he began to work very fast and efficiently. My boys and I connected the fifth wheel camper; we picked up all our camping equipment and withdrew the extended sides of the trailer.

Everybody was wet and tired as we loaded into the crew cab Toyota pickup truck. Then, we were on our way. I noticed as I drove past the Dell Lake dam that water was rushing by like a little river on both sides of the road. Some parts of the road were already flooded. We drove through the night. There were times we had to crawl because the rain was coming down so hard with fog and strong winds. All the way through Wisconsin, Illinois, Indiana, and Ohio the rain came. The weather was extremely violent as we saw eighteen wheelers turned over — lots of car accidents. Trees and debris were blowing everywhere, yet God was protecting us.

The next day when we finally arrived back in Pennsylvania, we discovered some shocking news. There had been hundreds of twisters and tornadoes right behind us which caused a huge amount of devastation in Wisconsin, Illinois, and Ohio. But that wasn't the only news. The dam at Dell Lake, Wisconsin had completely and collapsed. Dell Lake is the largest man-made lake in Wisconsin, and this had never happened before in all of its histories. The whole lake rushed out over the town. We would have been washed away in the storm. There is video footage of this disaster on the Internet. Thank God I had heard the still small voice of the Lord. Because I had obeyed His voice, my life and the life of my family was spared.

We need to practice godliness as we experience the school of hard knocks, learning to hear, and obey the voice of God. This will be a hit and miss proposition. As you begin to experience God's voice, you will begin to learn what it sounds like. Elijah knew the voice of God was not in the manifestations, of the **great and strong wind, the earthquake, or the fire**! I did not say God was not the author of this manifestation, but that God's voice was not in these manifestations. Yes, God is mighty and yet many times He is like a gentle dove.

Luke 3:22 and the Holy Ghost descended in a bodily shape like a

dove upon him, and a voice came from heaven, which said, Thou art my beloved Son; in thee, I am well pleased.

Now, what if the Lord doesn't tell you precisely what you should do? Just simply do what the word, the Bible tells you to do. Unless God gives you explicitly instructions, I do what Jesus and the word of God tells me to do. For instance, the Scripture tells us to pray, worship, to praise the Lord, to have a thankful heart, to gather together with other believers, to forgive. This list could go on, and on, and on. Simply begin to do what the word of God says, and you will begin to experience the voice of God speaking to you in many ways.

Isaiah 30: 21 and thine ears shall hear a word behind thee, saying, this is the way, walk ye in it, when ye turn to the right hand, and when ye turn to the left.

It is very important that we do not allow our imaginations to run wild with us. I have met many people to the years who declared up-and-down that it was God speaking to them, and no matter what you said you could not convince them otherwise. In the old covenant, the way you perceived whether a man was of God was by his fruits, and whether the prophetic word he spoke happened. That standard is still true today, for the God said I am the Lord and I change not.

Deuteronomy 18:22 when a prophet speaketh in the name of the Lord, if the thing follows not, nor come to pass, that is the thing which the Lord hath not spoken, but the prophet hath spoken it presumptuously: thou shalt not be afraid of him.

If at times we miss the will of God, we must be very quick to repent; otherwise a deceiving spirit will be able to wreak havoc in our lives. I have a simple illustration of this happening in my life at one time, and I believe this story will help you.

A Woman fell at my feet weeping!

Through the years, I have operated in the word of knowledge. The gift of the word of knowledge is when the Holy Spirit quickens to your heart information of which you have no natural knowledge. The Scriptures declare that we should desire spiritual gifts in order that we can see people set free. In the book of Galatians, it declares that the person who ministers to us through the spirit does it by faith. All the gifts of the spirit operate by faith in Christ Jesus. One of the major ways that faith comes is by the written word of God. Faith is when the word of God becomes more real to you than the natural world you live in. The Scripture that I decided to meditate on is discovered in first Corinthians chapter 14:

I Corinthians 14:24-25, But if all prophesy , and there come in one that believeth not, or one unlearned, he is convinced of all, he is judged of all: And thus are the secrets of his heart made manifest; and so falling down on his face he will worship God, and report that God is in you of a truth."

I took this Scripture and memorized it. Not only did I memorize it, but I meditated on it day and night. I kept speaking it to myself over and over very slowly and passionately. I did this until this Scripture was burning in my heart. It became more real to me than what was around me. This is a major key to the increasing of faith. It is very like the development and the building of physical muscles, and so it is with faith. Immediately I began to operate in a more precise word of knowledge.

Here's one illustration. At a midweek service as I was ministering, a lady walked into the back of our church. She was a first-time visitor, who I had never met before. This lady looked to be in her 50s. I was just finishing my message when the spirit of God quickened my heart to call her forward. When she came forward to the front of the church, I heard the still small voice of God! I simply repeated what I heard, and out of my mouth came these words, "You have one son, and two daughters. Your one

Daughter is married to a man who is physically abusing her. You are in tremendous fear for her life." I began to speak to her in detail about what was happening in her life and her family.

What is amazing is that when I operate in this realm, I remember very little of what I speak. As I continued to prophesy she began to weep and cry almost uncontrollably, as she literally threw herself to the floor. God brought about an amazing deliverance. She began to proclaim that everything I said was true. And that it was God speaking through me to her in a very precise way. I stood there in amazement as I witnessed first Corinthians 14 being fulfilled in exactly the way that it proclaimed it would, "And thus are the secrets of his heart made manifest; and so falling down on his face he will worship God, and report that God is in you of a truth."

God is not a respecter people, if we would give ourselves to the word of God, meditating upon it day and night, it will surely happen! I could write a book on just this way that God speaks. This is one of the major ways that I hear the voice of God in my life daily. It is the will of God for every one of his people to hear his still small voice. As you meditate upon these biblical truths, confessing, and agreeing with them, the voice of God will become very clear and precise.

Genesis 3:8 And they heard the voice of the Lord God walking in the garden in the cool of the day: and Adam and his wife hid themselves from the presence of the Lord God amongst the trees of the garden.

CHAPTER THREE

To know Him

Oh, the joy of the knowledge of it! We know if we look back how God has taken us on we love to shout “Hallelujah,” pressed out beyond measure by the Spirit, as He brings us face to face with reality, His blessed Holy Spirit dwelling in us and manifesting the works. I must know the sovereignty of His **GRACE** and the manifestation of His power.

Where am I? I am in Him; He is in God. The Holy Ghost, the great Revealer of the Son. Three persons dwelling in man. The Holy Spirit is in us to reveal the revelation of Jesus Christ to be manifest in us. “Therefore be it known unto you He that dwells in God does the works.” “The law of the Spirit of life having made us free from the law of sin and death.”

The Spirit working in righteousness, bringing us to the place where all unbelief is dethroned, and Christ is made the Head of the Corner. “This is the Lord’s doing, and it is marvelous in our eyes.” It is a glorious fact, we are in God’s presence, possessed by Him; we are not our own, we are clothed with another. What for? For the deliverance of the people. Many can testify to the day and hour when they were delivered from sickness by a supernatural power.

Some would have passed away with influenza if God had not intervened, but God stepped in with a his revelation, showing us we are born from above, born by a new power, God dwelling in us superseding the old. "If ye ask anything in My name, I will do it." Ask and receive, and your joy shall be full, if ye dare to believe. "What shall we do that we might work the works of God? Jesus answered and said unto them, 'This is the work of God that ye believe on Him whom He hath sent." God is more anxious to answer than we are to ask. I am speaking of faith based upon knowledge.

I was healed of appendicitis

Faith based upon the knowledge of the experience of it. Where I have ministered to others God has met and answered according to His will. It is in our trust and our knowledge of the power of God and the knowledge that God will not fail us if we will only believe. "Speak the word only, and my servant shall be healed." Jesus said unto the centurion, "Go thy way; as thou hast believed so be it done unto thee," and the servant was healed in the self-same hour.

An illustration. In one place where I was staying a young man came in telling us his sweetheart was dying; there was no hope. I said, "Only believe." What was it? Faith based upon knowledge. I knew that what God had done for me He could do for her. We went to the house. Her sufferings were terrible to witness. I said, "In the name of Jesus come out of her." She cried, "Mother, mother, I am well." Then I said that the only way to make her family to believe it was to get up and get dressed. Presently she came down dressed. The doctor came in and examined her carefully. He said, "This is of God; this is the finger of God." It was faith based upon knowledge.

If I received a check for £1,000, and only knew imperfectly the character of the man that sent it, I should be careful not to trust it until it was cashed in, and cleared the bank. Jesus did great works because of His knowledge of His Father. Faith begets knowledge, fellowship, and communion. If you see imperfect faith, full of doubt, a wavering condition, it always comes of imperfect knowledge.

Jesus said, "'Father, I know that You hear Me always, but because of the people that stand by I said it, that they may believe that Thou has sent Me.' He cried with a loud voice, 'Lazarus, come forth.' " "And God wrought special miracles by the hand of Paul, so that from his body were brought unto the sick handkerchiefs or aprons, and the diseases departed from them, and the evil spirits went out of them." For our conversation is in heaven from whence also we look for the Savior.

Who shall fashion anew the body of our humiliation that it may be conformed to the body of His glory, according to the working whereby He is able to subdue all things unto Himself? How God has cared for me these many years, and blessed me, giving me such a sense of His presence! When we depend upon God how wonderful He is, giving us enough and to spare for others.

Lately God has enabled me to take victory into new areas, a living-in-Holy-Ghost attitude in a new way. As we meet, immediately the glory falls. The Holy Ghost has the latest news from the Godhead, and has designed for us the right place at the right time. Events happen in a remarkable way. You find yourself where the need is.

There have been several mental cases lately. How difficult they are naturally, but how easy for God to deal with. One lady came, saying, "Just over the way there is a young man terribly afflicted, demented, with no rest day or night." I went with a very imperfect knowledge as to what I had to do, but in the weak places God helps our infirmities. I rebuked the demon in the name of Jesus, then I said, "I'll come again tomorrow." Next day when I went he was with his father in the field and quite well.

Another case. Fifty miles away there was a fine young man, twenty-five years of age. He had lost his reason, and could have no communication with his mother. He was always wandering up and down. I knew God was wanting to heal him. I cast out the demon-power, and heard long after he had become quite well. Thus the blessed Holy Spirit takes us on from one place to another. So many things happen, I live in heaven on earth. Just the other day, at Coventry, God relieved the people. Thus He takes us on, and on, and on. It's

Do not wait for inspiration if you are in need; the Holy Ghost is here, and you can have perfect deliverance as you sit in your seats.

I was taken to three persons, one in care of an attendant. As I entered the room there was a terrible quarreling, such a noise it seemed as if all the powers of hell were stirred. I had to wait for God's time. The Holy Ghost rose in me at the right time, and the three were instantly delivered. That night in our meeting they were singing praises to God.

There had to be activity and testimony. Let it be known unto you this man Christ is the same today. Which man? God's Man Who has all the glory, power and dominion. "For He must reign, till He hath put all enemies under His feet." When He reigns in you, you will obey, and you will know how to work in cooperation with His will, His power, His light, His life, having faith based upon his knowledge, and we know He has come. "Ye shall receive power, the Holy Ghost coming upon you." We are in the light and the experience of it.

Sometimes a living word comes unto me, in the presence of a need, a revelation of the Spirit to my mind, "Thou shalt be loosed." Loosed now? It looks like presumption to a carnal man, but God is with the man who dares to stand upon His word. I remember, for instance, a person who had not been able to smell anything for four years. I said, "You will smell now if you believe." This stirred another who had not smelled for twenty years. I said, "You will smell tonight."

She went about smelling everything, and was quite excited. The next day she gave her testimony. Another came and asked, "Was it possible for God to heal her ears?" The drums were removed. I said, "Only believe." She went down into the audience in great distress; others were healed but she could not hear. The next night she came again. She said, "I am going to believe tonight." The glory fell. The first night she came feeling; the second night she came believing.

At one place there was a man anointed for a terrible rupture. He came the next night, rose in the meeting saying, "This man is an impostor; he is deceiving the people. He told me last night I was healed; I am worse than ever today." I spoke to the evil power that held the man and rebuked it, telling the man he was indeed healed. He was a mason. The next day he testified to lifting heavy weights, and that God had completely healed him. "By His stripes we are healed." It was the Word of God that this man was coming against, not me.

What shall we do that we might work the works of God? Jesus said, "This is the work of God that ye believe on Him Whom He hath sent." Anything else? Yes. He took our infirmities, and healed all our diseases. I myself am a marvel of healing. If I fail to glorify God, the stones would cry out.

Salvation is for all,
Healing is for all.
Baptism of the Holy Ghost is for all.
Reckon yourselves dead indeed unto sin, but alive unto God.
By His GRACE get the victory every time. It is possible to live holy.
He breaks the power of canceled sin,
He sets the prisoner free;
His blood can make the foulest clean,
His blood avails for me.

What shall we do that we might work the works of God? "Jesus answered and said unto them, This is the work of God, that ye believe on Him whom He hath sent."

"God hath in these last days spoken unto us by His Son, whom He hath appointed heir of all things, by whom also He made the worlds."

By the Son of God, the Word of God, all things were created. The things which are seen were not made of things which do appear. The Son of God created everything that is seen out of things that were not there when He spoke.

I want you to see that as you receive the Son of God, as Christ dwells in your heart by faith, there is the incoming of divine ability, the power of limitless possibilities within you, and that as a result of this incoming Christ, God wants to do great things through you. If we receive and accept His Son, God brings us into son ship; and not only son ship, but joint heirship, into sharing together with Him all that the Son possesses.

Every day I live I am more and more convinced that very few who are saved by the **GRACE** of God have the right conception of how great is their authority over darkness, demons, death and every power of the enemy. It is a real joy when we realize our inheritance on this line.

I was speaking like this one day, and someone said, "I have never heard anything like this before. How many months did it take you to get that sermon?" I said, "Brother, God pressed my wife from time to time to get me to preach, and I promised her I would. I used to labor hard for a week to get something together. I would give out my text and then sit down and say, 'I am done.' O brother, I have given up getting things up.

They all come down, and the sermons that come down as He wants them. Then they go back to God, with fruitage, for the Word of God declares that His Word shall not return unto Him void. If you get anything worked up, it will not stay worked up very long. But when it comes down from heaven, it produces fruit, and eternal results."

The Son of God was manifested in this world to destroy the works of the devil; and it is His purpose that the sons of God should also be manifested on this present earth to destroy the works of the devil.

Do you remember the day when the Lord laid His hand on you? You said, "I couldn't do anything but praise the Lord at that moment." Well, that was only the beginning. Where are you today? The divine plan is that you increase until you receive the measureless fullness of God. You do not have to say, "It was wonderful when I was baptized with the Holy Ghost!"

If you have to look back to the past to make me know that you are baptized, then I fear you are in a back-slidden condition. If the beginning was good, it ought to be better day by day, until everyone is fully convinced that you are filled with the fullness of God! I don't want anything less than being full, and to be fuller and fuller until I am overflowing day by day. Do you realize that if you have been created anew and begotten again by the Word of God, that there is within you the same word of power, the same light and life that the Son of God Himself had? Actually it is Jesus Christ himself living inside of you doing the works.

God wants to flow through you in marvelous power with divine utterance and **GRACE**, until your whole body is a flame of fire. God intends each soul in Pentecost to be a live wire. So many people who have been baptized with the Holy Ghost came in because there was a movement, but so many of them have become monuments, and you cannot move them.

The Baptism in the Spirit should be an ever-increasing enlargement of **GRACE**. Jump in, stop in, and never come out; for this is the Baptism which is meant to be that we are lost in it, where you only know one thing, and that is the desire of God at all times. O Father, grant unto us a real look into the glorious liberty that Thou hast designed for the children of God who are delivered from this present evil world, separated, sanctified, and made meet for Thy use; whom Thou hast designed to be filled with all Thy fullness!

Nothing has hurt me so much as this: to see so-called believers have so much unbelief in them that it is hard to move them. Everything is possible to them that believe. God will not fail to fulfill His Word, wherever you are. Suppose that all the people in the world did not believe, that would make no difference to God or his Word. It would be the same. You cannot alter God's Word. It is from everlasting to everlasting, and they who believe in it shall be like Mount Zion which cannot be moved.

God heals by the power of His Word. But the most important thing is this: Are you saved? Do you know the Lord? Are you prepared to meet God? You may be an invalid as long as you live, but you may be saved by the power of God. You may have a strong, healthy body, but may go straight to hell because you know nothing of the **GRACE** of God and salvation. Thank God, I was saved in a moment, the moment I believed. And God will do the same for you.

The Spirit of God would have us understand there is nothing that can interfere stop us getting into God's perfect blessing except our unbelief. Unbelief is a terrible hindrance. As soon as we are willing to allow the Holy Ghost to have His way, we shall find great things will happen all the time. But oh, how much of our own human reason we have to get rid of, our carnality!

How much human planning we have to become to be divorced from! What would happen right now if everyone believed God? I love the thought that God the Holy Ghost wants to emphasize truth. If we will only yield ourselves to the divine plan, He is right here to do great things, and to fulfill the promise in Joel 2.21, "Fear not, O land; be glad and rejoice: for the Lord will do great things."

How many of us truly believe the Word of God? It is easy to quote it, but it is more important to believe it than to quote it. It is very easy for me to quote**, "Now are we the sons of God,"** but it is more important for me to know whether I am a son of God, When the Son of God was on the earth He was recognized by the people who heard Him. "Never man spake like this man." His word was with power, and that word came to pass. Sometimes you have quoted, "Greater is He that is in you, than he that is in the world," and you could not tell just where to find it. But, brother, is it so?

Can demons remain in your presence? You have to be greater than demons. Disease cannot lodge in your body when you are in fellowship with God. You have to be greater than the disease. Can anything in the world stand against you and resist you? It needs to be a fact a reality in your heart that Greater Is He That Is in You than He That Is in the World?

Have faith in the fact that Christ dwells in you, and dare to act in harmony with that glorious truth. Christ said, "Have faith in God. For verily I say unto you, That whosoever shall say unto this mountain, Be thou removed, and be thou cast into the sea; and shall not doubt in his heart, but shall believe that those things which he saith shall come to pass, he shall have whatsoever he saith."

If you have been begotten of the Word and the Word is in you, the life of the Son is in you, and God wants you to fully believe this reality. He says to you, "What things soever ye desire, when ye pray, believe that ye receive them, and ye shall have them."

Faith that comes from God

The Pentecostal Evangel, 16 September 1922.Preached at Glad Tidings Assembly, San Francisco.

Read Hebrews 11.1-11. I believe that there is only one way to all the treasures of God, and that is the way of faith. By faith and faith alone in Christ do we enter into a knowledge of the attributes, become partakers of the beatitudes, and participate in the glories of our ascended Lord. All his promises are yea and Amen [2Co 1.20] to them that believe.

God would have us come to him by his own way. That is through the open door of **GRACE**. A way has been made. It is a beautiful way, and all his saints can enter in by this way and find rest. God has prescribed that the just shall live by faith. [Ro 1.17] I find that all is a failure that has not its foundation on the rock Christ Jesus. He is the only way, the truth, and the life. [Jn 14.6] The way of faith is the Christ way, receiving him in his fullness and walking in him; receiving his quickening life that fills, moves, and changes us, bringing us to a place where there is always a loud Amen in our hearts to all the will of God.

As I look into the 12th chapter of Acts, I find that the people were praying all night for Peter to come out of prison. [Ac 12.5] They had a zeal but no faith. They were to be commended for their zeal in spending their time in prayer without ceasing, but there was one thing missing. It was faith. Rhoda had more faith than the rest of them.

When the knock came to the door, she ran to it, and the moment she heard Peter's voice, she ran back again with joy saying that Peter stood before the gate. And all the people said, "You are mad. It isn't so." [Ac 12.15] But she constantly affirmed that it was even so. But they had no faith, and conjectured, "Well, God has sent his angel." [Ac 12.15] But Peter continued knocking. They had zeal but no faith. And I believe there is quite a difference.

Zacharias and Elisabeth surely wanted a son, but even when the angel came and told Zacharias he was full of unbelief. And the angel said, "Thou shalt be dumb because thou believest not my words." [Lk 1.20] But look at Mary: When the angel came to her, Mary said, "Be it unto me according to thy word." [Lk 1.38] It was her Amen to the will of God.

And God wants us with an Amen in our lives, an inward Amen, a mighty moving Amen, a God-inspired Amen, that which says, "It is, because God has spoken. It cannot be otherwise. It is impossible to be otherwise." Let us examine this fifth verse, "By faith Enoch was translated that he should not see death; and was not found, because God translated him: for before his translation he had this testimony that he pleased God." [He 11.5]

When I was in Sweden, the Lord worked mightily. After one or two meetings the leaders called me and said, “We have heard very strange things about you, and we would like to know if they are true. We can see that God is with you, and that God is moving, and we know that this will be a great blessing to Sweden.” “Well,” I said, “what is it?” “Well,” they said, “we have heard from good authority that you preach that you have the resurrection body.”

When I was in France I had an interpreter that believed this thing, and I found out after I had preached once or twice through the interpreter that she gave her own expressions. And of course I did not know. I said to these brethren, “I tell you what my personal convictions are. I believe that if I had the testimony of Enoch I should be taken. I believe that the moment Enoch had the testimony that he pleased God, off he went.”

I pray that God will so quicken our faith, for translation is in the mind of God; but remember that translation comes on the line of holy obedience and a walk that is pleasing to God. This was true of Enoch. And I believe that we must have a like walk with God in the Spirit, having communion with him, living under his divine smile; and I pray that God by his Spirit may so move us that we will be where Enoch was when he walked with God.

There are two kinds of faith. There is the natural faith. But the supernatural faith is the gift of God. In Acts 26.18, Paul is telling Agrippa of what the Lord said to him in commissioning him: “To open their eyes, and to turn them from darkness to light, from the power of Satan unto God, that they may receive forgiveness of sins, and inheritance among them which are sanctified by faith that is in me.” [Ac 26.18]

Is that the faith of Paul? No, it is the faith that the Holy Ghost is giving. It is the faith that he brings to us as we press in and on with God. I want to put before you this difference between our faith and the faith of Jesus. Our faith comes to an end. Most people in this place have come to where they have said, “Lord, I can go no further, I have gone so far and I can go no further. I have used all the faith I have, and I have just to stop now and wait.”

I remember one day being in Lancashire, and going round to see some sick people. I was taken into a house where there was a young woman lying on a bed, a very helpless case. The reason had gone, and many things were manifested there which were satanic and I knew it. She was only a young woman, a beautiful child. The husband, quite a young man, came in with the baby, and he leaned over to kiss the wife. The moment he did, she threw herself over on the other side, just as a lunatic would do. That was very heart-breaking. Then he took the baby and pressed the baby's lips to the mother. Again another wild kind of thing happened.

I asked one who was attending her, "Have you anybody to help spiritually?" "Oh," they said, "we have had everything." "But," I said, "Have you no spiritual help?" Her husband stormed out and said, "Help? You think that we believe in God after we have had seven weeks of no sleep and maniac conditions? You think that we believe God? You are mistaken. You have come to the wrong house."

Then a young woman of about 18 or so just grinned at me and passed out of the door, and that finished the whole business. That brought me to a place of great compassion for the woman. Something had to be done, no matter what it was. Then with my faith I began to penetrate the heavens in prayer. I was soon out of that house looking a place to pray. I will tell you that I have never seen a man get anything from God who prayed on the earth. If you get anything from God you will have to pray into heaven, for it is all there.

If you are living in the earth realm and expect things from heaven, they will never come. I saw in the presence of God the limitations of my faith, but there came another faith, a faith that could not be denied, a faith that took the promise. It is a faith that believed God's word. And I came from that presence back again to earth, but not the same man under the conditions confronting me. God gave me a faith that could shake hell and everything in it.

I said, **"Come out of her in the name of Jesus!"** And she rolled over and fell asleep. She awakened 14 hours later, perfectly sane and perfectly whole. There is a process we must go through. Enoch walked with God. That was the result of all of those years as he was penetrating, and going through and laying hold, and believing and seeing and getting into perfect harmony with God. He began to move toward heaven. At last it was not possible for him to stop any longer. Oh hallelujah!

In the 15th chapter of 1 Corinthians we read of the body being "sown with dishonor," to be raised in power. [1Co 15.43] It seems to me that as we are looking for translation, that the Lord would have us know something of that power now on earth He would have us walk in that power, so that we should not be in dishonor.

Enoch walked with God. [Ge 5.24] God wants to change the condition of saints so that they walk with him and talk with him now. I don't want to build anything upon myself, but it is true that if you find me not having a conversation with man, you will most likely find me in conversation with God.

There is one thing that God has given me from my youth up: A taste and relish for my bible. I can say before God, I have never read a book but my bible, so I know nothing about books. It seems better to me to get the book of books for food for your soul, for the strengthening of your faith and the building up of your character in God, [1Th 3.13] so that all the time you are being changed and made meet to walk with God. "Without faith it is impossible to please him; for he that cometh to God must believe that he is, and that he is a rewarder of them that diligently seek him." [He 11.6]

I can see that it is impossible to please God on any position but faith, for everything that is not of faith is sin. [Ro 14.23] God wants us to see that the plan of faith is the heart and principle of God. In this connection I love to keep in my thoughts the beautiful words in the second verse of the 12th chapter of Hebrews: "Looking unto Jesus, the author and finisher of our faith." [He 12.2] He is the author of our faith. God worked through him for the forming of the worlds.

All things were made by him, and without him was not anything made that was made. [Jn 1.3] And because of the exceeding abundant joy of providing for us so great salvation, [He 2.3] he became the author of a living faith. And through this principle of living faith, looking unto him who is the author and finisher of our faith, we are changed into the same image from glory to glory, even by the Spirit of the Lord. [2Co 3.18]

God has something better for you than you have ever had in the past. Come out into all the fullness of faith and power and life and victory that he is willing to provide, as you forget the things of the past, and press right on for the prize of his calling in Christ Jesus. [Pp 3.13-14]

Smith - Don't ever indulge in unprofitable conversation. Feed on the Word of God.

"Show us the law."

You say, "Show us the law." I will, Come It is found in the seventh chapter of Romans, the 25th verse: "I thank God through Jesus So then with the mind I myself serve the the law of God; but with the flesh the law of sin."

Is it a sin to work? No, it is not a sin. Work is ordained by God. It is an honor to work. But I find that there are two ways to work. One is working in the flesh, but the child of God should not allow himself to come into the flesh when God leads him in the Spirit. God wants to show you that there is a place where you can live in the Spirit and not be subject to the flesh. Live in the Spirit till sin has no dominion. "That as sin hath reigned unto death, even so might **GRACE** reign through righteousness unto eternal life by Jesus Christ our Lord." (Rom. 5.) Reigning in life.

There is probably very few here who, if they are saved are reigning in life. There is satanic power reigning, and yet God wants you to know that you have to believe that God made you like Himself and Jesus bought back for us in the Garden of Gethsemane everything that was lost in the Garden of Eden, and restored it to us by his agony and suffering. He bought our blessed redemption. When we think of "redemption," I wonder if there is anything greater than the Garden of Eden, when Adam and Eve had fellowship with God, and He came down and walked with them in the cool of the evening. Is there anything greater?

Yes, redemption is greater. How? Anything that is local is never so great. When God was in the Garden Adam was local; but the moment a man is born again he is free, and lives in heavenly places. He has no destination except glory. Redemption is greater than the Garden and God wants you to know that He wants you to come into this glorious redemption, not only for the salvation of your soul, but also for your body to know that it is redeemed from the curse of the law. To know that you have been made free. To know that God's Son has set you free. Hallelujah!

Free from the law of sin and death! How is it accomplished? The third verse tells us. Let us look at it. It is a master verse. "For what the law could not do in that it was weak through the flesh, God, sending His Son in the likeness of sinful flesh and for sin, condemned sin in the flesh, that the righteousness of the law might be fulfilled in us who walk not after the flesh but after the Spirit." Righteousness fulfilled in us! Brother! Sister! I tell you there is a redemption and there is an atonement in Christ. The personality of Christ that dwells in you. There is a God-likeness for you to attain to and a blessed resemblance of Christ in you, if you will believe the Word of God. The Word is sufficient for you; eat it; devour it; it is the Living Word of God.

Jesus was manifested to destroy the works of the devil. God so manifested His fullness in Jesus that He walked this earth glorified and filled with God. In the first place, He was with God and was called "the Word." In the second place, He and God were so "One" in their operation that they said it was "God"; and then the harmony of oneness was so manifested that there was nothing done 'without the other. They co-operated in the working of power.

Then you must see that before the foundation of the world this plan of redemption was all completed, and set in order before the Fall; and then notice that this redemption had to be so mighty, and to redeem us all so perfectly, that there should be no lack in the whole redemption. Let us see how it comes about. First He became flesh and then with the power of the Holy Ghost He became the expression of the Word.

You and I are born of the incorruptible Word of God. By His personality and his nature. Ye are begotten of God and are not your own. You are now incarnated, and you need to believe you have passed from death unto life and become a joint heir with Christ, in the measure that you believe His Word. The natural flesh has been changed for a new order; the first order was the Adamic order, the last order is Christ in us which is the new order. And now you become changed by a power of Christ existing in our earthly body. A power which will never die: it can never see corruption, and it cannot be lost. If you are born of God, you are born by the power of the Word and not of man.

I want you to know that you are born of a power which exists in you, the power of which God took and made the world that we live in. It is the law of the Spirit of life in Christ that makes us free from the law of sin and death. Will you accept it? I want you all to see that what I have been preaching for the last two weeks in this place is all supernatural. Divine life, divine healing, satanic powers. If will only believe it you are secure, for there is a greater power in you than in all the world. Power over pain; power over death. Power over sickness and disease. Power over the natural world.

There are two laws. Let us look at the law without the Holy Spirit, the law of sin. Here is a man to-night who has never known regeneration, he is led captive by the Devil at his will. There is no power that can convert the heart of a man but Christ. Men try without Christ. Science tries without Christ. Many have tried without Christ; but all are left hopelessly headed to hell without Christ. Nothing can deliver you but the Blood of the Lamb. "Free from the law of sin and death by the Spirit of life in Christ Jesus."

Clean hearts, and pure lives are what God requires. Brothers, the carnal life is not subject to the will of God, neither indeed can be. Carnality is selfishness and uncleanness. It cannot be subject to God; it will not believe; it interferes in gets between you and God. It binds you and keeps you in bondage; but, beloved, God destroys carnality; He destroys the work of the flesh. How? By a new life which is so much better and by a peace that passes all understanding; by a joy which is unspeakable and full of glory which cannot be told our verbally expressed.

Everything that God does is too big to tell. His **GRACE** is too big. His love is too big. Why it takes all of heaven to even begin to reveal these truths. His salvation is too big to be told in which one cannot fully understand our grasp. It is so vast, mighty and wonderful, "in God;" but God gives us the power to understand it. Yes, of course, He does. Do you not know that ours is an abundant God? His love is far exceeding and abundant above all that we can ask or think. Hear!

After you were illuminated, enlightened (Glory to God) then you were quickened by the Spirit. Now we are looking forward to a day of rapture, when we will be caught up .and lifted into the presence of God. You cannot think of God on any small line. God's positions are magnificent and wonderful, glorious. God can manifest them in our hearts with a greater fullness than we are able to express.

Let me touch an important point; Christ Jesus has borne the Cross for us and there is no need for us to bear his cross. He has borne the curse, for "cursed is every one that hangeth upon a tree." The curse covered everything. When Christ was in the grave, the Word says that He was raised from the grave by the operation of God through the Spirit.

He was quickened by the Spirit in the grave, and so the same Spirit dwelling in you shall quicken your mortal bodies. Jesus rose by the quickening power of the Holy Ghost, "But if the Spirit of Him that raised up Jesus from the dead dwell in you, He that raised up Christ from the dead shall also quicken your mortal bodies." What does it mean? Now, it is not an immortal body you have received. Immortality can only be obtained in the resurrection, at the last trumpet.

He will quicken your mortal body. If you will allow Jesus to have control of your bodies, you will find that His Spirit will quicken you, will lose you; He will show you that it is the mortal body that has to be quickened. Talk about Divine Healing! You discover these realities within the Scriptures for they are full of divine healing.

Everyone that is healed by the power of God and especially the believers will take their healing as an incentive to make them purer and holier. If Divine Healing was only to make you whole, it would be worth nothing. Divine Healing is a Divine act of the providence of God coming into your mortal bodies and touching them with his Almightiness. Could you remain the same after his divine touch? No, me, you will go out to worship and serve God.

That is why I am here today preaching to you because of the healing of God in this mortal body. I am not here to build an organization. I see the fact that God would have me preach so that everyone who hears me should go back to his own home with energy and the power of God and the revelation of Jesus Christ. It is a simple fact that the more you are held in bondage, the more you shut your eyes to the truth. The Bible becomes meaningless instead of life and joy as it is meant to be. The moment you yield yourself, the Bible becomes a new Book; it becomes "Revelation," so that we have the fullness of redemption going right through our bodies in every fiber of our being. Filled with all the fullness of the Godhead bodily.

Filled with God! Yes, filled with God, Pardoned and cleansed and filled with God. Filled with God! Yes, filled with God, Emptied of self and filled with God!

"Mother," she said, "I am being healed. Take these things off please take them all off." The mother loosed the straps and bands and then the child said, "Mother, I am sure I am healed. Take these off." She had straps on her legs and an iron on her foot about 3½ inches deep. She asked her mother to unstrap her. Her mother took off the straps. There were no dry eyes in any of the people that were there that day as they saw that girl walk about with legs just as normal as when she was born. God healed her right away. What did it? She had cried, "Please, gentleman, come to me," and her longing was coupled with faith. May the Lord help us to be just like a simple child.

God has hidden these things from the wise and prudent, but He reveals them to babes. There is something in childlike faith in God that makes us dare to believe, and then to act. Whatever there is in your life that is bound, the name of Jesus and the power of that name will break it if you will only believe. Christ says, "If ye shall ask any thing in my name, I will do it." God will be glorified in Christ when you receive the overflowing life that comes from Christ in response to your faith.

Dare to believe. Do you think that the truth is put into the Word and revealed it is to mock you? Don't you see that God really means that you should live in this world to relieve those who were oppressed of the devil? God answers us so that we shall be quickened, be molded afresh, that the Word of God shall change everything that needs to be changed, both in us and in others, as we dare to believe and as we command things to be done in the name of Jesus. "Whosoever shall say unto this mountain, Be thou removed, and be thou cast into the sea; and shall not doubt in his heart, but shall believe that those things which he saith shall come to pass, he shall have whatsoever he saith."

"Have you received the Holy Ghost since you believed?" "Are you filled with divine power?"

This is the heritage of the Church, to be so endued with power that God can lay His hand upon any member at any time to do His perfect will. There is no stopping the Spirit-filled life: we begin at the Cross, the place of ridicule, terrible suffering, shame, and death, and that very death brings the power of resurrection life; and, being filled with the Holy Spirit, we go on "from glory to glory." Let us not forget that possessing the Baptism in the Holy Spirit, means there must be an "ever-increasing" holiness. How the Church needs divine unction—God's presence and power so manifested that the world will know it is God in us. The people know when the tide is flowing; they also know when it is ebbing.

The necessity that seven men be chosen for the position of "serving tables" was very evident. The disciples knew that these seven men were men ready for active service, and so they chose them. In the 5th verse, we read: "And the saying pleased the whole multitude, and they chose Stephen, a man full of faith and of the Holy Ghost, and Philip."

There were others, of course, but Stephen and Philip stand out most prominently in the Scriptures. Philip was a man so filled with the Holy Ghost that a revival always followed wherever he went. Stephen was a man so filled with divine power, that although serving tables might have been all right in the minds of the other disciples, yet, God had a greater vision for him—a baptism of fire, of power and divine unction, that took him on and on to the conclusion of his life, until he saw right into the open heavens.

Had we been there with the disciples at that time, I believe we should have heard them saying to each other, "Look here! Neither Stephen nor Philip are doing the work we called them to. If they do not attend to business, we shall have to get someone else!" That was the carnal way of thinking, but divine order is far above our fleshly planning. When we please God in our daily service, we shall always find in operation the fact "that everyone who is faithful in little, God will make faithful in much."

We have such an example right here—a man chosen to "serve tables," having such a revelation of the mind of Christ and of the depth and height of God, that there was no stopping in his experience, but a going forward with leaps and bounds. Beloved, there is a race to be run, there is a crown to be won; we cannot stand still! I say unto you, be vigilant! Be vigilant! "Let no man take thy crown!"

God has privileged us in Christ Jesus to live above the ordinary human plane of life. Those who want to be ordinary, and live on a lower plane, can do so; but as for me, I will not! For the same unction, the same zeal, the same Holy Ghost power is at our command as was at the command of Stephen and the apostles. We have the same God that Abraham had, that Elijah had, and we need not come behind in any gift or **GRACE**. We may not possess the gifts, as abiding gifts, but as we are full of the Holy Ghost and divine unction, it is possible, when there is need, for God to manifest every gift of the Spirit through us. As I have already said, I do not mean by this that we should necessarily possess the gifts permanently, but there should be a manifestation of the gifts as God may choose to use us.

This ordinary man Stephen became mighty under the Holy Ghost anointing, until he stands supreme, in many ways, among the Apostles—"And Stephen full of faith and power, did great wonders and miracles among the people." As we go deeper in God, He enlarges our conception and places before us a wide-open door; and I am not surprised that this man chosen to "serve tables" was afterwards called to a higher plane. "What do you mean?" you may ask. "Did he quit this service?" No! But he was lost in the power of God.

He lost sight of everything in the natural, and steadfastly fixed his gaze upon Jesus, "the author and finisher of our faith," until he was transformed into a shining light in the kingdom of God, Oh that we might be awakened to believe His word, to understand the mind of the Spirit, for there is an inner place of whiteness and purity where we can "see God." Stephen was just as ordinary a man as you and I, but he was in the place where God could so move upon him that he, in turn, could move all before him. He began in a most humble place, and ended in a blaze of glory. Beloved, dare to believe Christ!

As you go on in this life of the Spirit, you will find that the devil will begin to get restless and there will be a stir in the synagogue; it was so with Stephen. Any amount of people may be found in the "synagogue," who are very proper in a worldly sense—always correctly dressed, the elite of the land, welcoming into the church everything but the power of God. Let us read what God says about them:

"Then there arose certain in the synagogue, which is called the

Synagogue of the Libertines, and Cyrenians, and Alexandrians ... disputing with Stephen, and they were not able to resist the wisdom and the spirit by which he spake."

"The Libertines" could not stand the truth of God. With these opponents, Stephen found himself in the same predicament as the blind man whom Jesus healed. As soon as the blind man's eyes were opened they shut him out of the synagogue. They will not have anybody in the "synagogue" with their eyes open; as soon as you receive spiritual eyesight, out you go!

These Libertines, Cyrenians, and Alexandrians, rose up full of wrath in the very place where they should have been full of the power of God, full of love divine, and reverence for the Holy Ghost; they rose up against Stephen, this man "full of the Holy Ghost." Beloved, if there is anything in your life that in any way resists the power of the Holy Ghost and the entrance of His word into your heart and life, drop on your knees and CRY ALOUD for mercy! When the Spirit of God is brooding over your heart's door, do not resist Him but open your heart to the touch of God, There is a resisting "unto blood" striving against sin, and there is a resisting of the Holy Ghost that will drive you into sin.

Stephen spoke with divine Holy Ghost wisdom; where he was, things began to move. You will find that there is always a moving when the Holy Spirit has control. These people were brought under conviction by the message of Stephen, but they resisted, they did anything and everything to stifle that conviction. Not only did they lie, but they got others to lie against this man, who would have laid down his life for any one of them. Stephen was used to heal the sick, perform miracles, and yet they brought false accusations against him. What effect did it have on Stephen?

"And all that sat in the council, looking steadfastly at him, saw his face as it had been the face of an angel."

Something had happened in the life of this man, chosen for menial service, and he became mighty for God. How was it accomplished in him? It was because his aim was high; faithful in little, God brought him to full fruition. Under the inspiration of divine power by which he spoke, they could not but listen,—even the angels listened, as with holy prophetic utterance he spoke before that council.

Beginning with Abraham and Moses, he continued unfolding the truth. What a marvelous exhortation! Take your Bibles and read it, "listen in" as the angels listened in. As light upon light, truth upon truth, revelation upon revelation, found its way into their calloused hearts, they gazed at him in astonishment; their hearts perhaps became warm at times, and they may have said, "Truly, this man is sent of God,"—but when he hurled at them the truth:

"Ye stiffnecked and uncircumcised in heart and ears, ye do always resist the Holy Ghost; as your fathers did, so do ye. Which of the prophets have not your fathers persecuted? And they have slain them which showed before of the coming of the Just One; of whom ye have been now the betrayers and murderers; who have received the law by the disposition of angels, and have not kept it."—then what happened? These men were moved; they were "pricked to the heart, and gnashed upon him with their teeth."

There are two marvelous occasions* in the Scriptures where the people were "pricked to the heart." In the second chapter of the Acts of the Apostles, 37th verse, after Peter had delivered that inspired sermon on the Day of Pentecost, the people were "pricked to the heart" with conviction, and there were added to the Church three thousand souls.

Here is Stephen, speaking under the inspiration of the Holy Ghost, and the men of this council being "pricked to the heart" rise up as one man to slay him. As you go down through this chapter, from the 55th verse, what a picture you have before you. As I close my eyes, I can get a vision of this scene in every detail—the howling mob with their vengeful, murderous spirit, ready to devour this holy man, and he "being full of the Holy Ghost," gazed steadfastly into heaven. What did he see there? From his place of helplessness, he looked up and said:

"Behold, I see the heavens opened, and the Son of Man standing at the right hand of God."

Is that the position that Jesus went to take? No! He went to "sit" at the right hand of the Father; but in behalf of the first martyr, in behalf of the man with that burning flame of Holy Ghost power, God's Son stood up in honorary testimony of him who, called to serve tables, was faithful unto death. But is that all? No! I am so glad that it is not all. As the stones came flying at him, pounding his body, crushing his bones, striking his temple, mangling his beautiful face, what happened?

How did this scene end? With that sublime, upward look, this man chosen for an ordinary task but filled with the Holy Ghost, was so moved upon by God that he finished his earthly work in a blaze of glory, magnifying God with his latest breath. Looking up into the face of His Master, he said:"Lord Jesus, forgive them! Lay not this sin to their charge!" When he had said this, he fell asleep.

Friends, it is worth dying a thousand deaths to gain that spirit. My God! What a divine ending to the life and testimony of a man that was "chosen to serve tables." Without the Holy Ghost none of this would have been possible

Gifts of Christ, The

To each one of us, GRACE was given according to the measure of Christ's gift. Scripture reading: Ephesians 4:1-16

The apostle Paul spoke about the **GRACE** and the gifts of Christ, not the gifts of the Holy Spirit, but the gifts of Christ. You are joined to Christ's body the moment you believe. For instance, some of you may have children, and they have different names, but the moment they appeared in the world, they were in your family. The moment they were born, they became a part of your family and began to participate.

The moment you are born of God, you are in the family, and you are in the body, as He is in the body, and you are in the body collectively and particularly. After you come into the body, then the body has to receive the sealing of the promise, or the fulfillment of the promise, that Christ will be in you, reigning in you mightily. The Holy Spirit will come to unveil the King in all His glory so that He might reign as King there, the Holy Spirit serving in every way to make Him King.

You are in the body. The Holy Spirit gives gifts to the body. Living in this holy order, you may find that revelation comes to you and makes you a prophet. Some of you may have a clear understanding that you have been called into apostleship. Some of you may have perfect knowledge that you are to be pastors. When you come to be sealed with the Spirit of promise, then you find out that Jesus is pleased and gives gifts so that the church might come into a perfect position of being so blended together that there could be no division. Jesus wants His church to be a perfect body--perfect in stature, perfect in oneness in Him.

I have been speaking to this end: that you may see the calling that Paul was speaking about--humility of mind, meekness of spirit, knowing that God is in you and through you, knowing that the power of the Spirit is mightily bringing you to the place where not only the gifts of the Spirit but also the gifts of Christ have been given to you, making you eligible for the great work you have to do.

My purpose is not to tell what God has for you in the future. Press in now, and claim your rights. Let the Lord Jesus be so glorified that He will make you fruit-bearers--strong in power, giving glory to God, having "no confidence in the flesh" (Phil. 3:3) but being separated from natural things, now in the Spirit, living fully in the will of God.

Thought for today: Let your whole soul reach out unto God; dare to breathe in heaven; dare to be awakened to all God's mind; listen to the language of the Holy Spirit.

Gift of discerning of spirits

Subtitled, "Beware of deceiving voices."

I want to speak to you this morning on the subject of the Gifts. These are days when all the saints need to be furnished with the **GRACE**s and the gifts of the Spirit, and we must keep in mind that it is impossible to find the gifts of the Spirit made manifest without the **GRACE**s; they always work harmoniously, and the person filled with the power of the Spirit will find that the one will help the other to strengthen the person in the needy hour.

We need a clear knowledge of the Word of God; we cannot put too much emphasis on that. Then I want to say also that God demands of every believer who has been baptized in the Holy Spirit that he should have some "acts" and if you do not have them, you had better get face to face with God and demand from Him your acts.

When I was baptized in the Holy Ghost I received from God an utterance as all people do when they receive the Baptism; it was not an earthly language, but heavenly, and I was satisfied that God had granted unto me the Comforter, the Holy Ghost. But for nine months after that I never spoke in tongues and then God gave me the gift of tongues. I cannot say that I was very anxious or very hungry in asking for this as I was longing more that I might speak as the Spirit gave utterance, but God knew what I needed to be able to help others along this line.

The next evening after I had received the gift of tongues, I was walking down the road, loaded with bundles and God came upon me mightily, and tongues began to come forth in terrific force. I walked down the road without stopping, but soon I began to realize that this had no intelligence in it for me and neither was it a profit to anyone else. There were some men working in a garden nearby and as soon as they heard this peculiar noise they stuck their heads through the fence to find out where it was coming from. Right then I said to God,

“I will not leave till you give me the interpretation. You have poured forth a language, now you must interpret,” and suddenly God gave the interpretation, and that message has been fulfilled to the very letter over and over again. Since that time I have always claimed the right to have the interpretation. I believe God wants us to be definite and I don’t want you to run away with any wrong impression; if you come out on anything else but a definite side, then God has not spoken. I am not here to make children but men and women of you, men and women after the mind of God; in spirit, we must be children, but in understanding, we must be men and women.

So if God says to us that we must understand spiritual gifts you put your name right under that “must” and apply it as your very own. I believe as long as you dwell in the Spirit it is impossible for you ever to become twisted. You never heard of a Roman Catholic being filled with the Spirit as long as he was a Roman Catholic;* the same is true of a Russellite,* or a man who believes in New Theology.* Scripture is clearly against it for it says that no man can call Jesus, Lord except by the Holy Ghost and every man who has the Holy Ghost believes all the Bible. The man who is filled with the Holy Ghost is filled with that which gave the Bible; he is filled with the very matter of the Bible for the Word is Christ, and the Holy Ghost has come to manifest Christ.

You will always find that all the blessings and all the manifestations of the power, of God which you receive, always come on the line of faith; every saved person is saved by faith and saving faith is not something which you can take down and then hang up again. The saving faith of God is a permanent thing which God gave and which will remain with you.

It is a gift, and, because of that, I know that everyone in this place can choose that gift, but you have to come into that blessing under the shadow of the blood and claim your rights in the Scriptures. I want to say, however, that no man can come to God and claim His blessings if he knows that God can put His finger on any sin in his life. God never will hear sinners and if you expect any blessings don't come to Him with sin in your life. When a man repents God is gracious and full of mercy and forgives all sin and that man can begin from that moment with the knowledge that God has removed the past from him.

There are two points in this 12th chapter of Corinthians which have helped me more than anything else, and I am sure they will help you; one is this—Paul prayed for a keen conscience and also that he might not have his conscience seared. Do you know that a keen conscience is the greatest blessing anyone can have? A keen conscience is one which is easily disturbed, one which is easily broken and brought to repentance before God, one which will not permit you to sleep until everything is made right with your brother; a keen conscience is a place where God reigns supreme as a Refiner of fire.

What is a seared conscience? It is a conscience which once was keen, but the person got out of the will of God and failed to repent after sinning. God could not come in before that sin was undone, and the person went on sinning until he got to the place where he thought he had a right to sin. This is the most horrible place to be in. I pray that God will keep us in the place where we may hear His voice and heed it.

I want you to notice that I am trying to show you, by the **GRACE** of God, that if you keep in the fullness of the Spirit, you will have such a revelation of the Word of God in your life that it will save you and keep you from stumbling**. "The angel of the Lord encampeth round about them that fear Him and delivereth him."** And, **"The steps of a good man are ordered of the Lord."** He shall hide thee in the secret place, in the cleft of the rock, and in the time of adversity He shall raise a standard against the enemy. It is the Lord who reigns supreme over His household who's House ye are, His establishment, and ye shall not be moved. This means that God establishes His Kingdom in you and me. Oh, how we need to be filled with the joy of the Lord which is our strength and to have a fresh inflow of His life and love!

A man who is filled with the Spirit must have three things flowing through him; the ministration, operation, and manifestation of the Spirit. It is to your detriment if you have not these three working in your life. If you are to keep your path all clear and bright, you must remain steadfast, unmovable, always abounding in the work of the Lord.

We must abound in hope, rejoice in tribulation and then God will make straight paths for our feet. The man who has faith is never ruffled; he does not run off as if he had been shot, but he is always resting, knowing that God is over all. We must understand these principles because faith is God. Faith is the knowledge of God. Faith is that which lays hold, which will not let go. Faith is inwrought God; faith is God inwrought; faith is that which brings heaven on earth and lives in it.

The word which God would bring before us this morning is found in the 10th verse of the 12th chapter of 1st Corinthians: "To another the working of miracles; to another prophecy; to another discerning of spirits; to another divers kinds of tongues; to another the interpretation of tongues." The first we have to deal with is the discerning of spirits. Perhaps this is the most necessary thing in this present day.

In connection with this, we must speak on the different kinds of voices for so many people are disturbed by voices. They have an idea that it is the voice of God but begin to find themselves in difficulty as a result of obeying that voice. We are told in the 4th chapter of the Epistle of John that we must be able to discern the spirits. "Beloved, believe not every spirit but try the spirits, whether they are of God." So God would have us know the difference between false prophecy and the spiritual, divinely appointed prophecy.

There are voices of all descriptions. I have for some time had to deal with people along this line. If ever you find a person under the power of the evil one you will find that that spirit will never acknowledge that Jesus came in the flesh; so if you want to test any spirit you can tell by that, because often the voice will come right out and say, "No, Jesus did not come in the flesh," and every spirit that confesses not that Jesus came in the flesh is not of God. In the 4th chapter of Luke, we see how Jesus dispelled the power of Satan. If you test a false spirit by the inward presence, it will disturb the peace of God, and you will know it is of Satan. Make that thing worship the Christ with, and the devil will flee.

No person need to be captured at any time with an evil thought because we are to understand the wiles of the devil. Many people are disturbed with thoughts, evil thoughts which usually come early in the morning, but if these are tested the person will always find that they will deny that Jesus came in the flesh. Perhaps some will ask, "Is not that a gift of the Spirit to discern the spirits?"

Yes, it is a gift, but I want to say right here that if you are living in the fullness of the Spirit, you will have this gift at any moment when needed. It will not be an abiding gift, just a gift for the needy moment. Every one of you without exception will find that as you go on and on with God you will have to be in the Spirit of God or you will be a failure. It is not possible to love the present evil world and have the Holy Ghost within; you cannot love carnality and have the Holy Ghost. When the Holy Ghost comes in, every evil power will be dispelled until your whole body is free from sin and death. Oh you need to be filled with the Holy Ghost to be ready at any moment for Satan's power!

I want to show you how terribly deceiving these voices can be. One time when I was ministering in a certain place, two young ladies came into the room about five o'clock in the afternoon, and instantly we perceived that something had taken place. One of them had on white kid gloves which were spotted with blood. The excitement of these two ladies was such that one could see there was no peace abiding within.

If ever you get out of the will of God and Satan comes in you will find there is no rest. I have learned that if anything disturbs my peace, it is always Satanic. Neither one of these girls was willing to tell us what had happened. Now that is another way to test voices; God never reveals anything that you cannot tell on the housetop; everything God says to you, you can reach out and if you feel you dare not tell what you have heard this voice telling you, you may be sure it is evil.

I know people pride themselves that God speaks to them differently from everyone else; if ever you get to that place you are on the wrong track, you are going one notch downward. It is the false pride of the devil. Some people seem to believe that the devil comes around only with horns and a long tail, big ears, and big eyes. Don't you believe it; the devil cast out of heaven because of his pride, and you must never forget that he is called the "angel of light." He has never lost that pride. And to you ministers, I would say that whenever a person comes to you and says, "I never heard a man preach like you," you can make sure that is the voice of the devil every time.

These two girls were working in a telegraph station, and Satan came as an angel of light to one saying, "If you obey me, I will make you the biggest and the best preacher in the world." Now God never speaks that way. The girl became so excited about this and was sure it was the voice of God. She asked off from work for an hour, and she became more excited as the voice repeated those words over and over; she got so worked up that she dug her nails into her flesh until the blood came.

Then the voice further said to her, "You go to the station at 7:30 and, a train will come in. Buy two tickets. Don't tell anyone what I have said except your sister. You will find a train leaving for Glasgow at 7:32. When you have purchased the two tickets, you will have sixpence over." Sure enough, after she had the two tickets, she had the sixpence left. "Oh," you say, "that surely was the Lord speaking to her." Then another part of the message came true for the train came in exactly at 7:32.

She was to find in one of the coaches a gentleman sitting with his back to the engine and this man was to have all the money that the girl wanted and was to have it deposited in a certain bank. It needed only brains to think it out, but the people who get to that place do not use their brains and will not let anyone else think for them. They say, "Don't you try to stop me for no one can stop me.

You do not need to talk to me; you have not had the Lord speak to you." This is a dangerous place.

These two girls went up and down the coach, the full length of the railway train and failed to find anyone fitting that description. Someone said she had better come down for the next train, so they stayed there until nine o'clock. Then the voice said to her, "Now that I have found you will obey me, I will make you the best and biggest missionary in the world." You have no idea what it took to get those two girls out of that awful delusion, but God prevailed, and both are now on the mission field doing good work. Never be unwilling to take advice for God has other people who know His voice and you must be willing to learn.

While ministering in another place I had a letter from York, England, saying that they had about fourteen people who were seeking to be filled with the Holy Spirit. They were asking me to come and give them a few addresses on this important subject. So I went, and upon arriving, I heard the best news anyone could wish to hear. The people said, "We have had one of the finest men to join us that you have ever seen; he is a fine teacher. We will just wait and see if he receives the Baptism and then we are thinking of keeping him here as pastor." That was all very good. The preaching went on, and God manifested Himself; the power of God came down, and people began seeking. About 10:30 that night we saw this promising young man laid out under the power of God.

The Saints could hardly keep quiet; they rejoiced so over God's dealings. They would say, "Now we have him; when he receives his baptism we will have the best man," and they were so jubilant. Everything went well and then about 11:30 the power of God slew him, and divine utterance came forth, and we were all so glad and had a good time praising God. When he was getting ready to go home, the saints came around and said, "Oh, we are so glad you got through! You certainly are the best teacher." And then one woman went up to him and said, "I shouldn't wonder if you were not the second John the Baptist." That night, while on his way home, the devil came to this young man and said, "I shouldn't wonder if you were the second John the Baptist."

But he was able to throw it off and would have nothing to do with the voice. But listen, in the middle of the night, the devil awakened him, "You are John the Baptist. Arise." He was unable to shake that off, and the next day he went up and down the street shouting, "I am John the Baptist." Who spoiled him? The saints. Who was to blame for his downfall? Those people who should have had more sense. Never tell a preacher how wonderful he is. He knows he is nothing if he is in the right place, and don't you try to make him something.

If you do, you will get out of the will of the Lord and get him out, too. Is there deliverance for these people? Oh, how we need to distinguish the voice of God from that of Satan. We need to know that God the Holy Ghost has a better plan for us than that. I have met such wrecks. I came across one of the finest men in the ministry, such a good teacher who had been blessed to all the assemblies. It makes me weep now to think of it. You couldn't teach him anything, and if you spoke to him he would tell you that God had not spoken to you as to him, adding, and "Don't you know that God has made me a prophet?" You couldn't move him.

The important point is, how can we tell the difference between the voice of Satan and the voice of God? It is very simple. If you don't aspire to be something you will never get into that dangerous place; it is when your own heart desires it that the devil can switch you there.

Never desire to be anything. For in the true Christian's life no man wants to be anything but his only desire is to be one with Christ, to be his all and in all. It is to live only for the glory of God, to be filled with the power of God, to be kept at all times in that place where you know you are nothing and can do nothing but for the **GRACE** of God.

If you ever think you are anything of importance consider Jesus and if you consider Jesus you will find there is no room for exaltation, only brokenness of heart and contriteness of spirit. The Kingdom of God is brought forth in righteousness and truth. What is the truth? Truth says that Jesus is the Way; truth says that Jesus is the ideal for us, and we must be like Him; no man who truly follows Jesus and reads the words in Philippians can say any more about himself. Jesus who was the Son of God made Himself of no reputation, took on Himself the form of a servant and humbled Himself even to the death of the cross.

Discerning of Spirits. How much we need it! Sometimes I have been shut in for weeks with demon-possessed men, and in the middle of the night-watches these evil spirits have jumped upon me, but in the midst of it, I have held my ground for God and prayed for the man right into perfect deliverance. I am reminded of one man I knew. I was shut in for weeks with him and every time an evil spirit was cast out of him it leaped on me.

The last one to be cast laid hold of me so that I had to deliver myself first before I could deliver anyone else. In this situation, the evil spirits came out of this man and bound me so that I had to stand still. I couldn't move, and the man who was possessed would stand and look at me. As I commanded the evil spirit to leave I would be free again. That man today is perfectly delivered and preaching the Gospel.

It took someone who would lay hold of God and not let go until the work was completed. I have learned many things by experience, and if I can make you see this morning that you never will be anything I will be able to get something done here. Anything that is not for the glory of God is not worth having. God sees in secret and will reward openly. We will have to have secret power with God. We will have to meet God face to face in the closet, and then we can come out strong for Him.

From the author Dr. Michael H Yeager's

GRACE IS NOT SIMPLY ABOUT GOD's FAVOUR

People say: I'm God's favorite. But God does not have favorites based simply upon a prayer they prayed. The Bible says God is not a respect of people. That's what the Scripture says. So all of this teaching that Grace is God giving us favor simply because we have prayed a prayer of salvation is simply and completely wrong!

But Pastor Mike there are Scriptures that say that God respects his people. Now, this is where it is extremely important that we rightly discern the WORD of truth. God's word cannot contradict itself. So let's look at this truth first based upon the fact that the Scripture says **God is not a respecter of people**. The color of your skin, your education, your age, your sex, your position in life does not give you greater or lesser access to God. What gives us access to God then? Our faith in God, a faith that produces obedience. If you embrace the following Scriptures, they will give you a great understanding of what it is that God is looking for.

Acts 10:33 Immediately, therefore, I sent to the, and thou hast well done that thou art come. Now therefore are we all here present before God, to hear all things that are commanded thee of God.34 Then Peter opened his mouth, and said, Of a truth I perceive that God is no respecter of persons: 35 but in every nation he that feareth him, and worketh righteousness, is accepted with him.

Romans 2:10 but glory, honor, and peace, to every man that worketh good, to the Jew first, and also to the Gentile: 11 for there is no respect of persons with God.

Ephesians 6:9 And, ye masters, do the same things unto them, forbearing threatening: knowing that your Master also is in heaven; neither is there respect of persons with him

Colossians 3:24 knowing that of the Lord ye shall receive the reward of the inheritance: for ye serve the Lord Christ. 25 But he that doeth wrong shall receive for the wrong which he hath done: and there is no respect of persons.

James 2:8 If ye fulfil the royal law according to the scripture, Thou shalt love thy neighbour as thyself, ye do well: 9 but if ye have respect to persons, ye commit sin, and are convinced of the law as transgressors. 10 For whosoever shall keep the whole law, and yet offend in one point, he is guilty of all.

1 Peter 1:17 And if ye call on the Father, who without respect of persons judgeth according to every man's work, pass the time of your sojourning here in fear:

Now, if you listen to most grace preachers, they will say: Jesus shed his blood. Therefore, when I stand before the judge of all judges because Jesus shed his blood, I'll not be condemned for what I've done. They say: that all my sins are forgiven past, present, and future. This teaching and theology are so twisted and contrary to the Scriptures that it is hard to believe that people believe this. The previous Scriptures boldly declare that this teaching is entirely wrong.

The Bible says you will give an answer to every work you've done in the flesh that you willingly and knowingly committed and have not truly from your heart repented of. What does repentance? You turn away from it. You do not continue in it.

Many are teaching a gospel that says you can continue in your sin, but God does not see you sinning. All the Heavenly Father sees is Jesus. That is an absolute lie from the pit of hell inspired by demonic spirits. Actually it is the GRACE of God that takes away every excuse for his people to continue in their rebellion and their sin.

When the apostle Paul said: **by the grace of God I am what I am**, he was not talking about God's mercy. He was talking about divine enablement's that came into his heart through the person and deity of Jesus Christ. Even as Christ dwells in our hearts by faith, so grace is released in our lives by faith in Christ.

Romans 4:16 Therefore it is of faith, that it might be by grace; to the end the promise might be sure to all the seed; not to that only which is of the law, but to that also which is of the faith of Abraham; who is the father of us all,

---

Romans 5:2 by whom also we have access by faith into this grace wherein we stand, and rejoice in hope of the glory of God.

Romans 12:3 For I say, through the grace given unto me, to every man that is among you, not to think of himself more highly than he ought to think; but to think soberly, according as God hath dealt to every man the measure of faith.

Romans 12:6 Having then gifts differing according to the grace that is given to us, whether prophecy, let us prophesy according to the proportion of faith;

2 Corinthians 8:7 Therefore, as ye abound in every thing, in faith, and utterance, and knowledge, and in all diligence, and in your love to us, see that ye abound in this grace also.

Ephesians 2:8 For by grace are ye saved through faith; and that not of yourselves: it is the gift of God:

1 Timothy 1:14 And the grace of our Lord was exceeding abundant with faith and love which is in Christ Jesus.

1 Peter 5:12 By Silvanus, a faithful brother unto you, as I suppose, I have written briefly, exhorting, and testifying that this is the true grace of God wherein ye stand.

We apprehend the grace of God, the Charisma by faith. That means we take hold of the divine ability, the supernatural enablement's of God by faith. The grace of God is also multiplied and increased by the knowledge of God the Father And His Son Jesus Christ.

1 Peter 1:2 elect according to the foreknowledge of God the Father, through sanctification of the Spirit, unto obedience and sprinkling of the blood of Jesus Christ: Grace unto you, and peace, be multiplied.

2 Peter 1:2Grace and peace be multiplied unto you through the knowledge of God, and of Jesus our Lord,

OH such wonderful and amazing truths that will transform our human heart. We become partakers of God's divine nature by the exceeding great and precious promises of God.

The following stories is actually the grace of God at work in the human heart

Prodigal Son Coming Home

One day I was in downtown Gettysburg, taking care of some business. As I was walking across the square, I looked over to the other side of the square and immediately the Spirit caused me to look at a tall African-American man. The minute I put my eyes upon him, I **perceived** by the Spirit that God wanted me to go speak to this man. I'm not saying that I was guessing, or I was thinking, or I was assuming. I just knew that I needed to go talk to him right now. At that moment, I did not have any idea what I was going to say to him. I just knew, that I knew, that I knew I was to go speak to him.

That's how the Spirit of God leads, and guides, one baby step at a time. As you obey this divine perception, God will take care of the rest. As I walked up to him, the word of the Lord came to me. He was standing there minding his own business, so I stepped right in front of him. When I had his attention, I looked up into his face. This particular man was over 6 feet tall, and I'm only 5'8" and so my head was cranked back pretty far.

I looked him in the eyes and I told him that he was a backslidden preacher, that he was a Jonah. I told him that the Lord had revealed to me that God was calling him to come back to the work of the Lord to fulfill his calling. That God was not yet done with him. When I spoke these words to him his countenance completely changed. I could see complete shock fill his eyes. Immediately tears began to cascade down his cheeks. He began to audibly cry aloud, throwing his hands up into the air towards heaven. Yes, right there in downtown Gettysburg at the square.

This was the first and last time I have ever seen this man. As I left him, he was standing there on the square of Gettysburg with his hands lifted high towards heaven. He was weeping and praising the Lord. This all began by simply having a deep perception, impression of the spirit of the Lord that I was to go and speak to this man. This is one way how God leads and guides. One baby step after another.

The **fifth way** that we are teaching on how God speaks to us is by **perceiving** something in your heart. It is not coming from your head, or guessing, assuming, or being suspicious. By the spirit of the Lord you just know, that you know, that you know. This actually is also how all your prayers are answered. When faith is active in your heart you will simply know, that you know, that it is done.

Mark 11:23 For verily I say unto you, That whosoever shall say unto this mountain, Be thou removed, and be thou cast into the sea; and shall not doubt in his heart, but shall believe that those things which he saith shall come to pass; he shall have whatsoever he saith. 24 Therefore I say unto you, What things soever ye desire, when ye pray, believe that ye receive them, and ye shall have them.

An Unbelieving Man Healed

One day as I was preaching in a tent, a man who looked to be in his mid-thirties was hobbling by really slow on a pair of crutches. He was not even looking in the direction of our tent, but was looking straight ahead, minding his own business. As I looked at him, I **perceived** by the Spirit of God that the Lord would heal him right now if he would come up for prayer. At the same time the gift of faith rose up inside of me. When God quickens my heart in this way I do not even think what I'm about to do. I simply act upon this quickening and the witness in my heart. When I use, the word **perceive**, I am talking about knowing that I know what God wants to do. It is not coming from my head, but up out of my heart.

In this situation, I found myself calling out to this particular man who was walking by very slowly on his crutches. I kept calling out to him over the loudspeaker system. Everybody could hear me within a hundred feet, if not further. Probably the whole Huntington Fair could hear me as I called out to him! (The fire department was really upset with us because we were disturbing their bingo games.) When I first called out to this man he completely ignored me. Over and over I challenged him to come into the tent so God could heal him. He finally looked my way but kept hobbling along. I called out to him again, encouraging him to come and be healed of his problem.

After repeatedly calling him, he finally responded, and came hobbling into the tent. When he came to the front, I asked him if he had faith to believe that God would heal him. He looked at me as if I had lost my mind. He probably was thinking, you're the one who kept calling me up here. I don't even know what this is all about. Everybody was staring at me, so I had to come!

He did not respond to my question. I told him that I was going to pray for him now and God would heal him! I perceived this by the spirit of God, and by the gift of faith that was operating in me at that time. I asked him again if he believed that God would heal him when I prayed. Once again, he did not respond. I laid my hands on him and commanded him to be healed in the name of Jesus Christ of Nazareth.

After I was done praying, I told him to put down his crutches and to start walking without them. He stood there staring at me. Everybody else was also staring at me. This was okay because the gift of faith was at work in my heart. I reached forward and took away his crutches. I threw them on the ground and spun him around.

When I'm in this realm I'm not thinking, I'm simply acting. Then I pushed him on the back with my hands. He stumbled forward with his legs jerking unsteadily, but then he began to walk normally toward the back of the tent. He was picking his legs high up in the air, and high stepping it. When he got to the edge of the tent he spun back toward me. Tears were now streaming from his eyes and down his cheeks. He came back toward me walking perfectly normal with no limp whatsoever!

I gave him the microphone, and asked him to tell us what had just happened to him. He kept saying, "You don't understand" over and over. Once again, I encouraged him to tell us his story. I had him face the people in that tent and those outside of it who had been watching. He told us that last winter he had been walking on a very icy sidewalk and he lost his footing. Slipping and sliding, he fell forward onto the concrete and ice. He fell so hard on his right kneecap that he knew that he had done something terrible to it. He could not move his knee whatsoever, and it was extremely painful. He went to the doctor's office and they did x-rays. The x-rays revealed that his kneecap had literally been shattered and destroyed. In just two more days he was scheduled to have a major operation to replace his kneecap.

I encouraged him to go back to his doctor and get x-rays again. Sure enough, a couple of days later he came back to the tent filled with great joy and giving a wonderful testimony. He had gone to his doctor. He said when he walked into the doctor's office they could tell that he was walking normal. The doctor asked him what had happened. He told them about the encounter he had with Jesus at our tent meeting.

They did an x-ray his kneecap and discovered he had a brand-new kneecap! God had completely healed him. How did God do this? First there had to be a man who was so yielded and surrendered to the spirit of God that the Lord could speak to him. That once God spoke to him, he would respond in obedience no matter how it looked, or what people thought. This is how almost every miracle happens. Hearing the voice of God and obeying what the Lord is speaking.

Now there are well-known men that teach us that we should pray only one time, for those things which we desire. That is a biblical principle IF the conditions are met. One of the main conditions is that you **must believe** that when you pray, you have **received**. When do you receive? The minute you pray and believed you received.

If as a believer, you prayed and you did not believe that you received, then you need to keep praying until you believe that you receive. If when you prayed, you did believe that you received, but somehow the enemy has been able to get you to stop believing that you have received, then you need to pray again. Faith is knowing that when you prayed, God has heard your prayers. Now, because he has heard your prayers, you have received the petitions you have asked of him, because you know you are in his will.

Mark 11:24 Therefore I say unto you, What things soever ye desire, when ye pray, believe that ye receive them, and ye shall have them. 25 And when ye stand praying, forgive, if ye have ought against any: that your Father also which is in heaven may forgive you your trespasses.

We need to go back and meditate upon the truth of what God's word says, dealing with what we are asking for. Faith becomes alive as the word takes upon flesh and blood within our hearts. God has so many wonderful blessings for us, if we can simply believe that we receive them by faith.

Pastor Mike how do you know what you **perceived** was really of God? Because **number one**, it will never contradict the known will of God. **Number two**, it will never contradict his divine nature. **Number three**, there will be concrete evidence or you could say absolute proof that you heard from heaven as you act upon what you **perceived**.

The old saying is: the proof is in the eating of the pudding. If you are really hearing from God it will be manifested before everything is said and done. Through the years I have heard some well-known speakers make certain prophetic declarations. I've always watched to see if they happened, because that is the proof of whether they are really hearing from God. I am sorry to say that I have seen people prophesy about certain men that would become president, and it never happened. That is the evidence that what they proclaimed God told them, was not in fact really of God at all.

CHAPTER FOUR

God-given faith

Read Hebrews 11:1-11. I believe that there is only one way to all the treasures of God, and that is the way of faith. By faith and faith alone do we enter into a knowledge of the attributes and become partakers of the beatitudes, and participate in the glories of our ascended Lord. All His promises are Yea and Amen to them that believe.

God would have us come to Him in His way. That is through the open door of **GRACE**. God has made a way, and He is the WAY. It is a beautiful way, and all His saints can enter in by this way and find rest. God has prescribed that the Just shall live by faith. I find that all failure is because it was not based on the rock Christ Jesus. He is the only way, the truth, and the life. The way of faith is the Christ way, receiving Him in His fullness and walking in Him; receiving His quickening life that fills movees and changes us, bringing us to a place where there is always an Amen in our hearts to all the will of God.

As I look into the 12th chapter of Acts, I find that the people were praying all night for Peter to come out of prison. They had a zeal but seemed to have been lacking in faith. They were to be commended for their zeal in spending their time in prayer without ceasing, but their faith did not measure up to such a marvelous answer. Rhoda had more faith than the rest of them.

When the knock came to the door, she ran to it, and the moment she heard Peter's voice, she ran back again with joy saying that Peter stood before the gate. And all the people said, "You are mad. It isn't so." But she constantly affirmed that it was even so. Zacharias and Elisabeth surely wanted a son, but even when the angel came and told Zacharias that he should have a son, he was full of unbelief. And the angel said, "Thou shalt be dumb because you believe not my words."

But look at Mary. When the angel came to her, Mary said, "Be it unto me according to thy word." It was her Amen to the will of God. And God wants us with an Amen in our lives, an inward Amen, a mighty moving Amen, a God-inspired Amen, which says, "It is because God has spoken. It cannot be otherwise. It is impossible to be otherwise."

Let us examine this 5th verse, "By faith, Enoch was translated that he should not see death; and was not found, because God translated him: for before his translation, he had this testimony that he pleased God."

When I was in Sweden, the Lord worked mightily. After one or two addresses the leaders called me and said, "We have heard very strange things about you, and we would like to know if they are true. We can see that God is with you and that God is moving, and we know that it will be a great blessing to Sweden."

"Well," I said, "what is it?"

"Well," they said, "we have heard from good authority that you preach that you have the resurrection body." When I was in France, I had an interpreter that believed this thing, and I found out after I had preached once or twice through the interpreter, that she gave out her ideas. And of course, I did not know. I said to these brethren, "I tell you what my convictions are. I believe that if I had the testimony of Enoch, I should be off. I believe that the moment Enoch had the testimony that he pleased God, off he went."

I pray that God will so quicken our faith, for translation is in the mind of God; but remember that translation comes on the line of holy obedience and a walk that is pleasing to God. This was true of Enoch. And I believe that we must have a like walk with God in the Spirit, having communion with him, living under his divine smile, and I pray that God by His Spirit may so move us that we will be where Enoch was when he walked with God.

There are two kinds of faith. There is a natural faith. But the supernatural faith is the gift of God. In Acts 26:19, Paul is telling Agrippa of what the Lord said to him in commissioning him. "To open their eyes, and to turn them from darkness to light, from the power of Satan unto God, that they may receive forgiveness of sins, and inheritance among them which are sanctified by faith that is in Me."

Is that the faith of Paul? No, it is the faith that the Holy Ghost is giving. It is the faith that He brings to us as we press in and on with God. I want to put before you this difference between our faith and the faith of Jesus. Our faith comes to an end. Most people in this place have come to where they have said, "Lord, I can go no further. I have gone so far, and I can go no further. I have used all the faith I have, and I have just to stop now and wait."

I remember being one day in Lancashire and going round to see some sick people. I was taken into a house where there was a young woman lying on a bed, a very helpless case. The reason had gone, and many things were manifested there which were satanic, and I knew it. She was only a young woman, a beautiful child. The husband, quite a young man, came in with the baby, and he leaned over to kiss the wife. The moment he did, she threw herself over on the other side, just as a lunatic would do.

That was very heart-breaking. Then he took the baby and pressed the baby's lips to the mother. Again another wild kind of thing happened. I asked one who was attending her, "Have you anybody to help?" "Oh," they said, "We have had everything." "But," I said, "have you no spiritual help?" Her husband stormed out, saying, "Help? You think that we believe in God after we have had seven weeks of no sleep and maniac conditions."

Then a young woman of about eighteen or so just grinned at me and passed out of the door. That brought me to a place of compassion for the woman. Something had to be done, no matter what it was. Then with all my faith I began to penetrate the heavens, and I was soon out of that house, I will tell you, for I never saw a man get anything from God who prayed on the earth.

If you get anything from God, you will have to pray into heaven; for it is all there. If you are living in the earth realm and expect things from heaven, they will never come. And as I saw, in the presence of God, the limitations of my faith, there came another faith, a faith that could not be denied, a faith that took the promise, a faith that believed God's Word. And from that presence, I came back again to earth, but not the same man. God gave a faith that could shake hell and anything else.

I said, "Come out of her, in the name of Jesus!" And she rolled over and fell asleep and wakened in fourteen hours perfectly sane and perfectly whole.

There is a process on this line. Enoch walked with God. That must have been all those years as he was penetrating, and going through, and laying hold, and believing and seeing and getting into such close cooperation and touch with God that things moved on earth and he began to move toward heaven. At last, it was not possible for him to stop any longer. Oh, Hallelujah!

In the 15th chapter of 1st Corinthians, we read of the body being "sown in weakness," to be raised in power. It seems to me that, as we are looking for a translation, the Lord would have us know something of that power now, and would have us kept in that power so that we shall not be sown in weakness.

There is one thing that God has given me from my youth up, a taste and relish for my Bible. I can say before God, I have never read a book but my Bible, so I know nothing about books. It seems better to get the Book of books for food for your soul, for the strengthening of your faith, and the building up of your character in God, so that all the time you are being changed and made meet to walk with God.

"Without faith, it is impossible to please Him; for he that comes to God must believe that He is and that He is a rewarder of them that diligently seek him."

I can see that it is impossible to please Him on any line but faith, for everything that is not of faith is sin. God wants us to see that the plan of faith is the ideal and principle of God. In this connection, I love to keep in my thoughts the beautiful words in the 2nd verse of the 12th chapter of Hebrews: "Looking unto Jesus, the author, and finisher of our faith."

He is the author of faith. God worked through Him for the forming of the world. "All things were made by Him, and without Him was not anything made that was made." And because of the exceedingly abundant joy of providing for us so great salvation, He became the author of a living faith. And through this principle of living faith, looking unto Him who is the author and finisher of our faith, we are changed into the same image from glory to glory, even by the Spirit of the Lord.

God has something better for you than you have ever had in the past. Come out into all the fulness of faith and power and life and victory that He is willing to provide, as you forget the things of the past, and press right on for the prize of His high calling in Christ Jesus.

GRACE of Longsuffering

This morning we will move on to the "gifts of healing." "To another, faith by the same Spirit; to another the gifts of healing by the same Spirit." [1Co 12.9]

There is no use expecting to understand the gifts and to understand the epistles unless you have the Holy Ghost. All the epistles are written to baptized people, and not to the unregenerated. They are written to those who have grown into maturity as a manifestation of the Christ of God. Do not jump into the epistles before you have come in at the gate of the baptism of the Spirit. I believe that this teaching God is helping me to bring to you will move on you to become restless and discontented on every line till God has finished with you. If we want to know the mind of God through the epistles, there is nothing else to bring the truth but the revelation of the Spirit himself.

He gives the utterance: He opens the door. Don't live in a poverty state when we are all around, in and out, up and down, pressed out beyond measure [2Co 1.8] with the rarest gems of the latest word from God. "Ask, and it shall be given you; seek, and ye shall find; knock, and it shall be opened unto you. For every one that asketh receiveth; and he that seeketh findeth, and to him that knocketh it shall be opened." [Mt 7.7-8] There is the authority of God's word. And remember, the authority of God's word is Jesus. These are the utterances by the Spirit of Jesus to us this morning.

I come to you with a great inward desire to wake you up to your great possibilities. Your responsibilities will be great, but not as great as your possibilities. You will always find that God is over-abundance on every line he touches for you, and he wants you to come into mind and thought with him so that you are not trusting in yourselves. Be enlarged in God!

[Tongues and interpretation. "It is that which God hath chosen for us, which is mightier than we. It is that which is bottomless, higher than the heights, more lovely than all beside. And God in a measure presses you out to believe all things that you may endure all things, and lay hold of eternal life through the power of the Spirit."]

The "gifts of healings" are wonderful gifts. There is a difference between having a gift of healing, and "gifts of healings." God wants us not to come behind in anything. I like this word, "gifts of healing." To have the accomplishment of these gifts, I must bring myself to a conformity to the mind and will of God in purpose. It would be impossible to have "gifts of healing" unless you possessed that blessed fruit of "longsuffering." You will find these gifts run parallel with that which will bring them into operation without a leak.

But how will it be possible to minister the gifts of healing, considering the peculiarities there are in the Assemblies and the many evil powers of Satan which confront us and possess bodies? The man who will go through with God and exercise the gifts of healing will have to be a man of longsuffering; always have a word of comfort. If the one who is in distress and helpless doesn't see eye to eye in everything and doesn't get all he wants, longsuffering will bear and forbear. Longsuffering is a **GRACE** Jesus lived in and moved in. He was filled with compassion, and God will never be able to move us to the help of the needy one until we reach that place.

Sometimes you might think by the way I went about praying for the sick that I was unloving and rough; but oh friends, you have no idea what I see behind the sickness and the afflicted. I am not dealing with the person; I am dealing with the satanic forces that are binding the afflicted. As far as the person goes, my heart is full of love and compassion for all, but I fail to see how you will ever reach a place where God will be able definitely to use you until you get angry at the devil.

One day a pet dog followed a lady out of her house and ran all around her feet. She said to the dog, "I cannot have you with me today." The dog wagged its tail and made a great fuss. "Go home, pet," she said, but it didn't go. At last, she shouted roughly, "Go home!" and off it went. Some people play with the devil like that. "Poor thing!" The devil can stand all the comfort anybody in the world could give. Cast him out!

You are not dealing with the person; you are dealing with the devil. If you say, with authority, "Come out, your demons, in the name of the Lord!" they must come out. You will always be right when you dare to treat sickness as the devil's work, and you will always be near the mark when you treat it as sin. Let Pentecostal people wake up to see that getting sick is caused by some misconduct; there is some neglect, something wrong somewhere, a weak place where Satan has had a chance to get in. And if we wake up to the real facts of it, we will be ashamed to say that we are sick because people will know we have been sinning.

Gifts of healings are so varied in all lines you will find the gift of discernment often operated in connection in addition to that. The manifestations of the Spirit are given to us that we may profit withal. [1Co 12.7] You must never treat a cancer case as anything else than a living, evil spirit which is always destroying the body. It is one of the worst kinds I know. Not that the devil has anything good; every disease of the devil is bad, either to a greater or less degree, but this form of disease is one that you must cast out.

Among the first people, I met in Victoria Hall was a woman who had cancer in the breast. As soon as the cancer was cursed, it stopped bleeding because it was dead. The next thing that happened the body cast it off because the natural body has no room for dead matter. When it came out, it was like a big ball with thousands of fibers. All these fibers had spread out into the flesh, but the moment the evil power was destroyed they had no power. Jesus gave us the power to bind and power to loose; we must bind the evil powers and loose the afflicted and set them free. There are many cases where Satan has control of the mind, and those under the satanic influence are not all in asylums.

I will tell you what freedom is: No person in this place who enjoys the fullness of the Spirit with a clear knowledge of redemption should know that he has a body. You ought to be able to eat and sleep, digest your food, and not be conscious of your body; a living epistle of God's thought and mind, walking up and down the world without pain. That is redemption. To be fully in the will of God, the perfection of redemption, we should not have a pain of any kind.

I have had some experience along this line. When I was weak and helpless, and friends were looking for me to die, it was in that straitened place that I saw the fullness of redemption. I read and re-read the 91st Psalm and claimed long life: "With long life will I satisfy him." What else? "And show him my salvation." [Ps 91.16] This is greater than long life. The salvation of God is deliverance from everything, and here I am. At 25 or 30 they were looking for me to die; now at 63, I feel young. So there is something more in this truth that I am preaching than mere words. God hath not designed us for anything else than to be first fruits, sons of God with power over all the power of the enemy, [Lk 10.19] living in the world but not of it. [Jn 17.16]

We have to be careful in casting out demons, who shall give the command. A man may say "Come out," but unless it is in the Spirit of God, our words are vain. The devil always had a good time with me in the middle of the night and tried to give me a bad time. I had a real conflict with evil powers, and the only deliverance I got was when I bound them in the name of the Lord.

I remember taking a man who was demon-possessed out for a walk one day. We were going through a thickly crowded place, and this man became obstreperous. I squared him up, and the devil came out of him, but I wasn't careful, and these demons fastened themselves on me right on the street there, so that I couldn't move. Sometimes when I am ministering on the platform, and the powers of the devil attack me, the people think I am casting demons out of them, but I am casting them out of myself. The people couldn't understand when I cast that evil spirit out of that man on the street, but I understood.

The man who had that difficulty is now preaching and is one of the finest men we have. But it required someone to bind the strong man. [Mk 3.27] You must be sure of your ground, and sure it is a mightier power than you that is destroying the devil. Take your position from the first epistle of John and say, "Greater is he that is in me than he that is in the world." [1Jn 4.4] If you think it is you, you make a great mistake. It is your being filled with him; he is acting in place of you; your thought, your mouth, you're all becoming exercised by the Spirit of God.

At L----- in Norway, we had a place seating 1,500 people. When we reached there, it was packed, and hundreds were unable to get in. The policemen were standing there, and I thought the first thing I would do would be to preach to the people outside and then go in. I addressed the policemen and said, "You see this condition. I have come with a message to help everybody, and it hurts me very much to find as many people outside as in; I want the promise of you police officials that you will give us the marketplace tomorrow. Will you do it?" They put up their hands that they would.

It was a beautiful day in April, and there was a big stand in the woods about 10 feet high in the great park, where thousands of people gathered. After preaching, we had some wonderful cases of healing. One man came 100 miles, bringing his food with him. He hadn't passed anything through his stomach for over a month for there was a terrible cancer there. He was healed in the meeting, and opening up his lunch began eating before all the people.

Then there was a young woman who came with a stiff hand. I cursed the spirit of infirmity, and it was instantly cast out, and the arm was free. She waved it over her head and said, "My father is the chief of police. I have been bound since I was a girl." At the close of the meeting, Satan laid out two people with fits. That was my day! I jumped down to where they were and in the name of Jesus delivered them. People said, "Oh isn't he rough," but when they saw those afflicted stand up and praise God, that was a time of rejoicing.

Oh, we must wake up, stretch ourselves out to believe God! Before God could bring me to this place, he had to break me a thousand times. I have wept, I have groaned, I have travailed night after night till God broke me. Until God has mowed you down, you will never have this longsuffering for others.

When I was at Cardiff, the Lord healed a woman right in the meeting. She was afflicted with ulceration, and while they were singing she fell full length and cried in such a way, I felt something must be done. I knelt alongside the woman, laid my hands on her body, and instantly the powers of the devil were destroyed, and she was delivered from ulceration; rose up and joined in the singing.

We have been seeing wonderful miracles in these last days, and they are only a little of what we are going to see. When I say "going to see" I do not want to throw something out ten years to come, nor even two years. I believe we are in the "going," right on the threshold of wonderful things.

You must not think that these gifts fall upon you like ripe cherries. You must pay the price for everything you get from God. There is nothing worth having that you do not have to pay for, either temporally or spiritually. I remember when I was at Antwerp and Brussels. The power of God was very mighty upon me there. Coming through to London I called on some friends at C-----. To show you the leading of the Lord, these friends said, "Oh, God sent you here. How much we need you!"

They sent a wire to a place where there was a young man 26 years old, who had been in bed 18 years. His body was so much bigger than an ordinary body, because of inactivity, and his legs were like a child's; instead of bone, there was gristle. He had never been able to dress himself. When they got the wire, the father dressed him, and he was sitting in a chair. I felt it was one of the opportunities of my life.

I said to this young man, "What is the greatest desire of your heart?" "Oh," he said, "that I might be filled with the Holy Ghost!" I put my hands upon him and said, "Receive, receive ye the Holy Ghost." Instantly he became drunk with the Spirit and fell off the chair like a big bag of potatoes. I saw what God could do with a helpless cripple. First, his head began shaking terrifically; then his back began moving very fast, and then his legs, just like being in a battery.

Then he spoke clearly in tongues, and we wept and praised the Lord. His legs were still as they had been, by all appearances, and this is where I missed it. These "missings" sometimes are God's opportunities for teaching you important lessons. He will teach you through your weaknesses that which is not faith. It was not faith for me to look at that body, but human. The man who will work the works of God must never look at conditions, but at Jesus in whom everything is complete.

I looked at the boy, and there was no help. I turned to the Lord and said, "Lord, tell me what to do," and he did. He said, "Command him to walk, in my name." This is where I missed it. I looked at his conditions, and I got the father to help lift him up to see if his legs had strength. We did our best, but he and I together could not move him. Then the Lord showed me my mistake, and I said, "God forgive." I got right down and repented, and said to the Lord, "Please tell me again." God is so good, and he never leaves us to ourselves.

Again he said to me, "Command him in my name to walk." So I shouted, "Arise and walk in the name of Jesus." Did he do it? No, I declare, he never walked: He was lifted by the power of God in a moment, and he ran. The door was wide open; he ran out across the road into a field where he ran up and down and came back. Oh, it was a miracle!

There are miracles to be performed, and these miracles will be accomplished by us when we understand the perfect plan of his spiritual **GRACE**s which has come down to us. These things will come to us when we come to a place of brokenness, of surrender, of wholehearted yieldedness, where we decrease but where God has come to increase; and where we dwell and live in him.

Will you allow him to be the choice of your thoughts? Submit to him. **To the God of all GRACE, [1Pe 5.10] that you may be well-furnished with faith for every good work, [2Ti 3.17] that**

the mind of the Lord may have free course in you, run and be glorified; [2Th 3.1] that the heathen shall know, [Ek 37.28] the uttermost parts of the earth shall be filled with the glory of the Lord as the waters cover the deep. [Ha 2.14

Great GRACE upon the church

Preached at Pentecostal Union Meeting, Chicago October 31, 1922
Published in Latter Rain Evangel p. 18-20 August 23, 1923

And great **GRACE** was upon them all." Great **GRACE** is upon us when we magnify the Lord. If ever you want to see what God means when He gets a chance at His people, have a peep at the fourth chapter of Acts, and see what God did. Just because all the people shouted aloud to Him He imparted to them such blessing that every person was filled with the Holy Ghost, and I believe what God wants to do in these days is to give an inward manifestation of His divine presence within the body until the body is moved by the power of the Spirit. Beloved, we are accustomed to earthly things, but when God sends the heavenly, it is beyond our understanding. Oh, to have the revelation of the mind of God! It fills my soul, the thought of it! Oh, for the kind of loosening of the body that we will never be bound again! Just filled with God!

I believe God wants us to understand something of the words of this life. What life? The manifestation of the power of Jesus in the human body, a divine life, a divine power, a quickening, thrilling energy given to you. I was baptized with the Holy Ghost in 1907. If anyone had said to me: "Now, Wigglesworth, you will see such and such things," it would have been beyond my human comprehension, but the tide has risen for fifteen years, and it is still rising. Thank God, there has never been a black day, nor a blank day.

Often I think about the first Church and how God favored her, how He burst thru her. How He transformed Christians and made them

move with the power of apostles, it thrills my soul. That wherever they went, they transformed lives.
God did such wonderful things, and when I think of it, I think, that we should have something far greater, and say: **"Look up; your redemption draweth nigh!"** I want to take a perspective of what they were, and we must be. I am inwardly convinced of the power that awaits us, the installation of God's movement right in our hearts.

I notice in the first Church it wasn't possible for deception to live in that atmosphere. I want you to keep in mind that there is a time coming when nothing of uncleanness will be able to remain in His little flock. The first Church was so pure that God overshadowed it. He nursed it, brought it thru, and yet He has His hand upon us at this time also. How do we know? The Lord hath laid the foundation which is an immovable foundation. It is built upon the prophets, and it is built upon the apostles; it is built upon the Word of God, and the church will yet come into the fullness of the manifestation of the body of Christ.

God will keep His Word. The church will be ready like a bride adorned for her husband; the gifts will be a ministry clothed upon; the **GRACE**s will adorn the believer, and will be far beyond anything we have seen.

Now, Ananias and Sapphira were, I believe, baptized believers. I have a firm conviction in my heart that God in the first outpouring of the Spirit did His work so beautifully that those three thousand who that were pricked in their hearts met the condition of the Bible pattern. Peter said unto them: "Repent, believe, be baptized and ye shall receive the gift of the Holy Ghost."

They obeyed, and we have reason to believe they received the Holy Ghost. I cannot conceive of anything else but what the Early Church all received the outpouring of the Holy Ghost. And I believe today that we should press home to every soul the necessity of meeting the conditions and being filled with the Holy Ghost. Then I notice here in this fifth chapter of Acts that God had the particular oversight of the Church. I love to think of this. They gave of their substance; they gave willingly; they laid it down at the apostles' feet, and they were so eager to give that they began selling their property, and brought the proceeds to the apostles.

Now there were two people who had sold their land which began to talk over the thing at home, and this was the sense of their argument: "This thing may go down; it may leak out. If we give it all, we shall lose it all and have nothing left," and so they reserved for themselves a portion, but they missed it. Listen: God never wants anything from you but a spontaneous heart gift, and anyone who gives spontaneously to God will always get a big cup full. God is never in any man's debt.

I notice the moment God visited this people in showing up this sin and bringing death to Ananias and Sapphira; it instantly brought a tremendous fear over all the church, a fear that brought an answer. There is a fear that brings an answer. Were they afraid of God? No, it was something better than that. When they saw that God was there in judgment upon them, they turned with holy fear, with a reverence. It sobered things, and the people began to see that God was zealous for them. There are two kinds of fear, one that is afraid of God, and another fear that loves God, and that was the fear that came over them, the fear of grieving God, which the Lord wants us to have.

Oh, to fear Him in such a way that you would rather die than to grieve Him! That is it. This came over the people, and when it came, another thing happened. "No one durst join themselves to them." That was a wonderful time. May God so sanctify His church that no one durst come near without meaning business. Brother, did God have a hand in your plan? Did you join this people because you felt they were a choice people, or did you have the constraining power of God upon you?

I see more and more in this glorious life of God that there is a pure whiteness to be achieved, there is pure son ship without fear, and the saints of God shall rise in such confidence until they remove what people think are mountains, till they subdue what you call kingdoms.

I have had some wonderful times in Belfast and in fact all over Ireland. I was in Belfast one day, and a young man came to me and said: "Brother Wigglesworth, I am very much distressed," and he told me why. They had an old lady in their assembly who used to pray heaven down upon them.

She had an accident. Her thigh was broken, and they took her away to the infirmary. They put her in a plaster of Paris cast, and she was in that condition for five months. Then they broke the cast and lifted her on to her feet and asked her to walk. She fell again and broke her leg in another place. And they found out that the first break had never knit together.

They brought her home and laid her on the couch, and the young man asked me to go and pray for her. When I got into the house, I asked: "Do you believe that God can heal you?" She said "Yes. When I heard you had come to the city, I thought, 'This is my chance to be healed.' "An old man, her husband, was sitting in a chair, had been sitting there for four years; helpless. And he said: "I do not believe. I will not believe. She was the only help I had. She has been taken away with a broken leg, and they have brought her back with her leg broken twice. How can I believe in God?"

I turned to her and said: "Now is it all right?" Yes," she said, "it is all right." The right leg was broken in two parts. Physicians can join up bones beautifully, and make them fit together, but if God doesn't come in with His healing power, there is no physician can heal them.

As soon as the oil was placed upon her head and hands laid on, instantly down the right limb, there was a stream of life, and she knew it. She said: "I am healed." I said: "If you are healed, you do not need anybody to help you." J went out. She took hold of the mantle shelf above her head and pulled herself up and walked all around the room. She was perfectly healed.

The old man said: "Make me walk." I said: "You old sinner, repent." Then he began: "You know, Lord, I didn't mean it." I believe he was in earnest, and to show you the mercy and compassion of God, the moment I laid hands upon him, the power of God went thru him, and he rose up after four years being stiff and walked around the room. That day both he and his wife were made whole. Do you not believe now that God has a plan in all these things? I want you to realize that what God wants to do in us and thru us these days is to blend us together, and to give us one heart and one mind.

They were all of one heart and one mind, and they had such faith that the shadow of Peter worked a transformation in their bodies. Of course, it was God that did the healing. But as Peter came along, I can see the people moved by his presence. Beloved, we have one in the meeting tonight who is a million times mightier than Peter. His touch will set you free. It is the living virtue! "Go speak to the people the words of this life," the life of the Son of God, the quickening by the Word.

The first outpouring was of the Spirit, and the latter is to be the fullness of the Spirit. When God's mighty power shakes the foundation and purifies, there is a transformation. The Lord is the life, and where the life of the Spirit and the Word are together, they bring forth an issue of transforming and quickening until the man is possessed by Jesus. Jesus is the first fruits.

It is lovely to think that God sent Him in the likeness of sinful flesh, and for sin condemned sin in the flesh. Then we are here tonight with a clear conception of this thing, that the life of Jesus has come into our flesh and delivered us from the power of darkness and disease, from bitterness and covetousness, idolatry and lust; from the corruption of the present evil world, by the same Spirit, the same life.

I believe the Lord would have me take you to a moment in my life. I was having some meetings in Belfast, and this is the rising tide of what I believe was the move of the Spirit in a certain direction, to show the greatness of that which was to follow. Night after night the Lord had led me on certain lines of truth. There was so much in it that one felt they could not give up, and every night until ten o'clock we were opening up the Word of God. They came to me and said: "Brother, we have been feasting and are so full we are ready for a burst of some kind. Don't you think it is time to call an altar service?"

I said I knew that God was working and the time would come when the altar service would be called, but we would have to get the mind of the Lord upon it. There was nothing more said. They began early in the afternoon to bring sick people. We never had a thing said about it. The meeting came, and every seat was taken up, the window sills were filled and every nook and corner. The glory of God filled the place. It was the easiest thing in the world to preach; it came forth like a river, and the power of God rested mightily.

There were a lot of people who had been seeking baptism for years. Sinners were in the meeting and several sick people. What happened? God hears me say this: There was a certain moment in that meeting when every sick person was healed, every lame person was healed, and every sinner saved, and it all took place in five minutes. There comes into a meeting sometimes something we cannot understand, and it is amazing how things happen.

When I was on the ship, there was a man who had trained all his life, as it were, to be a physician. He got to be eminent and was looked up to as one of the leading physicians, an Indian. He had been over to England to lecture and was going back on the ship on which I was traveling.

When the Christian Science lady got healed, she saw the captain and told him what God had done. The Captain arranged a meeting, and I had a fine chance to preach to all on the ship. The Indian doctor was there, and he was struck with what happened. At the close of the meeting, people decided for Christ; some people followed me into my stateroom, where God healed them. This Indian doctor came to me. "I am done," he said. "I have no spirit left. You must talk to me."

For two hours we talked, and God dealt with him. He stood before me. “I will never have any more medicine,” he said. “God has saved me.” That physician saw the power of God and recognized it. You ask, What is that? That is where God plans a life in a moment, thru one act. God wants the way into our lives. He wants to transform you by His **GRACE**. He wants to make you know that you are only here to be filled with His power and His presence for His glory. The “seed of the woman” must “bruise the serpent’s head.”

Now, beloved, the Acts of the Apostles were written to prove to us that the power and manifestation of God were to be continuous. Have you read about the scattering of these people at Jerusalem, how God was with them? Do not be afraid of persecution. I am never at my best until I am in a spiritual fight, and until I fight with the enemy. They think I am rather unmerciful in my dealing with the sick, but I have no mercy for the devil and get him out at any cost. I resist him with all the power that is within me. God wrought mightily thru the persecution which came upon the church, and He could do the same today under similar circumstances.

We have a wonderful God

a God whose ways are past finding out, and whose **GRACE** and power are limitless. I was in Belfast one day and saw one of the brethren of the assembly. He said to me, “Wigglesworth, I am troubled. I have had a good deal of sorrow during the past five months. I had a woman in my assembly who could always pray the blessing of heaven down on our meetings. She is an old woman, but her presence is always an inspiration. But five months ago she fell and broke her thigh. The doctors put her into a plaster cast, and after five months they broke the cast. But the bones were not properly set, and so she fell and broke the thigh again.”

He took me to her house, and there was a woman lying in a bed on the right hand side of the room. I said to her, “Well, what about it now?" She said, "They have sent me home incurable. The doctors say that I am so old that my bones won't knit. There is no nutriment in my bones, and they could never do anything for me, and they say I shall have to lie in bed for the rest of my life."

I said to her, "Can you believe God?" She replied, "Yes, ever since I heard that you had come to Belfast my faith has been quickened. If you pray, I will believe. I know there is no power on earth that can make the bones of my thigh knit, but I know there is nothing impossible with God." I said, "Do you believe He will meet you now?" She answered, "I do."

It is grand to see people believe in God. God knew all about this leg and that it was broken in two places. I said to the woman, "When I pray, something will happen." Her husband was sitting there; he had been in his chair for four years and could not walk a step. He called out, "I don't believe. I won't believe it. You will never get me to believe." I said, "All right," and laid my hands on his wife in the name of the Lord Jesus. The moment hands were laid upon her the power of God went right through her, and she cried out, "I'm healed." I said, "I'm not going to assist you to rise. God will do it all." She rose and walked up and down the room, praising God.

The old man was amazed at what had happened to his wife, and he cried out, "Make me walk, make me walk." I said to him, "You old sinner, repent." He cried out, "Lord, You know I never meant what I said. You know I believe." I don't think he meant what he said; anyhow the Lord was full of compassion. If He marked our sins, where would any of us be? If we meet the conditions, God will always meet us. If we believe, all things are possible. I laid my hands on him, and the power went right through the old man's body; and those legs, for the first time in four years, received power to carry his body, and he walked up and down and in and out. He said, "O what great things God has done for us tonight!"

"What things soever ye desire, when ye pray, believe that ye receive them, and ye shall have them." Desire toward God, and you will have desires from God, and He will meet you on the line of those desires when you reach out in simple faith.

A man came to me in one of my meetings who had seen other people healed and wanted to be healed, too. He explained that his arm had been fixed in a certain position for many years and he could not move it. “Got any faith?” I asked. He said He had a lot of faith. After prayer, he was able to swing his arm round and round. But he was not satisfied and complained, “I feel a little bit of trouble just there,” pointing to a certain place. “Do you know what is the trouble with you?” He answered, “No.” I said, “Imperfect faith.” “What things soever ye desire, when ye pray, believe that ye receive there, and ye shall have them.”

Did you believe before you were saved? So many people would be saved, but they want to feel saved first. There was never a man who felt saved before he believed. God’s plan is always this; if you believe, you shall see the glory of God. I believe God wants to bring us all to a definite place of unswerving faith and confidence in Himself.

Jesus here uses the figure of a mountain. Why does He say a mountain? Because, if faith can remove a mountain, it can remove anything. The plan of God is so marvelous, that if you only believe, all things are possible.

There is one special phrase to which I want to call your attention, “And shall not doubt in his heart.” The heart is the mainspring. See that young man and young woman. They have fallen in love at first sight. In a short while, there is a deep affection, and a strong heart love, the one toward the other. What is the heart of love? A heart of faith. Faith and love axe kin. In the measure that that young man and that young woman love one another, they are true. One may go to the North and the other to the South, but because of their love they will be true to each other.

It is the same when there is a deep love in the heart toward the Lord Jesus Christ. In this new life into which God has brought us, Paul tells us that we have become dead to the law by the body of

Christ, that we should be married to another, even to Him who is raised from the dead. God brings us into a place of perfect love and perfect faith. A man who is born of God is brought into an inward affection, a loyalty to the Lord Jesus that shrinks from anything impure.

You see the purity of a man and woman when there is a deep natural affection between them; they disdain the very thought of either of them being untrue. I say that in the measure that a man has faith in Jesus, he is pure. He that believes that Jesus is the Christ overcomes the world. It is a faith that works by love.

Just as we have heart fellowship with our LORD, our faith cannot be daunted. We cannot doubt in our hearts. There comes, as we go on with God, a wonderful association, an impartation of His very life and nature within. As we read His Word and believe the promises that He has so graciously given to us, we are made partakers of His very essence and life. The Lord is made to us a Bridegroom, and we are His bride. His words to us are spirit and life, transforming us and changing us, expelling that which is natural and bringing in that which is divine.

It is impossible to comprehend the love of God as we think on natural lines. We must have the revelation from the Spirit of God. God giveth liberally. He that asketh, receiveth. God is willing to bestow on us all things that pertain to life and godliness. Oh, it was the love of God that brought Jesus. And it is this same love that helps you and me to believe. In every weakness, God will be your strength. You who need His touch, remember that He loves you. Look, the wretched, helpless, sick one, away to the God of all **GRACE**, whose very essence is love, who delights to give liberally all the inheritance of life and strength and power that you need.

When I was in Switzerland, the Lord was graciously working and healing many of the people. I was staying with Brother Reuss of Goldiwil, and two policemen were sent to arrest me. The charge was that I was healing the people without a license. Mr. Reuss said to them, "I am sorry that he is not here just now. He is holding a meeting about two miles away, but before you arrest him to let me show you something."

Brother Reuss took these two policemen down to one of the lower parts of that district, to a house with which they were familiar, for they had often gone to that place to arrest a certain woman, who was repeatedly put in the prison because of continually being engaged in drunken brawls. He took them to this woman and said to them, "This is one of the many cases of blessing that have come through the ministry of the man you have come to arrest.

This woman came to our meeting in a drunken condition. Her body was broken, for she was ruptured in two places. While she was drunk, the evangelist laid his hands on her and asked God to heal her and deliver her." The woman joined in, "Yes, and God saved me, and I have not tasted a drop of 'liquor since." The policemen had a warrant for my arrest, but they said with disgust, "Let the doctors do this kind of thing." They turned and went away, and that was the last we heard of them.

We have a Jesus that heals the broken-hearted, who lets the captives go free, who saves the very worst. Dare you, dare you, spurn this glorious Gospel of God for spirit, soul and body? Dare you spurn this **GRACE**? I realize that this full Gospel has in great measure teen hid, this Gospel that brings liberty, this Gospel that brings souls out of bondage, this Gospel that brings perfect health to the body, this Gospel of entire salvation. Listen again to this word of Him who left the glory to bring us this great salvation, "Verily I say unto you, That whosoever shall say unto this mountain, Be thou removed, . . . he shall have whatsoever he with." Whatsoever!

I realize that God can never bless us on the lines of being hardhearted, critical or unforgiving. This will hinder faith quicker than anything. I remember being at a meeting where there were some people tarrying for the Baptism-seeking for cleansing, for the moment a person is cleansed the Spirit will fall. There was one man with eyes red from weeping bitterly. He said to me, "I shall have to leave. It is no good my staying without I change things.

I have written a letter to my brother-in-law and filled it with hard words, and this thing must first be straightened out." He went home and told his wife, "I'm going to write a letter to your brother and ask him to forgive me for writing to him the way I did." "You fool!" she said. "Never mind," he replied, "this is between God and me, and it has got to be cleared away." He wrote the letter and came again, and straightway God filled him with the Spirit.

I believe there are a great many people who would be healed, but they are harboring things in their hearts that are as a blight. Let these things go. Forgive, and the Lord will forgive you. There are many good people, people that mean well, but they have no power to do anything for God. There is just some little thing that came in their hearts years ago, and their faith has been paralyzed ever since.

Bring everything to the light. God will sweep it all away if you let Him. Let the precious blood of Christ cleanse from all sin. If you will but believe, God will meet you and bring into your lives the sunshine of His love.

From the author Dr. Michael H Yeager's

Paul's Revelation That Grace Comes in Our Weakness

***2 Corinthians 11:22 Are they Hebrews? so am I. Are they Israelites? so am I. Are they the seed of Abraham? so am I. 23 Are they ministers of Christ? (I speak as a fool) I am more; in**

labours more abundant, in stripes above measure, in prisons more frequent, in deaths oft. 24 Of the Jews five times received I forty stripes save one. 25 Thrice was I beaten with rods, once was I stoned, thrice I suffered shipwreck, a night and a day I have been in the deep; 26 in journeyings often, in perils of waters, in perils of robbers, in perils by mine own countrymen, in perils by the heathen, in perils in the city, in perils in the wilderness, in perils in the sea, in perils among false brethren; 27 in weariness and painfulness, in watchings often, in hunger and thirst, in fastings often, in cold and nakedness.

28 Beside those things that are without, that which cometh upon me daily, the care of all the churches. 29 Who is weak, and I am not weak? who is offended, and I burn not? 30 If I must needs glory, I will glory of the things which concern mine infirmities. 31 The God and Father of our Lord Jesus Christ, which is blessed for evermore, knoweth that I lie not.

2 Corinthians 12:7 And lest I should be exalted above measure through the abundance of the revelations, there was given to me a thorn in the flesh, the messenger of Satan to buffet me, lest I should be exalted above measure. 8 For this thing I besought the Lord thrice, that it might depart from me. 9 And he said unto me, My grace is sufficient for thee: for my strength is made perfect in weakness. Most gladly therefore will I rather glory in my infirmities, that the power of Christ may rest upon me. 10 Therefore I take pleasure in infirmities, in reproaches, in necessities, in persecutions, in distresses for Christ's sake: for when I am weak, then am I strong.

Was it God causing Paul to have all these problems? No, he told us that it was the enemy who was behind all of these attacks.

Why? What was the enemy doing? The enemy was trying to kill him. The enemy was trying to snuff him out. Now, I want you to notice in verse 10 Paul says I therefore take pleasure in infirmities, in reproaches, in persecutions, in distresses, for Christ's sake. This is strange kind of theology. When most people go through hardships and problems and difficulties, they gripe, they complain, they grumble.

When a person is truly moved by faith and trust, confidence in God, they will never complain. That's why Paul said: In Everything Give Thanks, For This Is the Will of God in Christ Jesus concerning You.

Paul said I take pleasure in these adversities. Paul says, that when all hell breaks loose on me, I get excited. Do you know that wasn't just his theology? That was the motto of the early church when they were persecuted, when they were beaten, when they were attacked because of their love for Christ, they rejoiced. They actually considered it a great privilege to suffer because of Christ.

I'm telling you this that the apostle Paul had a hold of something that you and I need. James the brother of Jesus said, when the devil messes with you, count it all joy. No, I'm not implying that you let the devil mess with you. I'm not implying that you lay down and play dead like an opossum. I'm saying what Paul the apostle said: he was shipwrecked three times, whipped three times, and beaten with rods. He was stoned. He was in danger, he was in prison over and over.

He says, Man, This Is Exciting. **This Is An Adventure**. He said this is **Wonderful**. When's the last time you knew someone that got beat up for preaching the Gospel? The early church said, Oh man that was so wonderful. That was amazing. Wow. Come on, devil, and bring your worse.

Pastor Mike that's crazy! Oh, is it really? Pastor Mike has the devil ever attacked and afflicted you because of your love for Christ? Yes, more times than I can share with you. What was the end results? Amazing and supernatural, Divine Deliverances! Over, and over, and over. I literally have hundreds of testimonies of times I should have died, been murdered, been mortally wounded, but in my weakness, and sufferings, God Showed up!

My Wife and My Children Would have Died

Cutting Corners Almost Killed My Wife and My Children! We had built a homemade swimming pool at our new house. (I'm always trying to save money – which can lead to disaster.) The pool was 24 feet across and 4 feet deep. Now our house was built on the side of a small mountain. This pool was in the backyard, where right beyond it there is a very steep slope to the road below us. One day, my son Steven and my daughter Stephanie were swimming in this homemade pool. Stephanie was about 10 years old and Steven was 12. I was at my office when my wife called me on the phone. She said to me, Honey, something just doesn't look right with that swimming pool. There some water leaking out of the side. It must have been God who quickening both of us. A divine Holy Ghost **unction, urgency, a must right now** came upon me.

I told my wife, "Baby Doll Go get the kids out of the pool right now!" It is not in her nature or personality to do anything really quick, but in this instant the same Holy Ghost urgency, unction, this holy hurry up, came upon her. Thank the Lord, she did. She ran out and yelled for my son and daughter to come to her. They usually do not respond so quickly either, but his time they literally ran and swam to her. The pool up to this moment completely looked normal with no problems whatsoever.

Thank God, my wife was not standing at the part of the pool that is towards the steep slope. This in itself was a miracle. The kids swam, ran across the pool, and came to her right away. She reached over the 4-foot wall and pulled out our daughter first and then she help Steven get out. Now she will tell you that was a miracle in itself because of how much they weighed. It was like a supernatural strength came upon her, enabling her to lift them up, and pulled them out.

Now at that very instant, I mean at that very moment when she had both Steven and Stephanie out of the pool, the whole swimming pool completely broke loose and collapsed. The wooden walls and steel cables all came undone, swirling like a gigantic, uncontrollable snake. Over 13,500 gallons of water came flooding out; approximately 112,725 pounds of water broke loose. All of the boards, the four heavy steel cables that wrap around the pool, the pool lining and all the water broke loose. It rushed down the hill like a mighty flood onto the asphalt road over 80 feet below. It tore up the side of that hill creating great groups in the dirt and flooded the road below.

If my children would have still been in that pool, they would have been swept away, broken, and tumbling in the flood of the water, steel cables, pool lining and the retaining boards. They both would have surely been killed, along with my wife, if she had been standing on the down side of the pool. Thank God for his mercy and protection! When the divine unction of God hits us, a supernatural urgency, a Holy Ghost hurry up, we need to respond immediately. If we do not respond right away, then most likely something tragic and terrible will happen.

For as many as are led by the spirit of God they are the sons of God!

Christ and the Holy Ghost in us, gives us the ability to obey the will of the Father, to get up and go, to move on out. We are talking about a divine unction, Holy Ghost hurry up, supernatural urgency that will overtake you as you surrender your life, mind, heart, spirit, soul and body to the will of the Father. Many times through the years this divine urgency comes upon me like an invisible mantle. In these times of the divine flow of the unction of the Holy Ghost God enables me to do the supernatural and the miraculous. In one service I found myself in the situation where a young lady was about to be seriously hurt when the Holy Ghost unction overtook me.

Brittany would have been consumed by fire 1992

I have discovered through the years that when the spirit of God quickens my heart with the divine urgency, Holy Ghost unction to do something, it is not the time to think, but it is time to obey and act. I cannot tell you how many times I have immediately responded to the spirit of God to a certain situation. As I look back, I realize if I had not quickly done that which the spirit of God quickened to my heart, the end results would have been terrible and devastating. This is one of those situations.

Our youth had been practicing a wonderful Christmas Carol, in which we had a large children s choir. The men of the church had built small risers in which the youth and the children could stand upon. Starting from the front to the back, it took each child up approximately six inches. In one part of the production all the children held lit candles. Almost all the lights were turned off in the sanctuary during this time. It was a beautiful scene, with all the children having their candles lit and singing wonderful Christmas carols to the congregation.

One of our youth was a young attractive teenager who was approximately fourteen years old. Her name was Britney, who had long brown hair. She was standing approximately three rows deep on the third riser. I believe I was sitting on the front row of the chairs in a sanctuary, simply enjoying this wonderful performance of the youth. As I was watching the candlelight, singing performance I noticed something very peculiar.

A very light blue haze appeared over the top of Britney's head. Immediately I knew in my heart by the Holy Ghost that her hair was on fire. One of the teenagers behind her had accidentally put her candle up against Britney's hair. Britney must have used some type of hairspray to be prepared for tonight's performance, and this hairspray was extremely flammable. In my heart, I knew that this could be a very devastating situation. I discovered later, that this thought was truly from God. Here is some devastating information about the tragedies resulting from hair fires.

*One of the most common characteristics of hair fires is that they are unexpected. Rarely does anyone set his or her hair on fire intentionally. Therefore, when a hair fire happens, the person is caught completely off guard and very often their instinctive reactions make it worse. The most immediate preferred reactions would be to immediately douse the head with water or to smother the fire with a towel, blanket or other suitable material. However, what typically happens is that the person will run about or drop and roll, which only fans the fire with air.

Another reaction to a hair fire is to attempt to put out the fire by the use of hands, which typically results in hand and arm burns. – [Burns typical of a hair fire due to drop down]. Because burning hair will often "drop down," the person receives burns to the neck, shoulders and chest, sometimes to a greater degree than burns to the scalp. The individual's clothing may also catch on fire exacerbating these types of neck, shoulder and chest burns.

Another characteristic of a hair fire is that the person often believes they have successfully extinguished the fire and will stop their efforts to put out the fire only to find that it "re-ignites" In reality, the hair fire does not "re-ignite," but was never completely put out in the first place. If any small portion of the hair remains on fire, it will "re-ignite" the remaining hair. The final characteristic of hair fires is severe disfigurement requiring extensive plastic surgery to correct.

Of course, I had no knowledge of any of this at the time, all I had was a divine unction, a quickening, and a super natural urgency entering my heart to get to Britney. I immediately jumped up out of my chair, running for the choir, maneuvering pass all the other people in the play, and getting past all the props. In my supernatural rush to get to Brittany, not one time did I stumble, trip over a cord, bump into a person, or knock anything over. It is hard for me to explain to people this supernatural realm I enter in when the spirit of God takes me over.

When I finally reached the bleachers, Britney's hair was glowing bluer than ever. Somehow, I got in between the children, not knocking one of them off of the risers in order to get to Brittany. Of course, everybody saw all my actions, and had no idea what was happening. To this day many of them that were at this performance never knew what happened.

When I finally stood in front of Britney, in my heart I knew what I needed to do. I could not use my hands to put out her hair fire. Instead, somehow, I grabbed the back of her head, (with her hair all burning blue now) pulling her head down to my chest. I took my suit jacket and completely enveloped her head into my chest. Miraculously, yes supernaturally I was able to get her hair extinguished in a matter of seconds.

Britney had no idea what was going on until after the service. Once the fire was out, I did not even say a word to her or anyone. I just simply helped her stand back up straight, spun around, and went back to my chair. As I think back on this situation, I'm sure it looked a little bit comical. The performance never stopped. The play continued, with the choir singing, holding their candle lights. In the minds of the people it was just a little burp in the performance. Thank God for the Holy Ghost, the divine quickening, the unction of the spirit and divine intervention. It was even supernatural that neither one of us received any burns whatsoever.

Christ always responded immediately when the spirit of God put an urgency, an unction into his heart. One day he was walking along with a massive crowd of people when he came underneath a sycamore tree. When he looked up into that sycamore tree he saw a little man who was a local tax collector. Remember that Christ was in great demand at this period of his ministry, and that a lot of people were vying for his attention. Christ was never motivated by popularity, finances, and by people in upper political or spiritual positions. He was constantly being led and guided by the Holy Ghost. In this situation and unction of the Lord hit him to go to this particular man's house. He said:

Luke 19:5 And when Jesus came to the place, he looked up, and saw him, and said unto him, Zacchæus, make haste, and come down; for to day I must abide at thy house.

Did you notice that he used the word **must**? He said I **must come to your house today.** This was the divine unction of the Holy Ghost that was leading him, and guiding him. I have had similar situations in my own personal life. I wish I could tell you that I have always responded properly, but I have not. As a result of not responding to the unction of the Holy Ghost, people's lives have been lost for eternity.

Death & Destruction over the Mississippi! 2007

My family and I was saved from a terrible death at the Mississippi river! Many times, in my life I have had vivid experiences, perceiving that God is about to do something or that something is about to take place right before it happens!

On August 1, 2007, my wife, three sons, daughter and I were traveling on Highway I 35 West. We were in our Toyota crew cab pickup truck, pulling a 35 foot fifth wheel trailer. We were on vacation and headed for Yellowstone National Park. At the time, we were headed towards the downtown area of Minneapolis, Minnesota.

As I was driving, I sensed in my heart that we needed to get off this highway, even though our GPS was taking us the shortest route to where we were headed. I have discovered and personally experienced twenty major ways that God leads and guides. All twenty of these specific ways in which God leads and guides can be discovered in the Scriptures. What I felt is what I call a divine unction of the Holy Ghost. It is more than a perception or a feeling. It is more like an overwhelming urgency that flows up out of your belly.

I informed my family that something was wrong, that there was an urgency in my heart and we needed to get off I 35 West immediately. This is the only time I can remember having experienced this divine unction, urgency to get off a road or highway. I took the nearest exit off of I 35 W. and went north towards Canada. After a while, we connected to another highway that would take us West, over the Mississippi River towards Dakota. A little Later in the day, we pulled into a store to take a break from driving. As we entered this facility, we noticed that there were people gathered around the television.

We could see that some major disaster had taken place. The viewers informed us that a bridge had collapsed over the Mississippi River, when a lot of heavy traffic was loaded on top of it. We could see on the TV screen cars, trucks, buses everywhere that had fallen into the Mississippi. There is death and destruction everywhere.

The hair on the back of my neck stood up as I realized this bridge that had collapsed was on I 35 W. It was the same highway in which the spirit of God quickens my heart with a divine unction, urgency to get off. As we discussed this situation, and the precise time when the bridge collapsed, we discovered that we would've been on this bridge with our truck and our fifth wheel trailer.

If I had not left the highway at the unction, and the urging of the Holy Ghost most likely we would have found ourselves in the bottom of the Mississippi River. Thirteen people died that day and many were seriously injured, not including all the terrible destruction, and horrible nightmare that took place with all those who were a part of this tragedy. Thank God for the divine intervention and leading of the Holy Ghost.

For the spirit of the Lord to lead and guide us we must not have any other agenda, no other purpose, no other plan, just simply God's will to obey. John the Baptist said: but I must decrease, for Christ to increase. To be a disciple of Christ means to be led by the spirit. We become a nobody in our own eyes. For many years when I have perceived that people were beginning to look to me instead of Christ I told them I'm not your answer. If I can help it, I never let people think that I am there solution. If you allow people to put you on a pedestal you are simply an accident going somewhere to happen.

CHAPTER FIVE

The Holy Spirit is coming to take out of the world a church that is a perfect bride. He must find in us entirely yielded, with every desire subjected to Him.

We must be careful not to choose on our own, but to let God's Holy Spirit manage our lives. Not to smooth down and explain away, but to stir up the gift. To allow God's Spirit to disturb us, and disturb us, and disturb us until we yield, and yield, and yield. Until the possibility in God's mind for us becomes an established fact in our lives, with the rivers in evidence meeting the need of a dying world.

Oh, this Baptism of the Holy Spirit is an inward presence of the personality of God, which lifts, prays, takes hold, lives in, with tranquility of peace and power that rests and says, It is all right. God answers prayer because the Holy Spirit prays and your advocate is Jesus, and the Father, the Judge of all. There He is. Is it possible for any prayer to be missed on those lines?

You must be yielded to the Word of God. The Word will work out love in our hearts, and when practical love is in our hearts, there is no room to boast about ourselves. We see ourselves as nothing when we get lost in this divine love.

The Express Image of God

Christ, who is the express image of God, has come to our human weaknesses, to change us and to give us His divine likeness, to be partakers of His divine nature, so that by the power of His might we may not only overcome but rejoice in the fact that we are more than conquerors. God wants you to know by experience what it means to be more than a conqueror.

The Baptism in the Holy Spirit had come for nothing less than to empower us, to give the real power that Christ Himself had, so that you, a yielded vessel, may continue the same type of ministry that He had when He walked this earth in the days of His flesh. He purposes that we should come behind in no gift. There are gifts of healing and the working of miracles, but we must apprehend these. There is the gift of faith by the same Spirit which we are to receive.

The greatest need in the world today is that we should be burning and shining lights to reflect the Glory of Christ. We cannot do it with a cold, indifferent experience, and we never shall. His servants are to be flames of burning fire. Christ came that we might have life, and life more abundantly. And we are to give that life to others, to be ministers of the life and power and healing virtue of Jesus Christ wherever we go.

The faith which was in Christ was by the Holy Spirit to be given to those who believed. Henceforth, as Paul yielded his life to God, he could say, I am crucified with Christ: nevertheless I

live; yet not I, but Christ liveth in me: and the life which I now live in the flesh I live by the faith of the Son of God, who loved me and gave Himself for me. The faith of the Son of God communicated by the Holy Spirit to the one who puts his trust in God and in His Son.

Jesus Christ is glorified, as your faith in Him is quickened, from within you there will flow rivers of living water. The Holy Spirit will pour through you like a great river of life and thousands will be blessed because you are a yielded channel through whom the Spirit may flow.

Himself took our Infirmities

Bible reading, Matt. 8:1-17.

Here we have a wonderful word. All the Word is wonderful. This blessed Book brings such life and health and peace, and such an abundance that we should never be poor any more. This Book is my heavenly bank. I find everything I want in it. I want to show you how rich you may be, that in everything you can be enriched in Christ Jesus.

He has an abundance of **GRACE** for you and the gift of righteousness, and through His abundant **GRACE**, all things are possible. I want to show you that you can be a living branch of the living Vine, Christ Jesus and that it is your privilege to be right here in this world what He is. John tells us, "As He is, so are we in this world." Not that we are anything in ourselves, but Christ within us is our all in all.

The Lord Jesus is always wanting to show forth Ills **GRACE** and love in order to draw us to Himself. God is willing to do things, to manifest His Word, and let us know in a measure the mind of our God in this day and hour. There are many needy ones, many afflicted ones, but I do not think any present is half as bad as this first case that we read of in Matthew 8. This man was a leper. You may be suffering from consumption or cancers or other things, but God will show forth His perfect cleansing, His perfect healing if you have a living faith in Christ. He is a wonderful Jesus.

This leper must have been told about Jesus. How much is missed because people are not constantly telling what Jesus will do in this our day. Probably someone had come to that leper and said, "Jesus can heal you." And so he was filled with expectation as he saw the Lord coming down the mountain side. Lepers were not allowed to come within reach of people; they were shut out as unclean. And so in the ordinary way it would have been very difficult for him to get near because of the crowd that surrounded Jesus. But as He came down from the mount, He met this poor leper. Oh, this terrible disease!

There was no help for him humanly speaking, but nothing is too hard for Jesus. The man cried, "Lord, if thou wilt, thou canst make me clean." Was Jesus willing? You will never find Jesus missing an opportunity of doing good. You will find that He is always more willing to work than we are to give Him an opportunity to work. The trouble is we do not come to Him, we do not ask Him for what He is more than willing to give.

And Jesus put forth His band, and touched him, saying, "I will; be thou clean." And immediately his leprosy was cleansed. I like that. If you are definite with Him, you will never go away disappointed. The divine life will flow into yo, and instantaneously you will be delivered. This Jesus is just the same today, and He says to you, "I will; be thou clean." He has an overflowing cup for thee, a fullness of life. He will meet you in your absolute helplessness. All things are possible if you will only believe. God has a real plan. It is so simple. Just come to Jesus. You will find Him just the same as He was in days of old.

The next case we have in this chapter is that of the centurion coming and beseeching Jesus on behalf of his servant who was sick of the palsy and grievously tormented. This man was so in earnest that he came seeking Jesus. Notice this, that there is one thing certain; there is no such thing as seeking without finding. He that seeketh findeth. Listen to the gracious words of Jesus, "I will come and heal him." Most places that we go to there are so many people that we cannot pray for.

In some place, there are 200 or 300 who would like us to visit them, but we are not able to do so. But I am so glad that the Lord Jesus is always willing to come and heal. He longs to meet the sick ones. He loves to heal them of their afflictions. The Lord is healing many people today using handkerchiefs as you read that He healed people in the days of Paul. You can read of this in Acts 19:12.

A woman came to me in the city of Liverpool and said, "I would like you to help me. I wish you would join with me in prayer. My husband is a drunkard and every night comes into the home under the influence of drink. Won't you join me in prayer for him?" I said to the woman, "Have you a handkerchief?" She took out a handkerchief, and I prayed over it and told her to lay it on the pillow of the drunken man. He came home that night and laid his head on the pillow in which this handkerchief was tucked. He laid his head on more than the pillow that night. He laid his head on the promise of God. In Mark 11: 24, we read, "What things soever ye desire when ye pray, believe that ye receive them and ye shall have them."

The next morning the man got up and called at the first saloon that he had to pass on his way to work and ordered some beer. He tasted it and said to the bartender, "You have put some poison in this beer." He could not drink it, and went on to the next saloon and ordered some more beer. He tasted it and said to the man behind the counter, "You put some poison in this beer, I believe you folks have agreed to poison me." The bartender was indignant at being thus charged. The man said, "I will go somewhere else." He went to another saloon, and the same thing happened as in the two previous saloons. He made such a fuss that they turned him out.

After he came out from work, he went to another saloon to get some beer, and again he thought he had been poisoned and he made so much disturbance that he was thrown out. He went to his home and told his wife what had happened and said, "It seems as though all the fellows have agreed to poison me." His wife said to him, "Can't you see the hand of the Lord in this, that He is making you dislike the stuff that has been your ruin?" This word brought conviction to the man's heart, and he came to the meeting and got saved. The Lord has still power to set the captives free.

When I was in Australia, a lady came to me who was much troubled about her son who was so lazy. I prayed over a handkerchief which was placed on the boy's pillow. He slept that night on the handkerchief, and the next morning he got up and went out and secured a position and went to work. Oh, praise the Lord, you can't shut God out, but if you will only believe He will shut the devil out.

Jesus was willing to go and heal the sick one, but the centurion said, "Lord, I am not worthy that thou shouldest come under my roof; but speak the word only, and my servant shall be healed." Jesus was delighted with this expression and said to the man, "Go thy way; and as thou hast believed, so be it done unto thee." And his servant was healed the self-same hour.

When I was in Australia, a man came up to me. He was leaning on a big stick and said, "I would like you to help me. It will take you half an hour to pray for me." I said, "Believe God, and in one moment you will be whole." His faith was quickened to receive immediate healing, and he went away glorifying God for miraculous healing. The word of the Lord is sufficient today. If you dare to believe God's Word, you will see a performance of ills Word that will be truly wonderful. Here we have with the centurion an audacity of faith, a faith that did not limit God. Failures come when we limit the Holy One of Israel. I want to encourage you to a living faith to believe God's Word.

The next healing we read of here is the healing of Peter's wife's mother who was sick of a fever. Luke tells us that Jesus rebuked the fever. The fever could hear. The moment it could hear it went. Jesus had a new method. Today there are a lot of folks who try to sweat out a fever. You can't sweat the devil out. He can stand all the heat that you can apply to him. But if thou canst believe, deliverance is as sure and certain for you as it was for Peter's wife's mother.

I received a telegram once urging me to visit a case about 200 miles from my home. As I went to this place, I met the father and mother and found them broken hearted. They lead me up a staircase to a room, and I saw a young woman on the floor, and five people were holding her down. She was a frail young woman, but the power in her was greater than all those young men.

As I went into the room, the evil powers looked out of her eye, and they used her lips saying, "We are many, you can't cast us out." I said, "Jesus can." He is equal to every occasion. He is waiting for an opportunity to bless. He is ready for every opportunity to deliver souls. When we receive Jesus it is true of us, "Greater is He that is in you than he that is in the world." He is greater than all the powers of darkness. No man can meet the devil in his strength, but any man filled with the knowledge of Jesus, filled with His presence, filled with His power, is more than a match for the powers of darkness. God has called us to be more than conquerors through Him that loved us.

The living Word can destroy Satanic forces. There is power in the name of Jesus. I would say that every window in the street had the name of Jesus written large upon it. His name, through faith in His name. Brought deliverance to this poor, bound soul, and thirty-seven demons came out giving their names as they came forth. The dear woman was completely delivered, and they were able to give her back her child. That night there was heaven in that hom, and the father and mother and son and his wife were all united in glorifying Christ for His infinite **GRACE**.

The next morning we had a gracious time in the breaking of bread. All things are wonderful with our wonderful Jesus. If you dared rest your all upon Him, things would take place, and He would change the whole situation. In a moment, through the name of Jesus, a new order of things can be brought in.

In the world, they are always having new diseases, and the doctors cannot locate them. A doctor said to me, "The science of medicine is in its infancy, and we doctors have no confidence in our medicine. We are always experimenting." But the man of God does not experiment. He knows, or ought to know, redemption in its fullness. He knows, or ought to know, the mightiness of the Lord Jesus Christ. He is not, or should not be, moved by outward observation, but should get a divine revelation of the mightiness of the name of Jesus and the power of His blood. If we exercise our faith in the Lord Jesus Christ, He will come forth and get glory over all the powers of darkness.

At eventide they brought unto Him many that were possessed with devils; and He cast out the spirits with His word and healed all that were sick: that it might be fulfilled which was spoken by Esaias the prophet, saying, "Himself took our infirmities, and bare our sicknesses." The work is done if you only believe it. It is done. Himself took our infirmities and bared our sicknesses. If you can only see the Lamb of God as He went to Calvary!

He took our flesh that He might take upon Himself the full burden of all our sin and all the consequences of sin. There on the cross God laid upon Him the iniquities of us all. There on the cross of Calvary the results of sin were also dealt with. "As the children are partakers of flesh and blood, he also himself took part of the same; that through death he might destroy him that had the power of death, that is, the devil; and deliver them who through fear of death were all their life time subject to bondage." Through His death there is deliverance for you today.

Jesus is greater than all evil powers

There are evil powers, but Jesus is greater than all evil powers. There are tremendous diseases, but Jesus is a healer. There is no case too hard for Him. The Lion of Judah shall break every chain. He came to relieve the oppressed and to set the captive free. He came to bring redemption, to make us as perfect as the man was before the fall.

People want to know how to be kept by the power of God. Every position of **GRACE** into which you are led-forgiveness, healing, the deliverance of any kind, will be contested by Satan. He will contend for your body. When you are saved, Satan will come round and say, "See, you are not saved." The devil is a liar. If he says you are not saved, it is a sure sign that you are.

You will remember the story of the man who was swept and garnished. The evil power had been swept out of him. But the man remained in a stationary position. If the Lord heals you, you dare not remain in a stationary position. The evil spirit came back to that man and found the house swept, and took seven others worse than himself, and the last state of that man was worse than the first. Be sure to get filled with God. Get the Occupier. Be filled with the Spirit.

God has a million ways of undertaking for those who go to Him for help. He has deliverance for every captive. He loves you so much that He even says, "Before they call, I will answer." Don't turn Him away.

"I slipped and fell on Broadway, San Diego, in February 1921, and as was afterwards discovered, fractured the coccyx (the base of the spine), and so severely wrenched the hips and pelvic bones that I became a great sufferer. The broken bone was not discovered and set until about two months after the accident. The constant pain and irritation caused a general inflammation of the nervous system, and the long delay in getting the bone set made it impossible to heal. My condition steadily grew worse, and I was taken to the hospital, and the bone was removed about a month after it had been set.

Though the wound healed rapidly, the nervous inflammation remained, and so for many months longer, I was in constant pain and unable to get around without assistance. I was taken to the first service held by Mr. Wigglesworth on the 2nd of October, 1922. At the close of the service, all those who were sick and in pain and had come for healing were requested to rise if possible. My husband assisted me to my feet, and as those were prayed for by the speaker, I was instantly healed. Exactly how I do not know. I only know the Great Physician touched my body and I was made whole and freed from pain.

"After I got home I showed how I could sit down and rise with my hands above my head; when before it had taken both hands to push up my feeble body, and I had to have straps on my bed to pull up by. No more use for them now! I lay down and turned over for the first time without pain. I shall never cease to praise God for the healing of my body through the precious blood of Jesus and in His name. I walked to the street car alone the next day and attended the next service and have been "on the go" ever since. Can give names of friends who can substantiate all I have written. To Jesus be all the praise and glory." - Mrs. Sanders, 4051 Bay View Court, San Diego, Calif.

Immersed in the Holy Ghost

Published in Confidence p. 42-43 July-Sept 1920

The baptism of the Holy Ghost is a great beginning. I think the best word we can say is, "Lord, what wilt Thou have me to do?" The greatest difficulty today with us is to be held in the place where it shall be God only. It is so easy to get our own mind to work. The working of the Holy Ghost is so different. I believe there is a mind of Christ, and we may be so immersed in the Spirit that we are all the day asking, "What wilt Thou have me to do?"

This has been a day in the Holy Ghost. The last three months have been the greatest days of my life. I used to think if I could see such and such things worked I should be satisfied, but I have seen greater things than I ever expected to see, and I am hungrier to see greater things yet.

The great thing at conventions is to get us so immersed in God that we may see signs and wonders in the name of the Lord Jesus; a place where death has taken place and we are not, for God has taken us. If God has taken hold of us we will be changed by His power and might. You can depend on it, the Ethiopian will be changed. I find God has a plan to turn the world upside down, where we are not.

When I have been at my wit's end, and have seen God open the door, I have felt I should never doubt God again. I have been taken to another place that was worse still. There is no place for us, and yet a place where God is, where the Holy Ghost is just showing forth and displaying His **GRACE**s; a place where we will never come out, where we are always immersed in the Spirit, the glory of God being seen upon us. It is wonderful! There is a power behind the scenes that move things. God can work in such a marvelous way...

I believe we have yet to learn what it would be with a Pentecostal Church in England that understood truly the work of intercession. I believe God the Holy Ghost wants to teach us that it is not only the people on the platform who can move things by prayer. You people, the Lord, can move things through you. We have to learn the power of the breath of the Holy Ghost.

If I am filled with the Holy Ghost, He will formulate the word that will come into my heart. The sound of my voice is only by the breath that goes through it. When I was in a little room at Bern waiting for my passport, I found a lot of people, but I couldn't speak to them. So I got hold of three men and pulled them unto me. They stared, but I got them on their knees. Then we prayed, and the revival began. I couldn't talk to them, but I could show them the way to talk to Someone else.

God will move upon the people to make them see the glory of God just as it was when Jesus walked in this world, and I believe the

Holy Ghost will do special wonders and miracles in these last days. I was taken to see a young woman who was very ill. The young man who showed me the way said, “I am afraid we shall not be able to do much here, because of her mother, and the doctors are coming.” I said, “This is what God has brought me here for,” and when I prayed the young woman was instantly healed by the power of God. God, the Holy Ghost, says in our hearts today that it is only He who can do it. After that we got crowds, and I ministered to the sick among them for two hours.

The secret for the future is living and moving in the power of the Holy Ghost. One thing I rejoice in is that there need not be an hour or a moment when I do not know the Holy Ghost is upon me. Oh, this glorious life in God is beyond expression; it is God manifest in the flesh. Oh, this glorious unction of the Holy Ghost — that we move by the Spirit. He should be our continual life. The Holy Ghost has the last thoughts of anything that God wants to give. Glory to God for the Holy Ghost! We must see that we live in the place where we say, “What wilt Thou have me to do?” and are in the place where He can work in us to will and to do of His good pleasure.

Becoming ablaze for God

I see people from time to time very slack, cold, and indifferent; but after they get filled with the Holy Spirit, they become ablaze for God. I believe that God's ministers are to be flames of fire; nothing less than flames; nothing less than mighty instruments with burning messages.

With a heart full of love, with such a depth of consecration that God has taken full charge of the body and it exists only that it may manifest the glory of God. Surely, this is the ideal and the purpose of this great plan of salvation for man that we might be filled with all the fullness of God, and become ministers of life, God working mightily in us and through us to manifest His **GRACE**--the saving power of humanity.

Now let us turn to this wonderful Word of God. I want you to see the demonstration of this power in this man Paul--this man who was “born out of due time:” this Paul, who was plucked as a brand from the burning; this Paul whom God chose to be an apostle to the Gentiles.

See him first as a persecutor, mad to destroy those who were bringing glad tidings to the people. See how madly he rushed those people to prison, striving to make them blaspheme that holy name. Then see this same man changed by the power of God and the Gospel of Christ; see him filled with the Holy Ghost, becoming a builder for God and a revealer of the Son of God, so that he could say, “It is no longer I that live, but Christ liveth in me.” Gal. 2:20.

In the 9th chapter of Acts, we read that he was called to a special ministry. The Lord said to Ananias, “I will show him what great things he must suffer for my name's sake.” I don't want you to think that this means suffering from diseases; for it means suffering persecution, suffering from slander, from strife, from bitterness, from revilings, and many other evil things.

None of these things will hurt you; rather, they will kindle the fire of the holy ambition, because the scripture says, “Blessed are they that have been persecuted for righteousness' sake: for theirs is the kingdom of heaven.” Matt. 5:10. To be persecuted for Christ's sake is to be joined up with a blessed, blessed people; but, better still, it means to be united with our Lord Jesus in the closest of fellowship, the fellowship of His suffering. There is a day coming when we will rejoice greatly that we have been privileged to suffer for His name's sake.

Beloved, God wants witnesses, witnesses to the truth, witnesses to the full truth, and witnesses to the fullness of redemption--deliverance from sin and deliverance from disease--by the eternal power working in them, as they are filled with life through the Spirit. God wants us to believe that we may be ministers of that kind--of glorious things wrought in us by the Holy Spirit.

See in verse 7, how Paul was lost in his zeal for his ministry so that he "continued his speech until midnight." Then something happened that threatened to break up the meeting--a young man, becoming sleepy, fell out of the window. That was enough to break up any ordinary meeting. But this man, filled with the Spirit of God, was equal even to such an emergency even on the moment. He went down, picked up the young man, and brought life back into him by the Spirit of life that was in him, then returned to the upper room and continued the meeting until the break of day.

In Switzerland, the people said to me, "How long can you preach to us?" I said to them, "When the Holy Ghost is upon us, we can preach forever!" When I was in San Francisco, driving down the main street one day, we came across a crowd in the street. The driver stopped, and I jumped out of the car, and right across from where the tumult was, I found a boy lying on the ground apparently in the grip of death. I got down and asked, "What is amiss?" He replied in a whisper, "tramp." I put my hand underneath his back and said, "In the name of Jesus, come out." And the boy jumped up and ran away, not even stopping to say "Thank you."

So you will find out that, with the Baptism of the Holy Spirit, you will be in a position to act when you have no time to think. The power and working of the Holy Spirit is of divine origin. It is the supernatural, God thrilling and moving one with the authority and power of almightiness, and it brings things to pass that could not come to pass in any other way.

I had some things of this character happen on the ship as I was crossing the ocean. I want ever to be in Paul's position--that at any time, even at midnight, in the face of anything, even death itself, God may be able to manifest His power and do what He wants to do through me. This is what it means to be possessed by the Spirit of God. My heart is thrilled with the possibility of coming into the place where Paul was. Let us read verse 19, that we may get our mind perfectly fortified with this blessed truth that God has for us.

"Serving the Lord with all humility of mind." None of us is going to be able to be a minister of this new covenant of promise in the unction and power of the Spirit without humility. It seems to me that the way to get up is to get down. It is clear to me that in the measure that the dying of the Lord is in me, the life of the Lord will abound in me.

And to me, truly, a Baptism of the Holy Spirit is not the goal, but it is an inflow to reach the highest level, the holiest position that it is possible for human nature to reach by Divine power. The Baptism of the Holy Spirit is given to reveal and to make real Him in whom dwells "all the fulness of the Godhead bodily." Col. 2:9. So I see that to be baptized in the Holy Spirit means to be baptized into death, into life, into power, into fellowship with the Trinity, where the old life ceases to be, and the life of God possesses us forever.

No man can live after seeing God; and God wants us all to see Him in all His glorious, infinite sufficiency so that we shall joyfully cease to be--that He may become our life. Thus it was that Paul could say, "It is no longer I that live, but Christ liveth in me." I believe that God wants to make real to us all this ideal of humility where we so recognize human helplessness and human insufficiency that we shall rest no more on human plans and human devices and human energy, but continually look to God for His thought, for His voice, for His power, for His all-sufficiency in all things.

Now here is another word for us. Let us read it. It is found in verse 22. "Now, behold, I go bound in spirit." Is there a possibility of the human coming into oneness with the divine will? Let me give you two other versions of Scripture. Jesus was a man of flesh and blood like ourselves; though He was the incarnation of the authority and power and majesty of heaven, yet He bore about in His body our flesh, our human weakness, being tempted in all points like as we are, yet without sin. Oh, He was so lovely! Such a perfect Saviour!

Oh, that I could shout "Jesus!" so that all the world would hear. There is salvation, life, power, and deliverance through that name; but, beloved, I read in Mark 1:12, that the Spirit drove that body.

In the fourth chapter of Luke, it says "led" by the Spirit. And now here is Paul "bound" in the spirit.

Oh, what condescension that God should lay hold of humanity and so possess it with His holiness. His righteousness, with his truth, with His faith, that one can say: "I am bound in spirit.

I have no choice; my only choice is for God; my only desire, my only ambition is the will of God; I am bound with God." Is this possible, beloved? If you look into Galatians, first chapter, you will see how wonderfully Paul rose into this state of bliss. If you look in the third chapter of the Ephesians, you will see that he recognized himself as less than the least of all saints.

Then, if you'll look into the 26th chapter of Acts, you will find him saying, "I have never lost the vision, King Agrippa, I have never lost it." Then if you will look again in Galatians, you will see that, to keep the vision, he conferred not with flesh and blood.

God laid hold of him; God bound him; God preserved him. I ought to say, however, that it is a wonderful position to be in--to be preserved by Almightiness--and we ought to see to it that we leave ourselves to God. The consequences will be all right. "Whosoever shall seek to save his life, shall lose it, and whosoever shall lose his life for my sake the same shall save it."

Now, beloved, I am out for men. It is my business to be out for men. It is my business to make everybody hungry, dissatisfied. It is my business to make people either glad or mad. I have a message from heaven that will not leave people as I find them. Something must happen after they are filled with the Holy Spirit.

A man filled with the Holy Spirit is no longer an ordinary man. A man can be swept by the power of God in the first stage of the revelation of Christ so that from that moment he will be an extraordinary man. But to be filled with the Holy Spirit he has to become a free body for God to dwell in, and to use, and to manifest Himself through.

So I appeal to you, you people who have received the Holy Spirit. I appeal to you to let God have His way at whatever cost; I appeal to you to keep moving on with God into an ever increasing realization of His infinite purpose in Christ Jesus for His redeemed ones until you are filled unto all the fulness of God.

To remain three days in the same place would indicate that you have lost the vision. The child of God must catch the vision anew every day. Every day the child of God must be moved more and more by the Holy Ghost. The child of God must come into line with the power of heaven so that he knows that God has his hand upon him.

It is the same Jesus, the very same Jesus. He went about doing good. "God anointed Him with the Holy Ghost and with power: who went about doing good, and healing all that were oppressed of the devil; for God was with Him." Beloved, is not that the ministry God would have us see we are heir to? The mission of the Holy Ghost is to give us a revelation of Jesus and to make the Word of God life unto us as it was when spoken by the Son--as new, as fresh, as effective as if the Lord Himself were speaking.

The Bride loves to hear the Bridegroom's voice! Here it is, the blessed Word of God, the whole Word, not part of it, no, no, no! We believe in the whole of it. We have such effectiveness worked in us by the Word of life, that day by day we are finding out that the Word itself giveth life; the Spirit of the Lord, breathing through, revealing by the Word, giving it a fresh to us, makes the whole Word alive today. Amen.

So I have within my hands, within my heart, within my mind, this blessed reservoir of promises that can do so many marvelous things. Some of you most likely have been suffering because you have a limited revelation of Jesus, of the fullness of life there is in Him.

In Oakland, Calif., we had a meeting in a large theatre. God wrought in filling the place until we had to have overflow meetings. There was a rising tide of people getting saved in the meeting by rising voluntarily up and down in the place, and getting saved. And then we had a riding tide of people who needed help in their bodies, rising in faith and being healed.

One of this latter was an old man 95 years of age. He had been suffering for three years, till he got to the place where for three weeks he had been taking liquids. He was in a terrible state. I got him to stand while I prayed for him, and he came back, and with a radiant face, told us that new life had come into his body. He said, "I am 95 years old. When I came into the meeting, I was full of pain from cancer of the stomach. I have been so healed that I have been eating perfectly, and have no pain." Many of the people were healed similarly.

(After the telling of the above incident in the meeting in Wellington, New Zealand, where this address was given, a lady arose who had rheumatism in the left leg. After being prayed for, she ran the full length of the hall several times, then testified to partial healing. A young man with pain in the head was healed instantly. Another man with pain in the shoulder was healed instantly also.)

In the second chapter of Acts, you will see that when the Holy Ghost came, there was such a manifestation of the power of God that it wrought conviction as the Word was spoken in the Holy Ghost. In the third chapter, we read of the lame man healed at the Beautiful Gate through the power of the Spirit, as Peter and John went into the Temple.

And in the fourth chapter, we read of such a wonderful manifestation of miraculous power through the Spirit that five thousand men besides women and children became believers in the Lord Jesus Christ. God gives a manifestation of His Divine power, beloved, to prove that He is with us. Will you not, right now, open your heart to this wonderful God and let Him come into your life and make of you all that His infinite love has moved Him to provide in Christ Jesus and that His infinite power, through the Holy Ghost, has made possible to be wrought in sinful man.

Seek this vision from God, and keep it ever before you. Pray the prayer that the apostle Paul prayed for the Ephesian believers, as recorded in Ephesians 1:17, 18, 19,

"That the God of our Lord Jesus Christ, the Father of glory, may give unto you a spirit of wisdom and revelation in the knowledge of Him, having the eyes of your heart enlightened.

That ye may know what is the hope of His calling, what the riches of the glory of His inheritance in the saints, and what the exceeding greatness of His power to us ward who believe."

It is the word of God

"Never compare this book with other books. Comparisons are dangerous. Never think or never say that this book contains the word of God. It is the word of God. It is supernatural in origin, eternal in duration, inexpressible in value, infinite in scope, regenerative in power, infallible in authority, universal in interest, personal in application, inspired in totality. Read it through. Write it down. Pray it in. Work it out. And then pass it on."

And truly the word of God changes a man until he becomes an epistle of God. It transforms his mind, changes his character, moves him on from **GRACE** to **GRACE**, and makes him an inheritor of the very nature of God. God comes in, dwells in, walks in, talks through, and sups with him [Rv 3.20] who opens his being to the word of God and receives the Spirit who inspired it.

When I was going over to New Zealand and Australia, I had many to see me off. There was an Indian doctor who was riding in the same car with me to the docks. He was very quiet and took in all the things that were said on the ship. I began to preach of course, and the Lord began to work among the people.

In the second class of the ship there was a young man and his wife who were attendants on a lady and gentleman in the first class.

And as these two young people heard me talking to them privately and otherwise, they were very much impressed. Then the lady they were attending got very sick. In her sickness and her loneliness, she could find no relief. They called in the doctor, and the doctor gave her no hope.

And then, when in this strange dilemma—she was a great Christian Scientist, a preacher of it, and had gone up and down preaching it—they thought of me. Knowing the conditions, and what she lived for. That it was late in the day, that in the condition of her mind she could only receive the simplest word, I said to her. "Now you are very sick, and I won't talk to you about anything save this; I will pray for you in the name of Jesus, and the moment I pray you will be healed."

And the moment I prayed she was healed. That was this like precious faith in operation. Then she was disturbed. Now I could have poured in oil very soon. But I poured in all the bitter drugs possible, and for three days I had her on cinders. I showed her her terrible state and pointed out to her all her folly and the fallacy of her position. I showed her that there was nothing in Christian Science, that it is a lie from the beginning, one of the last agencies of hell. At best a lie, preaching a lie and producing a lie.

Then she wakened up. She became so penitent and broken-hearted. But the thing that stirred her first was she had to go to preach the simple gospel of Christ where she had preached Christian Science. She asked me if she had to give up certain things. I won't mention the things; they are too vile. I said, "No, what you have to do is to see Jesus and take Jesus." When she saw the Lord in his purity, the other things had to go. At the presence of Jesus, all else goes.

This opened the door. I had to preach to all on the boat. This gave me a great chance. As I preached, the power of God fell, conviction came, and sinners were saved. They followed me into my cabin one after another. God was working there.

Then this Indian doctor came. He said, "What shall I do? I cannot use medicine anymore." "Why?" "Oh, your preaching has changed me. But I must have a foundation. Will you spend some time with me?" "Of course I will." Then we went alone, and God broke the fallow ground. This Indian doctor was going right back to his Indian conditions under a new order. He had left a practice there. He told me of the great practice he had. He was going back to his practice to preach Jesus.

If you have lost your hunger for God, if you have not got a cry for more of God, you are missing the plan. There must come up from us a cry that cannot be satisfied with anything but God. He wants to give us the vision of the prize ahead that is something higher than we have ever attained. If you ever stop at any point, pick up at the place where you have dropped through, and begin again under the refining light and power of heaven and God will meet you. And while he will bring you to a consciousness of your frailty and brokenness of spirit, your faith will lay hold of him and all the divine resources. His light and compassion will be manifested through you, and he will send the rain. [Dt 11.14]

Shall we not dedicate ourselves afresh to God? Some say, "I dedicated myself last night to God." Every new revelation brings a new dedication. Let us seek him.

Our calling

Message given at Glad Tidings Tabernacle and Bible Training School, 1536, Ellis Street, San Francisco, California, August 18, 1922

I want to speak to you this morning from the fourth chapter of Ephesians. We will begin reading from the first verse:

I, therefore, the prisoner of the Lord, beseech you that ye walk worthy of the vocation wherewith ye are called, with all lowliness and meekness, with longsuffering, forbearing one another in love; Endeavoring to keep the unity of the Spirit in the bond of peace. There is one body, and one Spirit, even as ye are called in one hope of your calling; One Lord, one faith, one baptism, One God and Father of all, who is above all, and through all, and in you all. But unto every one of us is given **GRACE** according to the measure of the gift of Christ. Wherefore he saith, when he ascended up on high, he led captivity captive, and gave gifts unto men. (Now that he ascended, what is it but that he also descended first into the lower parts of the earth?

He that descended is the same also that ascended up far above all heavens, that he might fill all things.) And he gave some, apostles; and some, prophets; and some, evangelists; and some, pastors and teachers; For the perfecting of the saints, for the work of the ministry, for the edifying of the body of Christ: Till we all come in the unity of the faith, and the knowledge of the Son of God, unto a perfect man, unto the measure of the stature of the fullness of Christ. Ephesians 4:1-13

Beloved, we have for several mornings been speaking concerning the gifts. And I believe that the Lord would have us this morning further consider another side of the gifts. I shall be more or less speaking to preachers, and to those who desire to be preachers. I would like to utter those same words Paul utters in 1 Corinthians 14:5:

I would that ye all spake with tongues, but rather that ye prophesied…

I believe there is no way to make proclamation but by the Spirit. And I believe that they that are sent are called and chosen of God to be sent. And so as we go forth into this chapter, I trust that everyone will understand what his vocation is in the Spirit, and what the Lord demands of us as preachers.

We should be able in the face of God and the presence of His people to behave ourselves so comely and pleasing to the Lord that we always leave behind us a life of blessing and power without gendering strife.

It is a great choice to become a preacher of the Gospel, to handle the Word of life. We that handle the Word of life ought to be well built on the lines of common sense, judgment, and not given to anything contrary to the Word of God. There should be in us all the time such deep reverence towards God and His Word that under all circumstances we would not forfeit our principles on the lines of faith that God had revealed unto us by the truth.

Today I believe God will show us how wonderful we may be in the order of the Spirit for God wants us to be always in the Spirit so rightly dividing the Word of truth that all who hear it shall be like strength to weakness. It shall bring oil to the troubled heart. It shall bring rest. The Word of God shall make us know that having done all we may stand in the trial.

God would have us to know that there is strength by the power of the Spirit, of equipment of character to bring us into like-mindedness with the Lord. We must know to be baptized in the Holy Ghost is to leave your own life, as it were, out of all questioning; leave yourself out of all pleasing, and in the name of Jesus come into like-mindedness.

How He pleased God! How He brought heaven to earth, and all earth moved at the mightiness of the presence of heaven in the midst. We must see our vocation in the Spirit, for God hath chosen us. We must remember that it is a great choice. Turning to the tenth chapter of Romans, we read:

And how shall they preach, except they are sent?… How beautiful are the feet of them that preach the gospel of peace, and bring glad tidings of good things! Romans 10:15

We want to be sent. It is a great thing to be called of God to preach the unsearchable riches of Christ. You have in this land, and we have in our land, men of note and of authority, who are looked to on the lines of socialistic problems. I often think that Lloyd George has a wonderful time but not a time like a preacher. He only preaches of natural sources, but the man who handles the Word of God preaches life immortality that swallows up life. When we come into this blessed life, we know we are teaching principles and ideals which are for life eternal.

God has given to us in the Spirit, and behold, we are spiritual children today, and we must know that we have to be spiritual all the time. God forbid that we should ever be like the Galatian church after we have been in the Spirit, we could come in the flesh. You are allowed to go into the Spirit, but you are never allowed to come in the flesh after you have been in the Spirit.

And so God gives such an idea of this high order in the Spirit that we may be moved by its power to see how we may change the strength and come into all the line of faith in God. Let me turn to the first verse of this wonderful fourth chapter of Ephesians:

I, therefore, the prisoner of the Lord, beseech you that ye walk worthy of the vocation wherewith ye are called.

Here is Paul in prison. If I can take a word from anybody, I can take it from anyone who is in prison. I have never read a book but the Bible, but there are some things I have read out of Pilgrims Progress which have helped me very much. It was when he was in prison that God wakened him on so many wonderful lines of thought. How Paul must have read the Word right in the hearts of those who came and went when he was bound with chains for two full years. He could speak about a fullness, freedom, power, and joy although he was bound with chains.

My brothers, there is something in the Gospel different from anything else. And if these men could go through such hardships – read the first epistle of Peter and you will see how they were scattered. God says that the world wasn't worthy of such material as God was filling with His power that was in dens and caves of the earth.

Oh, brother and sister, there have been some wonderful gems passed through the world touched by the Master's hand. There have been some wonderful men in the world who have caught the glory as the rays have shone from His lips by the power of His expression. As they beheld Him, they have been fascinated with Him. And I can fairly see as Peter drew near the time of his departure, as Jesus said:

When thou wast young, thou girdedst thyself and walkedst whither thou wouldest: but when thou shalt be old, thou shalt stretch forth thy hands, and another shall gird thee, and carry thee whither thou wouldest not. John 21:18

And as Peter drew near to the portals of glory, he wished to die with his head downwards. My word! What **GRACE** incarnated in a human casket that it should have such ideals of worship.

Oh, beloved, God is a real essence of joy to us in a time when it seems barrenness when it seems nothing can help us but the light from heaven far above the brightness of the sun. Then that touches you, then that changes you, and you realize nothing is worthwhile but that.

How he speaks to us when he is in prison, about “the vocation wherewith ye are called, with all lowliness and meekness” (Ephesians 4:1,2). He speaks unto the preacher. Let no person in this place think that he cannot become a preacher. Let none think he cannot reach this ideal of lowliness and meekness. God can bring us there.

Some preachers get an idea that nobody ought to say a word until they are established. I like to hear the bleating of the lambs. I like to hear the life of the young believer. I like to hear something coming right from heaven into the soul as they rise the first time with tears coming down their eyes, telling of the love of Jesus.

The Holy Ghost fell upon a young man outside a church. He went into the church where they were all so sedate if anything had to move in that church out of the ordinary, my word! It would be extraordinary. And this young man with his fulness of life and zeal for the Master got into ejaculating and praising the Lord, and making manifest the joy of the Lord, and he disturbed the old saints.

An old man one day was reading the Psalms quietly. It touched a young man sitting behind him who was filled with the Holy Ghost, And the young man shouted, "Glory!" Said the old man, "Do you call that religion?"

The father of the young man to whom we referred was one of the deacons of the church. The other deacons got round him and said, "You must talk to your boy, and give him to understand that he has to wait till he is established before he manifests those things."

So his father had a long talk with the boy and told him what the deacons said. "You know," he said, "I must respect the deacons, and they have told me they wouldn't hate this thing. You have to wait till you are established."

As they neared their home, their horse made a full stop. He tried to make it go forward and back, but the horse would not move for anything.

What is up with the horse?" asked the father of the son. "Father," replied the boy, "this horse has got established."

I pray God the Holy Ghost that we will not get established in that way. God, loose us up from these old, critical, long-faced, poisoned kind of countenances, which haven't seen daylight for many days. They come into the sanctuary and are in a terrible way. May the Lord save Pentecost from going to dry rot. Yea, deliver us from any line of sentimentality, anything which is not reality. For remember, we must have reality of supernatural quickening till we are sane and active, and not in any way dormant, but filled with life, God working in us mightily by His Spirit.

We must always be on the transforming position, not on the conforming condition, always renewing the mind, always renovated by the mighty thoughts of God, always being brought into line with that which God has said to us by the Spirit, "This is the way, walk ye in it." "Walk in the Spirit, and ye shall not fulfill the lusts of the flesh."

Lord, how shall we do it? Can a man be meek and lowly, and filled with joy? Do they work together? "Out of the abundance of the heart the mouth speaketh." The depths of God come in, in lowliness and meekness and make the heart love. There is no heart that can love like the heart that God has touched.

Oh, that love that is made to love the sinner! There is no love like it. I always feel I can spend any time with the sinner. Oh, brother, there is a love which is God's love! There is a love which only comes by the principles of the Word of God. "He loved us and gave Himself for us."

When that meekness and lowliness of mind take hold, the preacher is moved by His Creator to speak from heart to heart and move the people. For without we are moved by an inward power and ideal of principles, we are never worth it. We must have ideals which come from the throne of God. We must live in the throne, live on the throne, and let Him be enthroned, and then He will lift us to the throne.

TONGUES AND INTERPRETATION: "Out of the depths He has called us, into the heights He has brought us, unto the uttermost He has saved us to make us kings and priests unto God. For we are His property, His own, His loved ones. Therefore He wants to clothe us upon, with the gifts of the Spirit, and make us worthy for His ministry."

Glory to God! Thank the Lord!

"With all lowliness and meekness, with longsuffering, forbearing one another in love" (Ephesians 4:2).

Oh, how it is needed, "forbearing one another in love." Oh, how this is contrary to the hardness of heart; how this is contrary to the evil powers; how this is contrary to the natural mind. It is a divine revelation, and you cannot forbear till you know how He has been with you in the same thing. It is God's love toward you that makes tender, compassionate love one toward another.

It is only the broken, contrite heart which has received the mark of God. It is only those in that secluded place where He speaks to thee alone and encourages thee when thou art down and out, and when no hand is stretched out to thee, He stretches out His hand with mercy and brings thee into a place of compassion. And now, you cannot think evil; now you cannot in any way act hard. God has brought you into long-suffering, with tenderness, with love.

Oh, this love, brother! Many a time my two brothers have been under conviction and have wept under conviction as I have tried to bring them into the light. But up till now, neither of them is in the light. I believe God will bring them.

In the church of God, where a soul is on fire, kindled with the love of God, there is a deeper love between that brother and me than there is between my earthly brother and me. Oh, this love that I am speaking about is divine love; it is not human love. It is higher than human love; it is more devoted to God. It will not betray. It is true in everything. You can depend upon it. It won't change its character. It will be exactly as He would act for you will act with the same spirit, for as He is so are ye in this world.

As you rise into association with Him in the Spirit, as you walk with Him in the light as He is in the Light, then the fellowship becomes unique in all its plan. I pray God that He will help us to understand it that we shall be able to put off and put on. We shall be able to be clothed upon as we have never been, with another majestic touch, with another ideal of heaven.

No one can love like God. And when He takes us into this divine love we shall exactly understand this Word, this verse, for it is full of entreaty, it is full of passion and compassion; it has every touch of Jesus right in it. It is so lovely:

"With all lowliness and meekness, with longsuffering, forbearing one another in love."

Speaking By the Grace of God

I am speaking this morning, by the **GRACE** of God, to the preacher. It should never be known that any preacher caused any distraction, or detraction, or any split, or disunion in a meeting. The preacher has lost his unction and his glory if he ever stoops to anything that would weaken the assembly in any way.

The greatest weakness of any preacher is to draw men to himself. It is a fascinating point, but you must be away from fascination. If you don't crucify your "old man" on every line, you are not going into divine lines with God. When they wanted to make Jesus king, He withdrew Himself to pray. Why? It was a human desire of the people. What did He want? His Kingdom was a spiritual Kingdom. He was to reign over demon powers. He was to have power over the passions of human life. He was to reign so supremely over everything earthly that all the people might know He was divine.

He is our pattern, beloved. When they want to make anything of us, He will give you the **GRACE** to refuse it. The way to get out is to find there is nothing in the earth which is worthy of Him; that there is no one in the world who can understand but He; that everything will crumble to the dust and become worthless. Only that which is divine will last.

"Be not afraid to ask, because God is on the throne waiting to answer your request."

Every time you draw anyone to yourself, it has a touch of earth. It does not speak of the highest realm of thought of God. There is something about it which cannot bear the light of the Word of God. Keep men's eyes off you, but get their eyes on the Lord. Live in the world without a touch or taint of any natural thing moving you. Live high in the order and authority of God, and see that everything is bearing you on to greater heights and depths and greater knowledge of the love of God.

You will help any assembly you go to, and everybody will get a blessing and will see how much richer they are because you brought them, Jesus. Only Jesus! And He is too big for any assembly, and He is little enough to fill every heart. We will always go on to learn of Him. Whatever we know, the knowledge is so small to what He has to give us. And so God's plan for us in giving us Jesus, is all things, for all things consist in Him.

"All things were made by him; and without him was not anything made that was made" (John 1:3).

"...in him we live, and move, and have our being..." (Acts 17:28).

And when it is a spiritual being and an activity of holiness, see how wonderfully we grow in the Lord. Oh, it is just lovely!

TONGUES AND INTERPRETATION: "Yea, it is the Lord Himself. He comes forth clothed upon to clothe thee in thy weakness, to strengthen thee in thy helplessness, to uphold thee in the limitation of thy knowledge, to unfold the mysteries of the Kingdom in the dire straits where two ways meet, and you know not where to go. He says, 'This is the way.' When thou art in such a straitened place that no hand but God can lead thee out, then He comes to thee and says, 'Be strong and fear not, for I am with thee.'"

Hallelujah! Praise the Lord of glory! He is the everlasting King and will reign forever and ever and ever. Glory! Glory! Amen!

TONGUES AND INTERPRETATION: "God has spoken, and He will make it clear, for He is in the midst of thee to open out thy mind and reveal unto thee all the mysteries of the Kingdom, for the God of **GRACE**, is with thee. For God is greater than all unto thee. He is making thy way straight before thee, for the Lord is He that comforteth thee as He comforted Israel, and will lead thee into His power, for His right hand is with thee to keep thee in all thy ways lest thou shouldst dash thy foot against a stone, for the Lord will uphold thee."

How beautiful is the Scripture coming to us this morning! How lively it appears to us! And now we can understand something about the fourteenth chapter of First Corinthians:

…I will pray with the spirit, and I will pray with the understanding also: I will sing with the spirit, and I will sing with the understanding also.

Verse 15

So God is bringing us right into the fullness of the Pentecostal power as given in the first days. God wants us t know that after we have been brought into this divine life with Christ, we can speak in the Spirit, and we can sing in the Spirit; we can speak with the understanding, and sing with the understanding also. Ah, hallelujah this good day!

I think I ought to say a few more words concerning: "Endeavouring to keep the unity of the Spirit in the bond of peace" (Ephesians 4:3).

Beloved, I want you, above all things, to remember that the church is one body. She has many members, and we are all members of that one body. At any cost, we must not break up the body but rather keep the body in perfect unity. Never try to get the applause of the people by any natural thing. Yours is a spiritual work. Yours has to be a spiritual breath. Your word has to be the Word of God. Your counsel to the church has to be so that it cannot be gainsaid. You have to have such solid, holy reverence on every line so that every time you handly anybody you handle them for God, and you handle the church as the church of God. By that means you keep the church bound together.

As the church is bound together in one Spirit, they grow into that temple in the Lord, and they all have one voice, one desire, and one plan. And when they want souls saved, they are all of one mind. I am speaking now about spiritual power. You get them into the mind of the Spirit with Christ, and all their desires will be the same desires of Christ the Head. And so nothing can break the church on those lines.

As preachers, you must never try to save yourself on any line. You must always be above mentioning a financial matter on your side. Always before God in the secret place mention your need, but never bring it to an assembly; if you do, you drop in the estimation of the assembly. You are allowed to tell any need belonging to the assembly or the church management, but on a personal line never refer to yourself on the platform.

If you preach faith, you must live it, and a man is not supposed to preach without he preach a living faith. And he must so impress it upon the people that they will always know God has taken us on for a special plan aand that we are not ordinary men. After we are called of God and chosen for Him, we are not again to have ordinary men's plans. We ought to have ideals of God only.

Another thing which I think is perhaps more essential to you than anything else: you preachers, never drop into an assembly and say the Lord sent you, because sometimes the assembly has as much on as she can manage. But it is right for you to get your orders from heaven, and for God to switch the same order somewhere else that will make the first call and you will be dropping into the call. Never make a call without you are sent. Be sure you are sent of God.

Brothers, can you be out of God's will when you hear His voice? "My sheep hear My voice, and they follow Me." Oh, that God today shall help us by the mind of the Spirit to understand. I believe God has a message on fire. He has men clothed by God. He has men sent by God. Will you be the men? Will you be the women?

You ask, "Can I be the man? Can I be the woman?" Yes, God says, "Many are called, but few are chosen." Are you the chosen ones? Those who desire to be chosen, will you allow God to choose you? Then He will put His hand upon you. And in the choice He will give you wisdom, He will lead you forth, He will stand by you in the straitened corner, He will lead you every step of the way, for the Lord's anointed shall go forth and bring forth fruit, and their fruit shall remain.

TONGUES AND INTERPRETATION: "Behold, now is the day of decision. Yield now while the moment of pressure by the presence of God comes. Yield now and make your consecration to God."

The altar is ready now for all who will obey.

From the author Dr. Michael H Yeager's

* GRACE flows to and through the Humblest soul.

Well, the Bible says, give no place to the devil. Do not open the door for the devil through disobedience and rebellion to God's word. **Let every one that names the name of Christ depart from iniquity.**

But what are we talking about? Paul says if I must need glory, if I'm going to boast about something, if I'm going to be proud about something, I will Glory of the things which concern my infirmities. He never boasted about how much he prayed, how much he fasted, how many devils he cast out, how many people that he raised from the dead. Why? Because he knew it was the grace of God at work in him by faith in Christ.

He boasted about his weakness. He bragged about he was persecuted. He said, I am the least of all apostles, and yet he became the greatest. I am going to show you what **GRACE really** is. Are you ready to find out what **GRACE** really is? Second Corinthians Chapter 12: for this thing, I sought the Lord thrice that it might depart from me. And he said unto me; my **GRACE** is sufficient for thee. Chapter 12 Second Corinthians verse nine, My **GRACE** is sufficient for thee. For My Strength. There it is. That is God's **GRACE**! Remember God said, My **GRACE** is sufficient for my **Strength** is made perfect in your weakness.

The GRACE Of God Is The Strength Of God. The **GRACE** of God is the **Strength of God**. My **GRACE** is sufficient for thee, for my strength is made perfect in weakness. There is the key that reveals what God's GRACE truly is!

My strength or my **GRACE** is made mature in your weakness Paul. You know how water flows to the lowest point. Water always flows to the lowest gravitational pull. It always goes to the lowest point. Anyone with even an elemental understanding of water and gravity knows this to be true. Do you know that's what **GRACE** is? **GRACE** flows to the lowest point.

Let me say this; **GRACE** will flow to and through the humblest soul.

The more humble you are (and that isn't walking around acting humble) looking and depending upon nobody, but God will cause His Grace to work mightily in your life. Jesus said you must become as a little child to enter into the Kingdom of heaven. You must humble yourself like a little child. Remember it says, humbles yourself under the mighty hand of God, and he will exalt you in due season. Do you know that **GRACE** flows to the humble? It says in First Peter Chapter five; God gives **GRACE** to the humble.

God Gives His Divine Ability To The Humble.

He doesn't give it to the proud. He doesn't give it to the egotistical. He doesn't give it to the boastful. Matter of fact, it says, let another man's lips praise you. What is humility**? Humility is The Foundation of the Power of God in His Church**. In the beatitudes, Matthew chapter five and verse three it says, blessed are the poor in spirit, for theirs is the Kingdom of Heaven. That means you recognize your true spiritual poverty. Lord There's nothing good in my flesh. My righteousness is as filthy rags. I need you more today, more than I needed you yesterday. God says to his people: My **GRACE** is sufficient for thee, for my strength is made perfect in your weakness.

Paul, the apostle, then says most gladly, therefore, will I rather glory in my infirmities that the **Power of Christ** may rest upon me. What is a child? A little child, a newborn infant, continually and consistently cries out for the need of its mommy. With absolutely no shame, no intimidation, no fear that newborn cries out I need mommy. I need daddy. I need help. This is a perfect illustration of a humble heart. This is where the divine rivers of God's Grace will flow freely.

You know the older a natural man gets, the more independent he becomes. It's a shame that in most of the modern day church preachers are propagating an egotistical me-ism Gospel. True faith in God will cause men to be humble and meek and kind and gentle. First Corinthians 13 is a perfect declaration and revelation of a heart that is filled with love and dependence upon God. It understands that, through the **GRACE** of God, because of Jesus, I can overcome because of Jesus living in me. I can conquer the devil because I totally submit to God.

The amazing experiences I've had with God has not created pride and arrogance in my heart. Actually it is the opposite. Literally hundreds of times since 1975 I have cried out to Jesus in desperation. And as I cried out to the Lord, he heard me and came to my rescue. I believe I am more dependent upon God today than I have ever been in the past. It is not even that I have confidence in the fact that I have memorized thousands of scriptures. The Scriptures simply bring me back to the reality that I need to have complete faith in Jesus. I do not trust or have any confidence in

Mike Yeager whatsoever. My confidence is in God. I realize I can only survive, live, and have victory through Jesus Christ.

Singing in Arabic by the Holy Ghost

During worship one Sunday morning in 1981, my wife Kathleen began to praise God in tongues. It was a very beautiful language. I love to listen to my wife speak and worship God in heavenly tongues because she operates in the what the Bible calls the gift of the diversity of tongues. On that Sunday morning, we had a first-time visitor that we had never seen before. He looked as if he was from the Middle East.

At the end of the service this gentleman came over to me with a look of amazement on his face. He asked me where my wife had learned to sing in such beautiful and perfect Arabic. I informed him that she did not know how to speak in Arabic, that this was the spirit of God singing through her. When he informed me that she had been singing in perfect Arabic, I asked him what she had said? He told me that she was giving worshiping, praising and giving glory to God. You can read in the book of acts you'll discover that this is nothing new.

Now when my wife speaks in diversity of tongues, and I give the interpretation, it is not what you would call and exact translation. What I am saying is that in my interpretation of the tongues, my voice inflections or body actions will not always be the same as hers. Sometimes my interpretation might be longer or shorter than her message of tongues. There are times though that I have operated so deeply in this gift of interpretation that even with my wife being behind me, when I cannot see her, I will move my hands and arms in the same way that she gave the tongues.

At times, some people have even came to us after the service asking if we had practiced before the meeting for this to happen. Her tongues and the moving of her body, is so matched by my interpretation and demonstration, even though I did not see it, they thought that we had practiced and manufactured this manifestation, but this is not the case. She was moving by the spirit of God in the tongues and in the moving of her hands and her body, and by the spirit I simply did the same things but with the interpretation.

Most times when my wife moves in diversity of tongues and I have the interpretation she is behind me, and I am not seeing what she is doing. These tongues, and the interpretation of these tongues is not coming from our heads or intellect, but from our hearts, by the spirit of God. Jesus said out of your belly would flow rivers of living water. This is pertaining to the baptism of the Holy Ghost. These gifts happen by the spirit and are manifested according to our faith in Christ.

How God Supernaturally Healed Me of Being Tongue-Tied!

Let me share an amazing story about how I was baptized in the Holy Ghost, and the difference it made in my life. After I gave my heart to Christ a divine hunger and thirst for the Word of God began to possess me. I practically devoured Matthew, Mark, Luke, and John. Jesus became my hero in every sense of the word, in every area of my thoughts and daily living. He became my soul reason for getting up every day and going to work, eating, sleeping, and living. I discovered that everything I did was based on a desire of wanting to please Him.

One day I was reading my Bible and discovered where Jesus said that it was necessary for him to leave. That because when he would go back to the Father, he would send the promise of the Holy Ghost to make us a witness. Furthermore, I learned it was His will for me to be filled to overflowing with the Holy Ghost and that the Holy Ghost would empower and equip me to be a witness an ambassador for God.

The Holy Ghost would also lead me and guide me into all truth. With all of my heart I desperately wanted to reach the lost for Jesus Christ in order for they could experience the same love and freedom that I was now walking in. I searched the Scriptures to confirm this experience. In the book of Joel, in the old covenant, the four Gospels and especially in the book of acts I discovered the will of God when it comes to this baptism.

I perceived in my heart that I needed to receive this baptism the same way that I had received salvation. I had to look to Christ and trust by faith that he would give to me this baptism of the Spirit. It declared in the book of acts that after they were baptized in the Holy Ghost they all began to speak in a heavenly language. I had not been around what we would call Pentecostal people, so I had never heard anybody else speak in this heavenly language. But that did not really matter to me, because it was within the Scriptures.

Acts 2:39 For the promise is unto you, and to your children, and to all that are afar off, even as many as the Lord our God shall call.

I remember getting on my knees next to my bunk bed where I cried out and asked God to fill me with the Holy Ghost so I could be a witness. As I was crying out to God something began to happen on the inside of me. It literally felt like hot buckets of oil was beginning to be poured upon me and within me. Something then began to rise up out of my innermost being. Before I knew what I was doing, a new language came out bubbling of my mouth which I had never heard before, or been taught to speak. I began to speak in a heavenly tongue.

Now up to this time I had a terrible speech impediment. You see I had been born tongue-tied. Yes they had operated on me, and I had gone to speech therapy, and yet most people could not understand what I was saying. I could not even pronounce my own last name YEAGER properly. My tongue simply refused to move in a way in which I could pronounce my Rs. After I was done praying in this new language, I discovered to my absolute surprise that my speech impediment was instantly and completely gone!

From that time on, I have never stopped preaching Jesus Christ. For almost 40 years I have proclaimed the truth of Jesus Christ to as many as I can.

For the First Time She Could Understand Me

About 4 months after I gave my heart to Christ I went back to my hometown, Mukwonago, Wisconsin, and I immediately went to see one of my best friends to share with him my conversion experience. Actually, it was his sister I had been dating for the last three years. I wrote her a letter telling her what happened to me, and how God gloriously had set me free from drugs, alcohol, and all of my worldly living. This caused her to cut me off completely, as if I had lost my mind. Praise God! I had lost my mind by receiving the mind of Christ. My friend's mother was listening while I was speaking to her son, and out of nowhere she said, "Mike, what happened to you?"

I told her how I had been delivered from drugs and immorality because I gave my heart to Jesus. She said, "No, that's not what I'm talking about. After many years of knowing you, this is actually the 1st time I can fully understand what you are saying." You see, my speech was so garbled that it was very difficult for people to truly understand exactly what I was saying. Those who know me now would not have recognized the old me. Before I was baptized in the Holy Ghost you would not have been able to understand most of what I said. I'm still trying to make up for the nineteen years when I could not speak properly.

Tattooed woman saved, filled with the Holy Ghost.

In July of 2015 my wife and I walked into a store where we knew the owner very well. The owner used to work for me as the principle of our Christian school. Standing in front of the counter was a lady who probably was in her late 30s. She was dressed in the style of a Gothic. She had a large tattoo of a human skull on her neck. She also had tattoos on her arms and her legs. This did not bother me in the least, because I came out of that kind of world. I knew that God is not moved by what he sees on the outer man.

Immediately my ears perked up because I heard this lady talking about the things of God. Instantly I perceived there was a spiritual hunger in her heart to know the Lord. I knew by the gift of the word of knowledge that she had been involved in new ageism. That she had been looking for something that was real her whole life, and yet she had not discovered it.

I heard the Lord say to me (in my heart) she is ready right now to be born again and filled with the Holy Ghost. When she had stopped to take a breath of air, I began to talk to her. I began to share with her what the Lord spoke to my heart about her life. She said that it was absolutely true. I asked her if she was ready to receive from the Lord? She said she absolutely was! At that moment, I told her that she needed to pray along with me, accepting Jesus Christ, and being filled with the Holy Ghost. She said she would.

I had her pray per that which God was quickening to my heart. She gave her heart to Jesus Christ right then and there. I asked my Heavenly Father to baptize her in the Holy Ghost, that the evidence of speaking in tongues. I told her that she needed to reach her hands towards heaven, in which she did. As I laid my hands upon her with my wife, instantly she began to speak in a heavenly language.

She is now attending church, and actively pursuing God with her children. Just last week, as I write this experience, she was water baptized for the glory of Jesus.

CHAPTER SIX

GOD'S WORD

(Smith Wigglesworth)

During three weeks thousands daily attended the meetings. Each morning two or three hundred were ministered to for healing. Each evening the platform was surrounded. Again and again, as each throng retired another company came forward seeking salvation. Here many were baptized in the Holy Ghost. The testimony meetings were excellent.

Now I will close with a vision a brother had who attended these meetings. He was lost in intercession for the hundreds of sick waiting to be ministered to for healing. He saw an opening from the platform, where the sick were, right into the glory. He saw wonderful beings in the form of men resting who, with interest, looked on.

Again he looked at the platform and saw a heavenly Being clothed in white, whom all the time was more active than any other in helping the sick, and when He touched them the effect was beautiful. Bent forms were made straight, and their eyes shone, they began to glorify and praise the Lord. A Voice said: Healings are the smallest of all gifts; it is but a drop in the bucket given what God has in store for His children. Ye shall do greater works than these.

We are given GRACE according to the measure of the gift of Christ

One God and Father of all, who is above all and through all and in you all. But unto every one of us is given **GRACE** according to the measure of the gift of Christ. Wherefore he saith, When he ascended up on high, he led captivity captive, and gave gifts unto men. (Now that he ascended, what is it but that he also descended first into the lower parts of the earth?

He that descended is the same also that ascended up far above all heavens, that he might fill all things.) And he gave some, apostles; and some, prophets; and some, evangelists; and some, pastors and teachers; For the perfecting of the Saints, for the work of the ministry, for the edifying of the body of Christ: Till we all come in the unity of the faith, and of the knowledge of the Son of God, unto a perfect man, unto the measure of the stature of the fullness of Christ. Ephesians 4:1-13

I believe the Lord, this morning as on the last morning, especially wants me to emphasize facts which will be a blessing and a strengthening to the preachers. If there is anything of importance, it is to the preachers because God must have us in the place of building and edifying the Church. And we must be in that order of the Spirit that God can work through us for the needs of the Church.

As it was only out of the brokenness of Paul's life that blessing came forth, so it is out of the emptiness, and brokenness, and yieldedness of our lives that God can bring forth all His glories through us to others. And as our brother said this morning on the platform, except we pass on what we receive, we shall lose it. If we didn't lose it, it would become stagnant.

Virtue is always manifested through blessing which you have passed on. Nothing will be of any importance to you except that which you pass on to others. So God wants us to be so in the order of the Spirit that when He breaks upon us the alabaster box of ointments of His precious anointing which He has for every child of His, He wants us to be filled with perfumes of holy incense that we may be poured out for others and that others may receive the **GRACE**s of the Spirit, and all the church may be edified. And there shall never be known in Glad Tidings Tabernacle one dry day, but there shall always be freshness and life which makes all hearts burn together as you know the Lord has talked with you once more.

We must have this inward burning desire for more of God. We must not be at any stationary point. We must always have the highest power telescopes looking and hasting unto that which God has called us to that He may perfect that forever.

Oh, what a blessed inheritance of the Spirit God has for us in these days, that we should be no longer barren, nor unfruitful, but rather filled with all fullness, unlimited, increasing with all increasings, with a measureless measure of the might of the Spirit in the inner man, so that we are always like a great river pressing on and healing everything that it touches. Oh, let it be so today!

TONGUES AND INTERPRETATION: "The Lord has awakened in us the divine touches of His spiritual favor to make us know He is here with all you require if you are ready to take it."

But are we ready to take it? If we are, then God can give us wonderful things. We must always be in that hunger ready for every touch of God.

Last week you remember we were dwelling on verse three: "Endeavouring to keep the unity of the Spirit in the bond of peace."

It was a very precious word to us because it meant that under any circumstances we would not have our way but God's way. We have it for the person and the Church.

Whatever God means us to be, He means us to be peacemakers. Yes, love without alloy; that which, always at its own expense, goes to help another and pays the price for it. I shall not find a Scripture which will help me so much on this line as Matthew 5:23,24:

Therefore if thou bring thy gift to the altar; and there rememberest that thy brother hath aught against thee; Leave there thy gift before the altar, and go thy way; first be reconciled to thy brother, and then come and offer thy gift.

Most Christians are satisfied with the first line of it, but the second line is deeper. Most people believe it is perfectly right if you have offended another, to go to that one and say, "Please forgive me," and you gain your brother when you take that part. But this is a deeper sense: "If thou...rememberest that thy brother hath ought against thee," go forgive him his transgressions. It is so much deeper than getting your side right, to go and get their side right by forgiving them all they have done.

That will be a stepping stone to very rich **GRACE** on the line of "keeping the unity of the Spirit in the bond of peace." Someone says, "I cannot forgive her because she did that, and the brother said that. You know the brother didn't recognize me at all. And he has never smiled at me for at least six months." Poor thing! God help you through evil report and good report. God can take us right through if we get to the right side of **GRACE**.

My brother, when you get to the place of forgiving your brother who hath ought against you, you will find that is the greatest ideal of going on to perfection, and the Lord will help us "to keep the unity of the Spirit in the bond of peace."

I like that "bond of peace." It is an inward bond between you and the child of God. "Bond of peace." Hallelujah! Oh, glory to God!

There is one body, and one Spirit, even as ye are called in one hope of your calling. Ephesians 4:4

We must recognize there is only one body. It seems to me that God would at one time have made such an inroad into all nations on the lines of the truth through the Plymouth brethren if they had only recognized that there was more in the body than just the Plymouth brethren. You will never gain interest without you see that in every church there will be a nucleus which has as real a God as you have.

It is only on these lines I believe that the longsuffering of God waiteth for the precious fruit. And the longsuffering of God is with the believers who have an idea that only those in Glad Tidings Hall are right, or those in Oakland, or those in England. It is all foolishness.

Fancy people are sitting round the table and reckoning that that table is the only table. What about hundreds of people I know who are sitting round the table every day and taking the bread and the wine? Brother, the body of Christ consists of all who are in Christ.

While we know the Holy Ghost is the only power that can take the Church up, we know the Holy Ghost will go with the Church. The Scriptures are very definite in saying that all that are Christ's at His coming will be changed. It doesn't seem to be that we can be all Christ's without something is done, and God will sweep away so many things which are spoiling things. We must get to perfect love, and we will see that God can make even those in Caesar's household our souls, glory to God!

TONGUES AND INTERPRETATION: "It is the Spirit that joins us and makes us one. It is the health of the Spirit that goes through the body that quickens the body and makes it appear as one."

Oh, the body appearing as one body! The same joy, the same peace, the same hope! No division, all one in Christ! What a body! Who can make a body like that? It seems to me that this body is made deep in the cross. Hundreds of people are carrying a cross on watch guard, or around their necks. I could never carry a cross; He has carried the cross, He has borne the shame. I find right there in that atoning blood there is cleansing and purifying, and taking away every dross, and everything that will mar the vessel, and He is making a vessel unto honor fit for the Master's use, joined up in that body, one body.

Let us be careful that we do not in any way defile the body because God is chastening the body and fitly framing it and bringing it together. The body of Christ will rise. You ask, "How will it rise?" It will rise in millions, and billions and trillions, more than any man can number. It will be a perfect body.

Oh, there is one body! Ah, it is a lovely body. I look at you; I see you. I look in your faces, and I know there is a closer association than one can tell or speak about. Oh, brother, there is something deeper down in the spirit of the regenerated person when the dross of life and the flesh falls off.

Oh, there will be a similitude, a likeness, a perfection of holiness, of love! Oh God, take away the rudiments, the weaknesses, all the depravities.

"Now ye are the body of Christ, and members in particular" (1 Corinthians 12:27).

I like the word, particular, meaning to say there is just the right place for us. God sees us in that place. He is making us fit in that place so that for all time we shall have a wonderful place in that body. Ah, it is so lovely!

Oh, these exhaustless things! Brothers, sisters, it isn't the message; it is the heart. It isn't the heart; it is the Christ. It isn't the Christ; it is the God. It isn't the God; it is the whole Body. Deeper and more precious than we have any conception of!

There is one body, and one Spirit, even as ye are called in one hope of your calling. Ephesians 4:4

I feel that God would have me say a word about the calling. Many people get called, and they have missed because they are dull of hearing.

There is something in the call, beloved. "Many are called, but few are chosen." I want a big heart this morning to believe that all shall be chosen. You ask, "Can it be so?" Yes, beloved, it can, not a few chosen, but many chosen.

And how shall the choice be? The choice is always your choice first. You will find that gifts are your choice first. You will find that salvation is your choice. God has made it all, but you have to choose. And so God wants you especially this morning to make an inward call, to have a great intercessory condition of beseeching the Holy One to prepare you for that wonderful mystical Body.

Called! Beloved, I know some people have an idea (and it is a great mistake), because they are not successful in everything they touch. It is because they have failed in so many things they have been desirous to go forward in, because they don't seem to aspire in prayer as some. Perhaps they don't enter into the fullness of tongues, that there is no hope for them in this calling.

Satan comes and says, "Look at that black catalogue of helpless infirmities! You never expect to be in that calling!" Yes, you can, brother! God has it in the Scriptures. Oh, my brother, it is the weakness made strong! " It is the last that can be made first. What will make the whole different? When we confess our helplessness. He says He feeds the hungry with good things, but the satisfied He sends away empty.

If you want to grow in **GRACE** and the knowledge of the **GRACE** of God, get hungry enough to be fed, be thirsty enough to cry, be broken enough you cannot have anything in the world without He comes Himself. I was reading last night in my Bible, it was so lovely, "And God shall wipe away all tears from their eyes..." (Revelation 21:4).

Ah, you say, that will be there. Thank God there are two "theres." Hallelujah! Let God do it this morning. Let Him wipe away all tears. Let Him comfort thy heart. Let Him strengthen thy weakness. Let Him cause thee to come into the place of profit. Let Him help thee into the place God has chosen for thee, for "many are called, but few are chosen." But God has a big choice.

He is a big Jesus! If I could measure Him, I would be very small. But I cannot measure Him, and I know He is very large. I am glad I cannot measure Jesus, but I am glad I can touch Him all the same. The fifth verse: One Lord, one faith, one baptism. Ephesians 4:5.

I must touch the thought of baptism this morning. We must get away from the thought of water baptism when we are in the epistles. If water baptism is at all mentioned in any way, it is always mentioned as a past tense. We must always remember this, beloved, which while water baptism, in my opinion, is essential, "He that believeth, and is baptized, shall be saved." I wouldn't say for a moment a man could not be saved without he was baptized in water, because it would be contrary to Scripture. I see there is a blending. If we turn to the third chapter of John's gospel we find:

…Except a man is born of water, and of the Spirit, he cannot enter into the kingdom of God. John 3:5b

I believe God would have us to know that we never ought to put aside water baptism, but believe it is in perfect conjunction and operation with the working of the Spirit that we may be buried with Him.

But oh, the baptism in the Holy Ghost! The baptism of fire! The baptism of power! The baptism of oneness! The baptism of the association! The baptism of communion! The baptism of the Spirit of life which takes the man shakes him through, builds him up, and makes him know he is a new creature in the Spirit, worshipping God in the Spirit.

If my preaching and the preaching of those who come on this platform emphasizes the facts of being baptized with the Holy Ghost, and you only have touches of it, if you stop at that, you will be almost as though you were missing the calling. John said by the Spirit:

...He that cometh after me is preferred before me... John 1:15

I indeed baptize you with water unto repentance: but he that cometh after me is mightier than I…he shall baptize you with the Holy Ghost, and with fire. Matthew 3:11

By all means, if you can tarry, you ought to tarry. If you have the Spirit's power upon you, go into that room or somewhere else and never cease till God finishes the work. Outside the Pentecostal church where there isn't a revival spirit, and where people are not born again, you will find the church becomes dead, dry, and barren, and helpless. They enter into entertainments and all kinds of teas. They live on a natural association and lose their grand, glorious hope.

I come to the Pentecostal church. Without the Pentecostal church is having an increase on the lines of salvation, without it has continuous baptisms in the Holy Ghost, and a continuous pressure into the Kingdom, that church will become dry, lukewarm, helpless, and you will wonder what church it is.

But every night if somebody rises in testimony saying they received the Holy Ghost, and others say, "Oh, last night I was saved," that church is ripening. She will not flounder. She is ripening for greater things, for God will take that church.

Beloved, you are responsible for this, the platform is not responsible. The whole Church is responsible to keep this place on fire. If you have come into this meeting, and if you are baptized with the Holy Ghost, without an unction upon you and ready so that you feel like bursting into tongues, or having a psalm, hymn, or some spiritual song, without you have a tongue or interpretation, without something is taking place on these lines you have fallen from the **GRACE** of the Pentecostal position.

You talk about a message. God has given us a message this morning if you dare hear it. We dare say in the open air and everywhere that we are Pentecostal. If we are Pentecostal, we shall be Biblical Pentecostal. What is Biblical Pentecost? It is found in the fourteenth chapter of First Corinthians, 26th verse:

How is it then, brethren? When ye come together every one of you hath a psalm, hath a doctrine, hath a tongue, hath a revelation, hath an interpretation. Let all things be done unto edifying.

It is an injunction for a Pentecostal continuance in the Corinthian church. Supposing that was the case of this Pentecostal church, it would not be possible for sinners to come in without being saved, or for people coming in not having the baptism without having a hunger and thirst to come into that fulness. It must be so. God must bring us to a place where we have not a name but have the position that brings the name.

How many of you felt speaking in tongues as you came into the room this morning? Praise God; there are some. How many of you have a psalm burning through you and feel like rehearsing it in the streets? Praise God that is very well. How many of you sung a hymn as you came along? Praise the Lord, glory to God! You are going on very well. But don't you see this is what we have to continue. There has to be a continuance of such things.

TONGUES AND INTERPRETATION: "The hope of the Church is springing up of the Spirit through the Word. Therefore, as many of you as are living in the Spirit are putting to death the flesh. You are quickened by the Spirit and live in the realms of His **GRACE**."

Praise the Lord; it is the **GRACE** of our Lord Jesus. Hallelujah! We can sing, "'I will never be cross anymore." Beloved, it is the most wonderful thing on earth when God touches you with this new life in the Spirit. Oh, then whether you are on the streets, or roadways, or trains, it doesn't matter where you are in the Spirit, you are ready to be caught up.

Oh, beloved, here we are this morning, "one body," praise the Lord! One spirit, one baptism. I am crying to God for these meetings because I believe God can do a great thing in a moment when we are all brought into the line of the Spirit. It wouldn't surprise me whatever happened.

I have been in meetings for ten days when the attention has been on the gifts, and the people have gotten so worked up, as it were, in the Spirit that they felt something had to happen on a new line else they couldn't live. And it has happened. I believe these and other meetings are bringing us to a place of great expectancy. "One Lord, one faith, one baptism" (Ephesians 4:5).

Just in the proportion that you have the Spirit is unfolding to you, "One Lord, one faith, one baptism," you have the Holy Ghost so incarnated in you bringing into you a revelation of the Word. Nothing else can do it, for the Spirit gave the Word through Jesus. Jesus spoke by the Spirit that was in Him, He is the Word. The Spirit brought out all the Word of this life. Then we must have the Spirit.

If you take up John's gospel, you will find that when He came it wasn't to speak about Himself but to bring forth all He said. Just as we have the measure of the Spirit, there will be no measure of unbelief. We shall have faith. The Church will rise to the highest position when there is no schism in the Body of the lines of unbelief. When we all, with one heart, and one faith, believe the Word as it is spoken, then signs, and wonders, and divers miracles will be manifested everywhere. One accord: "One Lord, one faith, one baptism." Hallelujah!

The next verse I think probably is one of the primary verses of all:

One God and Father of all, who is above all, and through all, and in you all. Ephesians 4:6

If this spiritual life is in us, we will find we have no fear. We would have no nervous debility; it would vanish. Every time you have fear, it is imperfect love. Every time you have nervous weaknesses, you will find it is departing from an inner circle of true faith in God. We read in 1 John 4:18:

There is no fear in love; but perfect love casteth out fear: because of fear hath torment. He that feareth is not made perfect in love.

Then you can get a very good word in the sixteenth verse of the same chapter:

...**God is love, and he that dwelleth in love dwelleth in God, and God in him.**

Where is the man? He is swallowed up in God. And when God takes hold of us on these lines, it is remarkable to see we are encircled and overshadowed by Him.

TONGUES AND INTERPRETATION: "I feel we must magnify the Lord in the Spirit."

When the believer sees that God is over all, take a real glance at that. Think about God is through all. See if any satanic powers can work against you. But just think about another step; He is in you all. How can the devil have a chance with the body when God is "in you all"? Hallelujah! Glory!

Don't you see the groundwork, the great base, the rock of the principles of these Scriptures, how they make us know that we are not barren, we cannot be unfruitful, but we must always be abounding and in the joy of the Lord. We lack because we are short of the truth.

When this truth of God lays hold the man, he is no longer a man. What is he? He is a divine construction. He has a new perception of the ideals of God. He has a new measurement. Now he sees God is over all things. Now he sees that God is through all things. The whole world can join in a league of nations, they can do as they like, but the Word of God abideth forever.

"In you all." Think of that; God is in you all. Who is God? Who is the Holy Spirit? Who is Jesus? Is it possible to have any conception of the mightiness of the power of God? And yet you take the thoughts of Jesus, and see that all the embodiment of the fulness was right in Him. And I have Him. I have the Holy Ghost also which is as great in equality for those three are one, and joined equally in power. They never twaddle on their conditions but are perfectly one.

When the Spirit comes in the body, how many are there in the body? You have Jesus already. When you are baptized you have the Holy Ghost. And now God is in you all. Hallelujah! Talk about Samson carrying the gates, if you know your position you will take both the city and the gates. Go in and possess every part of the land, for surely there is a land of gladness, a land of pleasure, a land of peace, And remember, brothers; when the Holy Ghost gets an end of us, and we just utter the Spirit's power and the Spirit's words, we find out it is always more and more and more. Oh, yes, we will magnify the Lord on all these lines. If we don't the stones will begin to cry out against us.

But unto every one of us is given **GRACE** according to the measure of the gift of Christ. Ephesians 4:7

This is a great summing up. Oh, brother, I wish you to see Jesus this morning because if we don't see Him we miss a great deal. **GRACE** and gifts are equally abounding there. It is as you set your strength on Jesus, it is as you allow the Holy Ghost to penetrate every thought bringing always on the canvas of the mind a perfect picture of holiness, purity, righteousness, that you enter into Him and become entitled to all the riches of God.

How do you measure up this morning? God gives a measure. Oh, this is a lovely word:

But unto every one of us is given **GRACE** according to the measure of the gift of Christ.Ephesians 4:7

I know that salvation, while it is a perfect work, is an insulation which may have any amount of volts behind it. In the time when they laid bare wires, when they were getting electric power from Niagara, they tell me there was a city whose lights suddenly went out.

Following the wires they came to a place where a cat had gotten on the wires, and the lights were stopped. I find that the dynamo of heaven can be stopped with a less thing than a cat. An impure thought across the mind stops the circulation. An act stops the growth of the believer. I like Hebrews 4:12:

For the word of God is quick, and powerful, and sharper than any twoedged sword, piercing even to the dividing asunder of soul and spirit, and of the joints and marrow, and is a discerner of the thoughts and intents of the heart.

Then I find in 2 Corinthians 10:5 these words:

Casting down imaginations, and every high thing that exalteth itself against the knowledge of God, and bringing into captivity every thought to the obedience of Christ.

So I find if I am going to have all the revelations of Jesus brought to me, I am going to attain to all that God has for me through a pure heart, a clean heart, right thoughts, and an inward affection towards Him. Then heaven bursts through my human frame, and all the rays of heaven flow through my body. Hallelujah! My word, it is lovely!

The measure of the gift of Christ remains with you. I cannot go on with inspiration without I am going on with God in perfection. I cannot know the mind of the natural and the mysteries of the hidden things with God without I have power to penetrate everything between me and heaven. And there is nothing goes through but a pure heart, for the pure in heart shall see God.

Oh, it is lovely! And I see that the pure heart can come into such closeness with God that the **GRACE**s are so enriched, and the measure of Christ becomes so increased that you know you are going on to possess all things.

Nothing comes up in my mind so beautiful as a soul just developing in their first love to want to preach to all people. In Revelation, one church is reproved for having lost its first love. And I believe that God would have us to know that this first love, the great love which Jesus gives us with which to love others, is the primary stepping stone to all these things that we had this morning. I don't know whether there is such a one here who has never lost that first love.

The preacher, I love him. The young man I love. Oh, how I love the youth who is developing in his character and longing to become a preacher. If you ask me if I have a choice in my whole life, I say, yes, I have a choice for a young preacher. I love them. God has perfect positions of development for the preacher.

The young preacher may have greater inward longings to get people saved than he has power over his depravities. And they are hindered in their pursuit into this grandeur of God. I want to take you to a place where there is wonderful safety and security.

God will take into captivity him who is captive to weaknesses, and to failures, and to the power of Satan which has interfered with the young or old life that is longing to preach the glories of Christ. God will take him into captivity if he will let Him for God has gifts for him. He takes the captive into captivity and surrounds him, keeps him, chastens him, purifies him, cleanses him, washes him. And He is making prophets of such, and apostles of such, and evangelists of such.

God has never been able to make goodness only out of helplessness lest we should glorify through the flesh. God destroys every line of flesh that no flesh can glory in His sight. If we have any glory, we will glory in the Lord.

Do you want to be preachers? Nay, verily, I know you do. There isn't a child in this place who does not want to bear the glad tidings.

...**How beautiful are the feet of them that preach the gospel of peace, and bring glad tidings of good things!Romans 10:15**

Oh, glad tidings! What does it mean? Eternal salvation. You talk about gold mines, and diamonds, and precious stones! Oh, my brother, to save one soul from death! Oh, to be the means of saving many! God has for us a richer treasure than we have any idea of. Don't say you cannot reach it, brother, sister. Never look at yourself, get a great vision of the Master. Let His love so penetrate you that you will absolutely make everything death but Him. And as you see Him in His glory, you will see how God can take you.

I believe that there are many in this place that God is taking hold of this morning. My brother, don't fail God, but by the measure of faith in Christ let your hand be outstretched, let your eye be fixed with an eternal fixedness, let an inward passion grip you with the same zeal that took the Lord. And let your mind forget all the past, come into like-mindedness with Jesus and let Him clothe you.

Wherefore he saith, When he ascended up on high, he led captivity captive, and gave gifts unto men. Ephesians 4: 8

He has gifts for men. You ask, what kind of men? Rebels also. Did they desire to be rebels? No. Sometimes there are transgressions who break our hearts and make us groan and travail. Was it our desire? No. God looks right through the very canvas of your whole life history, and He has set His mind upon you. I would like you, preachers, to know:

...Eye hath not seen, nor ear heard, neither have entered into the heart of man, the things which God hath prepared for them that love him. 1 Corinthians 2: 9

Your weakness has to be riddled through like the chaff before the wind, and every corn shall bring forth pure grain after God's mind.

So the fire will burn as an oven, and burn up the stubble, but the wheat shall be gathered into the garner, the treasury of the most High God, and He Himself shall lay hold of us.

What is it for? The perfecting of the saints. Oh, to think that that brokenness of thine is to be so made like Him, that weakness of thine to be made so strong like Him! Thou hast to bear the image of the Lord in every iota. We have to have the mind of Christ in perfection, in beauty.

Beloved, don't fail and shrivel because of the hand of God upon thee, but think that God must purify thee for the perfecting of the saints. Oh, Jesus will help us this morning. Oh, beloved, what are you going to do with this golden opportunity, with this inward pressure of a cry of God in thy soul? Are you going to let others be crowned, and you lose the crown? Are you willing to be brought into captivity today for God?

Verily, this morning must decide some things. If you are not baptized, you must seek the baptism of the Spirit of God. And if there is anything which has marred the fruit, or interfered with all His plan, I beseech you this morning to let the blood so cover, let the anointing of Christ so come, let the vision of Christ so be seen that you will have a measure that shall take all that God has for you.

Called by his GRACE

"When it pleased God, who separated me from my mother's womb, and called me by his **GRACE**, to reveal his Son in me, that I might preach him among the heathen; immediately I conferred not with flesh and blood." [Ga 1.15-16] Now read together with the words: "Therefore I was not disobedient to the heavenly vision," [Ac 26.19] and "I conferred not with flesh and blood."

There is no man here this afternoon who can be clothed in the Spirit, and catch the fire and zeal of the Master every day and many times in the day, without he ceases in every way to be connected with the "arm of flesh" [2Ch 32.8] which would draw him aside from the power of God. Many men have lost the glory because they have been taken up with the natural. If we are going to accomplish in the Spirit the thing God has purposed for us, we can never turn again to the flesh. If we are Spirit-filled God has cut us short and brought us into a relationship with himself, joined us to Another, and now he is all in all to us.

You may have a vision of the Lord all the time you are on a railway train, or in a tramcar, or walking down a street. It is possible to be lonely in the world and to be a Christian, without what? Without you cease to be a natural man. I mean that the Christian ought to have such an unction as to realize at any moment, whether in the presence of others or alone, that he is with God. He can have a vision in the tramcar, or the railway train, even if he has to stand with others in front or behind him; or he can have a vision if he is there alone.

Nehemiah stood before the king because of trouble in Jerusalem which had nigh broken his heart. He was sorrowful, and it affected his countenance; [Ne 2.1-3], but he was so near to God that he could say: "I have communed with the God of heaven." And if we believers are to go forth and fulfill God's purpose with us, the Holy Spirit must constantly be filling us and moving upon us until our whole being is on fire with the presence and power of God. That is the order of the baptism of the Holy Ghost. The man is then ready for every emergency.

Now it is a most blessed thought struck me as I was reading at our assembly on Sunday morning. That in the holy, radiant glory of the vision that was filling Paul's soul, [Ac 20] the people became so hungry after it that until midnight they drank in at the fountain of his life, and as he was pouring forth a young man fell from the third loft, [Ac 20.9] and Paul, in the same glorious fashion, as always, went down and embraced him and pressed the very life from himself into the young man, and brought him back to life. [Ac 20.10-11]

Always equipment for emergency, blessed, holy equipment by God! Someone calls at your door and wants to see you particularly, but you cannot be seen till you are through with God. Living in the Holy Ghost, walking in the divine likeness, having no confidence in the flesh, but growing in the **GRACE** and knowledge of God, and going on from one state of glorious perfection unto another state of perfection—that is it.

You cannot compare the Holy Ghost to anything less, but something more, than ever you thought about with all your thoughts. That is the reason why the Holy Ghost has to come into us to give us divine revelations for the moment. The man that is a "partaker of the divine nature" [2Pe 1.4] has come into a relationship where God imparts his divine mind for the comprehension of his love andthe fellowship of his Son. We are only powerful as we know that source, we are only strong as we behold the beatitudes and all the wonderful things and **GRACE**s of the Spirit.

It was a necessity that Jesus should live with his disciples for three years, and walk in and out amongst them [Ac 1.21] and manifest his glory, and show it forth day by day. I will show you why it was a necessity. Those men believed in God. But this Messiah had continually, day by day, to bring himself into their vision, into their mind, into their very nature. He had to press himself right into their life to make them success after he had ascended to heaven. He had to show them how wonderfully and **GRACEFULLY** and peacefully he could move the crowds.

You remember that the house to which they brought the sick of the palsy, and in which he was speaking to the people, was so crowded that they could not come nigh unto him except by uncovering the roof and dropping the man through. [Mk 2.4] The way to the cities was so pressed with the people [Mk 3.10] who were following Jesus and his disciples, which he and they could hardly get along, but he always had time to stop and perform some good deed on the journey thither. What he had to bring home to the minds and hearts of the disciples was that he was truly the Son of God.

They never could accomplish what they had to accomplish until he had proved that to them, and until he had soared to the glory. They could only manifest him to others when he had imparted his life into the very core of their nature, and make others confess that they were astonished, and that "we never saw things like this." [Mk 2.12] It was the Son of God traveling in the greatness of his strength to manifest before those disciples the keynote of truth that no one could gainsay. They had been with him and seen his desire, his craving, and his lust to serve God. Yes, he lusted to be like God in the world manifesting him so that they might see what Philip had missed when Jesus said to him, **"Hast thou not seen the Father?" [Jn 14.9]** He wanted them to be clothed with the Spirit, baptized by the Spirit.

Some people get the wrong notion of baptism. The baptism is nothing less than the third person of the blessed trinity coming down from the glory, the executive Spirit of the triune God indwelling your body, revealing the truth to you, and causing you sometimes to say "Ah!".

Our bowels yearn with compassion, as Jesus yearned, to travail as he travailed, to mourn as he mourned, to groan as he groaned. It cannot be otherwise with you. You cannot get this thing along a merely passive line. It does not come that way. But, glory is to God; it does come. Oh that God might bring from our hearts the cry for such a deluge of the Spirit that we could not get away till we were ready for him to fulfill his purpose in us and for us.

I had a wonderful revelation of the power of God this last week. If there is anything I know about this baptism it is this: That it is such a force of conviction in my life that I am carried, as it were, through the very depths of it. Sometimes we have to think; at other times we have not time to think, and it is when we are at our wits' end that God comes and brings deliverance. When you are at your wits' end, and you throw yourself on the omnipotent power of God, what a wonderful transformation there is in a moment.

An incident.

I went to a house where they were very much distressed. It is a peculiar thing, but it is true, that the Spirit of the Lord upon one either binds people together or makes them tremendously fidgety or restless, that they have to come to some place of decision. I know nothing like the mighty power of the Spirit; it works so harmoniously with the will of God. I was talking to the people in that house, and a young woman was there, and she said, "Oh, Father, I ought to have relief today. I am sitting here, and I do know what to say, but somehow I feel that this whole trouble ought to go today." "What trouble?" I said. "For six years I have not been able to drink. I cannot drink. I go to the tea-table and cannot drink. My body has gone down."

I knew what it was. It was a devil in the throat. You say, "You must be very careful." Well, I don't care whom I affront by saying that; I believe the devil is the root of all evil, and it is a serious thing for a beautiful young woman who had perfect health, otherwise to be, as a result of that one thing, so disorganized in her mind and body.

I knew it was the power of Satan. How did I know? Because it attacked her at a vital point, and it got her mind on that point, and when it got her mind on that point she went downhill, and she said, "I dare not drink; if I do I shall choke." I asked the father and mother to go out, and then I said to the young woman, "You will be free, and you will drink as much as you want as soon as I have done with you if you will believe. As sure as you are there, you will drink as much as you want."

Our brethren are going out into the streets tonight, and I may be amongst them, and they will be preaching, and they will say definitely, "Everyone that believeth can be saved." [Mk 16.16] They will mean, everyone that believeth can be healed. The same truth. They will emphasize it over and over again. They have no more right to emphasize that than I have a right to say "He was wounded for my transgressions, he was bruised." [Is 53.5] So I said to her, "Now, dare you to believe?" "Yes, I believe that in the name of Jesus you can cast the evil power out." I then laid my hands upon her, and I said, "It's done; you drink." She went laughingly, praise God, and drew the first glass of water and drank. "Mother! Father! Brother!" she said, "I've drunk one glass!" There was joy in the house.

What did it? It was the living faith of the Son of God. Oh, if we only knew how rich we are, and how near we are at the fountain of life! "All things are possible to him that believeth." [Mk 9.23] When Aeneas, who had kept his bed eight years, was told by Peter to "Arise and make thy bed, and he arose immediately," [Ac 9.34] what did it? A life clothed with the Spirit.

[Tongues (by Wigglesworth) and interpretation: "The living water is falling and making manifest the Christ mission to those who will enter in by living faith. Nothing can hinder the life-flow to those who believe, for all things are possible to them that believe."]

I wonder how many people there are here this afternoon who have missed the point. If I talked to you for a short time, you would probably say to me, "I had a wonderful vision when I was baptized." I want you to notice that this vision that Jesus gave to Paul was right on the threshold of his baptism. An inspired life is always on the very open door of the quickening of that life by the Spirit.

I want you to notice also that when a man is born of God, or when, as it were, God is born into the man, and he becomes a quickened soul to carry out the convictions of the life of the Spirit of God in him—when he is born of God, instantly on the threshold of this new birth there comes a vision of what his life is to be. The question is whether you dare go through with it, whether you are going to hold on to the very thing the Holy Ghost brought to you, and never lose sight of it, but press on in a life of devotion to God and of fellowship and unity with him.

A warning.

That is what Paul did, that is what Jesus did, and that is what we all have to do. In this connection, I want to say advisedly that when we are baptized with the gift of tongues, we must not allow tongues to entertain us, nor he entertained with speaking in tongues. When you have accomplished one thing in the purpose of God for you, he means you to go forward and accomplish another. As soon as you accomplish one thing, it is no more to you, and God will enlarge you and fit you for the next thing he wants you to do.

When I was baptized in the Holy Ghost, there was the unfolding of a new era of my life, and I passed into that and rejoiced in the fact of it, and others with me. But the moment I reached that, God has been ready with another ministry for me. If you are careful to watch for God, God is always caring for you. Jesus said: "If you honor me here, I will honor you yonder." [1Sa 2.30, Mt 10.32] Whatever it may be that you are working out for God here, he is working out a far greater, a divine, glory for you. You have no need to be constantly talking about what you are going to appear like in the glory.

The chief thing you are to watch is that you realize within yourself a deeper manifestation of the power of God today than yesterday, that you have something more clear today of the mind of the Spirit than you had the day before, that nothing comes between you and God to cloud your mind. You are to see a vision of the glory of God more today than yesterday and to be living in such a state of bliss that it is heavenly to live. Paul lived in that ecstasy because he got into a place where the Holy Ghost could enlarge him more and more. I find that if I continually keep my mind upon God, he unfolds things to me, and if I obediently walk before God and keep my heart pure and clean and holy and right, he will always be lifting me higher than I have ever expected to be.

How does it come?

On this line. In Romans 12.1, Paul speaks about a certain place being reached—he speaks about an altar on which he had laid himself. [Ro 12.1] When he had experienced the mercies of the Lord he could do no other than make a presentation of his body on the altar, and it was always to be on the altar and never to be taken off.

As soon as he got there, he was at the place where the Holy Ghost could bring out of him "things new and old," [Mt 13.52] and, as we read in his epistles, "things" which Peter said were "hard to be understood." [2Pe 3.16] How was that?

Because he so lived in the Spirit that God brought his mind into Paul's mind, so that the apostle could write and speak, as an oracle of the Holy Ghost, things which had never been in print before, things portraying the mind of God; and we read them today and drink them in like a river, and we come out of the epistles, as it were, clothed with mighty power, the power of God himself.

How does it come? It comes when we are in a place low enough, and where God can pour in, pour in, pour in. Paul could say that not one thing that God had spoken of him had failed. In Acts 26 and Romans 15, you will find that he accomplished the whole of what Jesus said he would accomplish, when he was re-organized, or filled, or in-filled by the mighty power of God. God wants to do the same for you and me, according to the gifts he has bestowed upon us.

Shall we stop short of what he says we ought to be?—shall we cease to come into line with the mind which is always thinking for our best?—shall we cease to humble ourselves before him who took the way of the cross for us?—shall we cease to withhold ourselves from him who could weep over the doomed city, [Lk 13.34-35] from the Lord Jesus Christ who "trod the winepress alone"? [Is 63.3] —shall we cease to give him our all?

To what profit it will be if we hold back anything from him who gives us a thousand times more than ever he asks from us? In Hebrews 2 he says he is going to bring many sons to glory. [He

2.10] Let that be your vision. If you have lost the vision, he is tender to those who cry to him; from the broken heart he never turns away, [Ps 15.17] and they that seek him with a whole heart will find him. [Ps 119.2]

As I speak to you this afternoon, I feel somehow that my heart is very much enlarged, that my compassion for my Lord is intensified, that nothing is too hard. The people in the days of the apostles took joyfully the spoiling of their goods, [He 10.34] and I feel there is a measure of **GRACE** given to the man who says, "I will go all the way with Jesus." What is that measure of **GRACE**? It is a girding with hopefulness in pressing forward to the goal that God would have us reach. But it is important that we forget not Paul's words, "Let no man take thy crown." [Rv 3.11] He saw there was a possibility lest any man who had been the means of sowing the good seed of the gospel should lose that for which God had apprehended him.

• • •

In closing, let me remind you that the Holy Ghost has brought us here. For what purpose has he brought us? Can anyone have come here, either seeker or speaker, without a cry to God to make some men today, as it were, flames of fire? [He 1.7]

My passion is that God shall endue this convention with such unction and cry that you won't be satisfied until you feel the very members of your body all on fire with a Spirit-kindled unity. It is not too late to don the girdle today; it is not too late to put on the armor of God, [Ep 6.11] to put on the shield, [Ep 6.16] to put on the sandals [Ep 6.15] better than ever before.

This afternoon God wants me to know, and you to know, that experimentally we have only touched the very frill, the very edge, of this outpouring of the Spirit. If we do not allow God to fill us with himself, he will choose somebody else. If we do not fall into line with the will of God, there will be somebody else who will. God can raise up men to carry out his behests. The children were crying out one day, and the disciples rebuked them. "No," he said, “if these were to hold their peace, the very stones,” [Lk 19.40] of which he could make bread [Mt 4.3] —he could make them cry out.

I have a Jesus like that, who can speak the word, and the thing is done; I have a Jesus indwelling me and vitalizing me with a faith that believes it is true; I have a Jesus within me who has never let me get faint-hearted or weary. Let us press on in faith along the line of God’s will, and the outpouring which we have longed to see will come.

Cheer up, hold on, never let go the vision; be sure it is for you just as much as for anybody else, and God will surely make it come to pass. Never look down, because then you will only see the ground and miss the vision. All blessings come from above; [Jm 1.17] therefore keep your eye on Jesus. Never weary. If you do not fall out, by the way, he will be with you to strengthen you in the way. Hallelujah!

From the author Dr. Michael H Yeager's

GOD’s GRACE WORKS

When David said about Goliath, let no man's heart be filled with fear about this uncircumcised Philistine, he's nothing because the God who delivered the lion and a bear in my hands, God will deliver Goliath into my hands. He wasn't bragging about his faith. He wasn't bragging about his walk. He was bragging about the God of Israel who gave the lion and the bear to him.

It's in your weakness. It's in your brokenness God's GRACE works. Jesus said: Blessed are those who mourn. He said blessed are the meek. Blessed are those who hunger and thirst after God's righteousness, and they will be filled. The **GRACE** of God flows into a humble heart and causes them to become mighty warriors in the kingdom. God takes nothing to make everything Paul says, therefore will I rejoice for when I am weak then I am Strong. See, brothers and sisters, you might think your weakness, your lack of education, your lack of good looks, your bad upbringing are a millstone around your neck, but they can be used for quite the opposite. What the devil meant for evil, God can turn it to Good.

All things work together for good to them that love God, which are called according to his purpose. So some people walk around, and they're proud of their pedigree, and some of you say, oh Lord, I'm just nothing but a mud puppy. I don't have a pedigree, and I do not need one!

Not many wise men after the flesh, not many mighty, not many noble, but God has chosen the foolish things of this world to confound the wise. God has chosen the weak things of this world to confound the mighty things, and base things of the world, and things which are despised. Has God chosen yea, things which are not to bring to not things that are? No flesh will glory in his presence. God is not going to have Braggadocios, egotistical, proud; I'm special, people in Heaven. We brag and boast about Jesus and not about who we are! Paul said we are those who have no confidence in the flesh. If any other man thinks of where he can trust in the flesh. He said, I am circumcised the eighth day of the stock of Israel, the tribe of Benjamin, a Hebrew of Hebrews, touching the law blameless, but what things were gained to me, that counted loss for Christ.

1 Corinthians 1:25 Because the foolishness of God is wiser than men, and the weakness of God is stronger than men. 26 For ye see your calling, brethren, how that not many wise men after the flesh, not many mighty, not many noble, are called: 27 but God hath chosen the foolish things of the world to confound the wise; and

God hath chosen the weak things of the world to confound the things which are mighty;

Yea, I count lost all things, but for the excellence of the knowledge of Christ Jesus, for whom I have suffered the loss of all things and do count them, but dung. What is Dung? Manure. What's manure? Poop. He said all of this pedigree of being a Benjamite of being a Pharisee, of keeping the law. I did this, and I did that. He said it's all poop. He said I don't have confidence in my flesh. He said I am the least of all apostles.

Jesus picked nobodies. That's why the somebodies despise him. Why didn't you pick the teachers of the law? Why didn't you pick the doctors of the law? Why didn't you pick the cream of the crop? The shakers and movers of the time? No, because my **GRACE** will not work in them. See, they are depending upon themselves. They're not looking to God. The deeper and more mature you are in God, the more you know how lost you are without him. I need him. I need him to be the man that God has called me to be.

He chose me. I didn't do it myself. I need God. Oh, I need God. Oh, I need God every moment. I need God every minute I need God. Every second. I need God every hour. That's why it may seem like God never gives you more money than what you really need at the moment. God kept the people of Israel in the wilderness for forty years was that they might learn to be dependent upon him and that they live upon nothing but God's Word. God is trying to teach you how to become totally dependent upon him.

The financial system of this world is going to come tumbling down. People have their confidence in the materialism of this world. It is going to crumble. Why? Because God is saying to his people, I want you to learn how to depend upon me for your money, your needs, your daily living!

Hebrews 12:26 whose voice then shook the earth: but now he hath promised, saying, Yet once more I shake not the earth

only, but also heaven. 27 And this word, Yet once more, signifieth the removing of those things that are shaken, as of things that are made, that those things which cannot be shaken may remain. 28 Wherefore we receiving a kingdom which cannot be moved, let us have grace, whereby we may serve God acceptably with reverence and godly fear:

Demonic power tried to kill me

Here I was as a 21-year-old kid on-fire for God! I knew in my heart I was stirring things up in the satanic realm and the demonic world would try to find a way to destroy me. I did not have any fear in my heart because I had discovered the truth that "greater is He that is in me, than he that is in the world!"

Now I had a very realistic experience one night as I was sleeping. I saw this dark, faceless demon come running down the long hallway of the house I was staying in. It was just a tiny house that had been a chicken house converted into a small house with a guest quarters. I shared this house with an evangelist and his wife. I slept all the way down on the other side of this long narrow building. I'm not complaining (faith never grumbles or gripes).

I could handle it even if it was not heated or air conditioned. The night, I saw in a very tangible dream this demonic spirit come running down this long hallway through the door and into my bedroom. When it came into my bedroom, it immediately jumped on top of me and began choking me. I could not physically breathe at that moment. Panic and fear overwhelmed me! Then I heard the voice of God speak to my heart, telling me to be at peace.

The Lord's presence came flooding in upon me at that very moment. I cried out to Jesus with a whisper and rebuked this demon that was choking me, in the name of Jesus. At this point I was fully awake by this time. As this dark image continued choking me, I saw a gigantic hand come down through the ceiling of my room. It grabbed this faceless, dark demonic power around the neck and ripped it off me. This gigantic hand shook it like a cat would a mouse and threw it out of the room. God’s presence overwhelmed me as I was sitting up in my bed crying and weeping with joy and praising God! This experience was not just my imagination running wild, but it was literal and real!

God wants to open our eyes, guide and lead us to give us instruction through dreams. Like I said this doesn't mean every dream is of the Lord. That's why we must look at the dreams we have experienced through Christ and through the word of God. There are many examples of God giving men warnings and instructions using dreams. God gave a message to King Abimelech about Abraham's wife:

We must learn how to live in the realm of faith, not only a faith that opens the door for God to speak to us, but also a faith that will cause us to hearken and obey. I have said from the time I gave my heart to Christ, I can hear the voice of God! I say this to myself all the time, I can hear the voice of God. So many believers make the mistake by saying: God never talks to me! They say: I'm so confused, I don't know what to do. When you contradict what the word of God says, it opens the door for your enemy the devil to send you confusing signals. Jesus boldly declared when he said:

John 10:27My sheep hear my voice, and I know them, and they follow me:

Dreams are a major way that God was speak to us by the prophets.

I the Lord will make myself known unto them(Prophets)in the vision and will speak unto him in a dream.

I experienced an amazing dream not too long ago. God used this dream to bring direction, and peace of mind to my heart. I know it was of the Lord because I was not in the natural thinking upon this subject. I have had many such like dreams through the years. Now how do we know if these dreams are of the Lord? First, they will never be contradictory to the divine nature of Christ, his will, or his word. Time also will tell whether we have really heard from the Lord.

Bye-Bye Obama!

I had an amazing dream NOVEMBER 13, 2014. In this amazingly vivid dream my wife and I were in a very large outdoor meeting. A Minister I know was just finishing his message. A holy hush fell upon this large gathering of thousands of believers. As we were all waiting upon God for what was to happen next, my wife Kathleen who is at my side, stood to her feet, got out of our aisle and went to the front of the gathering.

She stood behind the podium and began to speak in a wonderful heavenly language (this is a spiritual gift called diversity of tongues). During her speaking in this tongues scattered throughout the tongues were the words Bye-Bye Obama, Bye-Bye Obama, Bye-Bye Obama. On three different occasions, she would stop speaking in tongues and say: Bye-Bye Obama, Bye-Bye Obama, Bye-Bye Obama.

To be honest in this dream I became extremely intimidated with what my wife was doing, because I knew that I was going to have to give the interpretation. When she finished with this tongues, immediately I sensed a very strong quickening of my spirit. A divine boldness came upon me and I stood to my feet. I stepped out of the row of people I was in and went up front. My wife had stepped aside, and I boldly stepped behind the pulpit and began to give the interpretation. As I gave this interpretation my physical, and voice inflections matched that which my wife had spoken as she was flowing in the gift of the diversity of tongues. At the exact same place in her tongues where she had said Bye-Bye Obama, Bye-Bye Obama, Bye-Bye Obama I spoke the exact same thing.

I watched myself give this interpretation in this dream, and I was amazed at what I heard the spirit of the Lord saying to his people. I cannot exactly give you word for word everything that was spoken, but the meaning was that Obama was leaving. I am not speaking about him being impeached, but that he will be leaving at the end of 2 years, is my understanding from the interpretation of the tongues. Many conservatives, well-known people, believers, and even so-called profits have been saying that Obama would declare martial law and stay in office longer than normal.

If you did a search on Google about Obama, and martial law, you would see thousands of posts. Even well-known people like Dr. Ben Carson believes that this might be the case. Dr. Ben Carson is a very well-known black neurosurgeon, who has repeatedly stated that he believes there is a chance that the 2016 elections may not be held at all. Many believe that widespread anarchy gripping the country could be reason enough for the Obama administration to announce the implementation of martial law and the suspension of some, if not all, of Americans' constitutionally protected rights — including the right to vote and hold national elections. People's hearts are being filled with fear that Obama is going to orchestrate some type of disaster in order to stay in power. As a result of this divine dream I had, I no longer fear this.

In the mist of this interpretation I heard the Lord say that Obama was like a Nebuchadnezzar that had God had used to bring judgment to America. That everything that was shaken and going to be shaken was in order to separate those who truly love Christ, from those who did not. That the division that was and is happening in our nation right now was simply the revealing of people's hearts. That now those who put their trust in God, and those who put their trust In Man has been revealed. That from here on out our nation will never be the same, but that this dividing between light and darkness will grow ever wider. The revealing and manifestation of this spiritual war and division has begun.

Daniel 12:10 Many shall be purified, and made white, and tried; but the wicked shall do wickedly: and none of the wicked shall understand; but the wise shall understand.

Amazing Dream I Had: Creation Held Together by a Divine Song!

I had an amazing dream. It's very hard to describe in human terms. I was sleeping peacefully when, at about three o'clock in the morning, I was suddenly smack dab in the middle of heaven, close to the throne of God. It was so real and tangible; it literally felt as if I was in heaven physically. God gave me eyes to see all of existence. It was as if I was omnipresent. All of creation lay before me. My mind and emotions, and all five of my senses perceived all things. I embraced everything at one time.

It was the most amazing experience you could imagine. It was so beautiful and magnificent that it is beyond precise description. It could be likened to being in the eye of a storm with everything spinning around you. With this supernatural, imparted ability I could perceive the spiritual and angelic. I saw angels of all types and ranks. I saw and felt the nature and the physical realms. I saw the planets, moons, stars, solar systems, and the whole universe. I saw animal life, plant life, oceans, seas, lakes, and rivers. I even saw the microscopic molecular realm. God supernaturally expanded my capacity mentally and emotionally to perceive all things. If it had not happened to me personally, I would be skeptical myself of someone saying these things.

In the midst of this experience I began to be overtaken by an absolute sense of incredible harmony. It was a unity and oneness of a mind-boggling proportion. It resonated through my whole being. I could feel it in my bones, flesh, emotions, and mind. My heart resonated with His harmony. My whole being was engulfed in this unbelievable symphony. All creation, the universe, and spiritual realm was in complete and total harmony and unity. Instantly I perceived everything was at one with God. Not one molecule, not one atom or proton was out of sync with God. As I was looking at creation, suddenly I perceived an invisible force permeating and saturating all of it. God literally gave me eyes to see this invisible force. I could see it moving, flowing, and penetrating everything. With this ability to see, He also gave me spiritual understanding. I realized at that moment that it was this incredible invisible force which was causing all things to exist and flow and move as one living, breathing creation.

What I am sharing with you was a progressive revelation unfolding before me like a flower blossoming. In the midst of this experience my ears opened, and I heard the most incredible music, a breathtaking song. This invisible force was literally a song that was being sung. Instantly I perceived that it was this music, this song, which was holding all of creation together. This song was permeating every animate and inanimate thing together. Not only was it holding everything together but also everything was singing along with it. It was the most incredible music and song you could ever imagine. Actually, it is beyond comprehension or human ability to describe this song and what it was doing. All of creation was being upheld and kept together by this song. I could see it and feel it. It was inside of me. I was a part of it. No maestro, psalmist, no Beethoven or Mozart could ever produce such a majestic masterpiece.

As I watched and listened, I was overwhelmed with the reality that it was this song that was causing everything to be in harmony and unity. It was this song causing everything to live, move, exist, and have being. During this experience a curiosity took a hold of me. I began to wonder, where is this music, this song, coming from?

I began to look high and low, trying to discover where this song had originated. I finally looked behind me, and on a higher elevation I saw God sitting upon His throne. I did not see the clarity of God's form or face. He was covered in a glistening mist, somewhat like fog. But as I looked upon His form, it was as if my eyes zoomed in on His mouth. I was looking intently at the mouth of God. Out of His mouth was coming this amazing, beautiful, awesome song.

This song that God was singing was holding everything together and in perfect harmony. God the Father was making everything one with Himself through this song, this music coming out of His mouth. I literally could see, feel, and experience the song coming out of God's mouth. In my heart I said to the Father, "Father, how long will you sing this song?" And He spoke to me in my heart, "Throughout eternity, my voice will never cease to sing. My voice will never cease to be heard." I could see letters streaming from God's mouth. Words were coming forth from His mouth. They were swimming in a river of transparent life, like fish swimming in a river. These words seemed to be alive. They were spreading throughout the entire universe, causing everything to exist and to be in harmony. They were permeating all of creation, visible and invisible, spiritual and natural.

I knew in my heart that this was the Word of God, the divinely inspired Scriptures. The Word was swimming as if in an invisible transparent river. I knew that this river was a living, quickening force. I knew that it was this river which was causing the Word of God to be alive. The Word of God was being carried forth by this river. I said to the Father, "Father, what is this river that the Word is flowing, swimming, and living in?" And He said to my heart, "It is the Holy Ghost!"

I was stunned into silence. After a while I repeated my question. Once again, He said to me, "It is the Holy Ghost. It is the breath of My mouth coming from the voice of My lips. And this voice is My Son, Jesus Christ. My voice is My Son, Jesus Christ. And out of His voice comes the Holy Ghost and My Word." Further He said to me, "My Word would not sustain, heal, deliver, or bring life unless it is quickened and made alive by My Spirit." Then the Father confirmed this to me by quoting the Scripture where Jesus said, "My Words are Spirit, and they are life." (See John 6:63.) The Father spoke to me again and said, "You can quote, memorize, and declare the whole Bible, but it will be dead and lifeless until you yield, surrender, move, flow, and come into complete harmony with the Word of God and the Holy Ghost."

This I believe, to some extent, reveals God's eternal purpose for you and I: to be in complete oneness and harmony with God, the Father, the Son, and the Holy Ghost!

One dream can change the whole perspective of your life.

It can open your eyes to truths and realities that you could never obtained by worldly knowledge or wisdom. Another amazing dream I experienced.

CHAPTER SEVEN

Surrender

Out of the emptiness, brokenness & surrender of our lives, God can bring forth all His glories through us, and to others.

Our living hope

Preached at Bowland Street Mission, March 1917.

"Being begotten again unto a living hope, by the resurrection of Jesus Christ from the dead." [1Pe 1.3]

In 1 Corinthians 15, we read of the great fact of Christ the first-fruits. A farmer goes over his land eagerly scanning the first ears of corn that show themselves above the soil because he knows, as the first beginnings, so may the harvest be. And just in the measure as Jesus Christ is risen from the dead, so are we.

As he is, so are we in this world. [1Jn 4.17] Christ is now getting the church ready for translation. Here, we read in Peter, "We are begotten again into a living hope by the resurrection of Jesus Christ from the dead." [1Pe 1.3] Oh, to be changed—a living fact in the body. Just as in the flesh Jesus triumphed by the Spirit. Oh, to be like him! What living hope it is!

Paul and Peter were very little together, but both were inspired to bring before the vision of the church this wonderful truth of the living being changed. If Christ rose not, our faith is vain; we are yet in our sins, [1Co 15.17] it has no foundation. But Christ has risen and become the first-fruits, [1Co 15.20] and we have now the glorious hope that we shall be so changed. We who were not a people are now the people of God. [1Pe 2.10]

Born out of due time, [1Co 15.8] out of the mire, [Ps 69.14] to be among princes. Beloved, God wants us to see the preciousness of it. It will drive away from the dullness of life; it is here set above all other things. Jesus gave all for this treasure. He purchased the field because of the pearl, the pearl of great price [Mt 13.44-46] —the substratum of humanity. Jesus purchased it, and we are the pearl of great price for all time. Our inheritance is in heaven, [1Pe 1.4] and in 1 Thessalonians 4.18, we are told to comfort one another with these words. [1Th 4.18]

What can you have better in the world than the hope that in a little while the change will come? It seems such a short time since I was a boy; in a little while, I shall be changed by his **GRACE** and be more than a conqueror [Ro 8.37] in an inheritance incorruptible, undefiled, that fadeth not away. [1Pe 1.4]

The inheritance is in you, something that is done for you, accomplished by God for you; a work of God wrought out for us by himself, an inheritance incorruptible. When my daughter was in Africa, she often wrote of things "corroding." We have a corruptible nature, but, as the natural decays, the spiritual man is at work. As the corruptible is doing its work we are changing.

When will it be seen? When Jesus comes. Most beautiful of all, we shall be like him. What is the process? **GRACE**! What can work it out? Love! Love! Love! It cannot be rendered in human phrases. God so loved that he gave Jesus. [Jn 3.16]

There is something very wonderful about being undefiled, there in the presence of my king to be undefiled, never to change, only to be more beautiful. Unless we know something about **GRACE** and the omnipotence of his love, we should never be able to grasp it. Love, fathomless as the sea. **GRACE** flowing for you and me.

He has prepared a place for us, [Jn 14.3] a place which will fit in beautifully, with no fear of anyone else taking it; reserved. When I went to a certain meeting, I had a seat reserved and numbered. I could walk in any time. What is there in the reserving? Having a place where we can see him; the very seat we would have chosen. He knows just what we want! There will be no brokenness or jar or wish to have come sooner. He has made us for the place. The beginning of all joys. He loved me so; no sorrow throughout all eternity. Will you be there? Is it possible for us to miss it? We are kept by the power of God, through faith, unto a salvation ready to be revealed in the last time. [1Pe 1.5]

What is there peculiar about it? The fullness of perfection, the ideal of love—the beatitudes worked in. The poor in spirit, the mourners, the meek, the hungry and thirsty, the merciful, the pure [Mt 5.3-8] —all ready to be revealed at the appearing of Jesus Christ. [1Pe 1.7] You could not remain there but for the purifying, the perfecting, the establishing; working out his perfect will when ready! Refined enough, you will go. But there is something to be done yet to establish you, to make you purer.

A great price has been paid. The trial of your faith is more precious than gold that perisheth. [1Pe 1.7] Men are losing their heads for gold. And we must give all, yield all, as our Great Refiner puts us again and again in the melting pot; what for? To lose the chaff, that the pure gold of his presence is so clearly seen and His glorious image reflected from glory to glory even by the Spirit of the Lord. [2Co 3.18] We must be steadfast, immovable until all his purposes are wrought out.

Praising God on this line in a meeting is a different thing to the time when you are faced with a hard career: there must be no perishing though we are tried by fire. [1Pe 1.7] What is going to appear at the appearing of Jesus? Faith! Faith!

The establishing of your heart by the **GRACE** of the Spirit, not to crush, but to refine; not to destroy, but to enlarge you. Oh, beloved, to make you know the enemy as a defeated foe, and Jesus not only conquering but displaying the spoils of conquest. The pure in heart shall see God. [Mt 5.8] If thine eye is single, thy whole body shall be full of light. [Mt 6.22]

What is it? Loyalty to the word by the power of the blood. You know your inheritance within you is more powerful than all that is without. How many have gone to the stake and through fiery persecution? Did they desire it? Faith tried by fire had power to stand all ridicule, all slander. The faith of the Son of God who, for the joy that was set before him, endured the cross. [He 12.2] Oh, the joy bf pleasing him. No trial, no darkness; nothing is too hard for me.

If only I may see the image of my Lord in it again and again. He removes the skimmings until in the melting pot his face is seen. When it reflects Him, it is pure. Who is looking into our hearts? Who is the refiner? My Lord. He will only remove that which will hinder. Oh, I know the love of God is working out in my heart a great purpose of reality.

I remember going to the Crystal Palace when General [William] Booth had a review of representatives of the Salvation Army from all nations. It was a grand sight as company after company with all their peculiar characteristics passed a certain place where he could view them. It was a wonderful scene.

We are going to be presented to him. The trials are getting us ready for the procession and the presentation. We are to be a joy to look at, to be to his praise and glory. [Ep 1.14] No one will be there, but they tried by fire. Is it worth it? Yes, a thousand times. Oh, the ecstasy of exalted pleasure. God thus reveals himself to our hearts.

Verse 22 speaks of unfeigned faith and unfeigned love. [1Pe 1.22] What it means to have unfeigned faith! When ill-used, put to shame, or whatever the process, it never alters, only to be more refined, more like unto him. Unfeigned love is full of appreciation for those who do not see eye to eye with you. “Father, forgive them.” [Lk 23.34] Remember Stephen: “Lay not this sin to their charge.” [Ac 7.60] Unfeigned love is the greatest thing God can bestow on my heart.

Verse 23 shows we are saved by a power incorruptible [1Pe 1.23] —a process always refining, a **GRACE** always enlarging, a glory always increasing. Thus we are made neither barren nor unfruitful, in the knowledge of our Lord Jesus Christ. [2Pe 1.8] The spirits of just men made perfect [He 12.23] are garnered in the treasury of the Most High and purified as sons. To go out no more.

To be as he is—holy, blameless. Through all eternity to gaze upon him with pure, unfeigned love. God glorified in the midst, as the whole company of heaven cries out: “Holy, Holy, Holy, Lord God Almighty.” [Rv 4.8] Verse 35: And this is the word which by the gospel is preached unto you. [1Pe 1.35]

How can we be sad, or hang our heads or be distressed? Oh, if we only knew how rich we are! Blessed be the name of the Lord.

Transform us by His GRACE

God has promised to pour out His Spirit upon all flesh, and His promises never fail. Our Christ is risen. His salvation was not a thing done in a corner. Truly He was a man of glory who went to Calvary for us so that He might free us from all that would mar and hinder, that He might transform us by His **GRACE**, and bring us out from under the power of Satan into the glorious power of God. One touch of our risen Christ will raise the dead. Hallelujah!

Oh, this wonderful Jesus of ours! He comes and indwells us. He comes to abide. He it is who baptizes us with the Holy Ghost, and makes everything different. We are to be a kind of firstfruits unto God and are to be like Christ who is the first fruit, walking in His footsteps, living in His power. What a salvation this is, having this risen Christ in us. I feel that everything else must go to nothingness, helplessness, and ruin. Every thought of advantage for ourselves must be on the decrease so that Christ may increase, that we may live in another state, where all things are under the power of the Spirit.

Dare you take your inheritance from God? Dare you believe God? Dare you stand on the record of His Word? What is the record? If thou shalt believe thou shalt see the glory of God. You will be sifted as wheat. You will be tried as though some strange thing tried you. You will be put in places where you will have to put your whole trust in God. There is no such thing as anyone being tried beyond what God will allow.

There is no temptation that will come, but God will be with you right in the temptation to deliver you, and when you have been tried, He will bring you forth as gold. Every trial is to bring you to a greater position in God. The trial that tries your faith will take you on to the place where you will know that the faith of God will be forthcoming in the next test. No man can win any victory save through the power of the risen Christ within him. You will never be able to say, "I did this or that." You will desire to give God the glory for everything.

If you are sure of your ground, if you are counting on the presence of the living Christ within, you can laugh when you see things getting worse. God would have you settled and grounded in Christ, and it is only as you are filled with the Holy Ghost that you become steadfast and unmoveable in Him.

The Lord Jesus said, "I have a baptism to be baptized with; and how am I straitened till it is accomplished." He was assuredly straitened in the way, at Gethsemane, at the judgment hall, and, after that, at the cross, where He, through the eternal Spirit, offered Himself without spot to God. God will take us right on in like manner, and the Holy Spirit will lead every step of the way. God led Him right through to the empty tomb, to the ascension glory, to a place on the throne; and the Son of God will never be satisfied until He has us with Himself, sharing His glory and sharing His throne.

Paul's conversion and his baptism

Published in the Pentecostal Evangel, April 26, 1924.

Read Acts 9:1-22.

Saul was probably the greatest persecutor that the early Christians had. We read that he made havoc of the church, entering into every house, and haling men and women, committed them to prison. At this time we find him breathing out threatening and slaughter against the disciples of the Lord.

He was on his way to Damascus to destroy the church there. How did God deal with such a one? We should have dealt with him in judgment. God dealt with him in mercy. Oh, the wondrous love of God! He loved the saints at Damascus and the way He preserved them was through the salvation of the man who purposed to scatter and destroy them. Our God delights to be merciful, and His **GRACE** is vouchsafed daily to both sinner and saint. He shows mercy to all. If we would but realize it, we are only alive today through the **GRACE** of our God.

More and more I see that it is through the **GRACE** of God that I am preserved every day. It is when we realize the goodness of God that we are brought to repentance. Here was Saul, with letters from the high priest, hastening to Damascus. He was struck down, and there came to his vision a light, a light that was brighter than the sun. As he fell speechless to the ground, he heard a voice saying to him, "Saul, Saul, why persecutest thou Me?" He answered, "Who art thou, Lord?" And the answer came back, "I am Jesus whom thou persecutes." And he cried, "Lord, what wilt thou have me to do?"

I do not want to bring any word of condemnation to anyone, but I know that there are many who have felt very much as Saul felt against the children of God, especially those who have received the Pentecostal Baptism. I know that many people tell us, "You are mad;" but the truth is that the children of God are the only people who are glad.

We are glad inside, and we are glad outside. Our gladness flows from the inside. God has filled us with joy unspeakable and full of glory. We are so happy about what we have received that if it were not for the desire to keep a little decent, we might be doing awful things. This is probably how Paul himself felt when he refers to being "beside ourselves" in the Lord. This joy in the Holy Ghost is beyond anything else. And this joy of the Lord is our strength.

As Saul went down to Damascus, he thought he would do wonderful things with that bunch of letters he had from the high priest. But I think he dropped them all on the road, and if he ever wanted to pick them up, he was not able for he lost his sight. And the men that were with him lost their speech—they were speechless—but they led him to Damascus.

There are some people who have an idea that it is only preachers who can know the will of God. But the Lord had a disciple in Damascus, a man behind the scenes. Who lived in a place where God could talk to him. His ears were open. He was one who listened in to the things from heaven. Oh, this is so much more marvelous than anything you can hear on earth. It was to this man that the Lord appeared in a vision. He told him to go down to the street called Straight and inquire for Saul. And He told him that Saul had seen in a vision a man named Ananias coming in and putting his hand on him that he might receive his sight.

Ananias protested, “Lord, I have heard by many of this man, how much evil he hath done to Thy saints in Jerusalem: and here he hath authority from the chief priests to bind all that call on Thy name.” But the Lord reassured Ananias that Saul was a chosen vessel, and Ananias, nothing doubting, went on his errand of mercy.

The Lord had told Ananias concerning Saul, “Behold, he prayeth.” Repentant prayer is always heard in heaven. The Lord never despises a broken and contrite heart. And to Saul was given this vision that was soon to be a reality, the vision of Ananias coming to pray for him that he might receive his sight.

I was at one time in the city of Belfast. I had been preaching there and had a free day. I had received several letters, and I was looking through them. There were about twenty needy cases in that city, cases that I was asked to visit. As I was looking through my letters, a man came up to me and said, “Are you visiting the sick?” He pointed me to a certain house and told me to go to it and there I would see a very sick woman. I went to the house, and I saw a very helpless woman propped up in bed. I knew that humanly speaking she was beyond all help.

She was breathing with short, sharp breaths as if every breath would be her last. I cried to the Lord and said, “Lord, tell me what to do.” The Lord said to me, “Read the fifty-third chapter of Isaiah.” I opened my Bible and did as I was told. I read down to the fifth verse of this chapter, when all of a sudden the woman shouted, “I am healed! I am healed!”

I was amazed at this sudden exclamation and asked her to tell me what had happened. She said, “Two weeks ago I was cleaning the house, and I strained my heart very badly. Two physicians have been to see me, but they both told me there was no help. But last night the Lord gave me a vision. I saw you come right into my bedroom. I saw you praying. I saw you open your Bible at the fifty-third chapter of Isaiah. When you got down to the fifth verse and read the words, ‘With His stripes we are healed,’ I saw myself wonderfully healed. That was a vision; now it is a fact.”

I do thank God that visions have not ceased. The Holy Ghost can give visions, and we may expect them in these last days. God willeth not the death of any sinner and He will use all kinds of means for their salvation. I do praise God for this gospel. It is always so entreating. That is such a wooing message, "Look unto Me and be ye saved, all ye ends of the earth." Oh, what a gospel! Whatever people say about it, it is surely a message of love.

Ananias went down to the house on Straight Street, and he laid his hands on the one who had before been a blasphemer and a persecutor. He said to him, "Brother Saul, the Lord, even Jesus, that appeared unto thee in the way as thou camest, hath sent me, that thou mightest receive thy sight, and be filled with the Holy Ghost." He recognized him as a brother, that already his soul had been saved and that he had come into relationship with the Father and with all the family of God, but there was something necessary beyond this.

The Lord had not forgotten his physical condition, and there was healing for him. But there was something beyond this. It was the filling with the Holy Ghost. Oh, it always seems to me that the Gospel is robbed of its divine glory when we overlook this marvelous truth of the Baptism of the Holy Ghost. To be saved is wonderful, to be a new creature, to have passed from death unto life, to have the witness of the Spirit that you are born of God, all this is unspeakably precious.

But whereas we have the well of salvation bubbling up, we need to go on to a place where from within us shall flow rivers of living water. The Lord Jesus showed us very plainly that, if we believe in Him, from within us should flow rivers of living water. And this He spake of the Spirit. The Lord wants us to be filled with the Spirit, to have the manifestation of the presence of His Spirit, the manifestation that is indeed given to profit withal, and for us to be His mouthpiece and speak as the very oracles of God.

God chose Saul. What was he? A blasphemer. A persecutor. That is **GRACE**. Our God is gracious, and He loves to show His mercy to the vilest and worst of men. There was a notable character in the town in which I lived who was known as the worst man in the town.

He was so vile, and his language was so horrible, that even wicked men could not stand it. In England, they have what is known as the public hangman who has to perform all the executions. This man held that appointment, and he told me later that he believed that when he performed the execution of men who had committed murder that the demon power that was in them would come upon him and that in consequence he was possessed with a legion of demons.

His life was so miserable that he purposed to make an end of life. He went down to a certain depot and purchased a ticket. English trains are much different from the American. In every coach, there are several small compartments, and it is easy for anyone who wants to commit suicide to open the door of his compartment and throw himself out of the train. This man purposed to throw himself out of the train in a certain tunnel just as the train coming from an opposite direction would be about to dash past and he thought this would be a quick end to his life.

There was a young man at the depot that night who had been saved the night before. He was all on fire to get others saved and purposed in his heart that every day of his life he would get someone saved. He saw this dejected hangs man and began to speak to him about his soul. He brought him down to our mission and there he came under a mighty conviction of sin. For two and a half hours he was sweating under conviction, and you could see vapor rising from him. At the end of two and a half hours, he was graciously saved.

I said, “Lord, tell me what to do.” The Lord said, “Don’t leave him; go home with him.” I went to his house. When he saw his wife, he said, “God has saved me.” The wife broke down, and she too was graciously saved. I tell you there was a difference in that home. Even the cat knew the difference. Previous to this that cat would always run away when that hangs man came into the door.

But that night that he was saved the cat jumped on to his knee and went to sleep.

There were two sons in that house, and one of them said to his mother, "Mother, what is up in our house? It was never like this before. It is so peaceful. What is it?" She told him, "Father has got saved." The other son was struck with the same thing.

I took this man to many special services, and the power of God was on him for many days. He would give his testimony, and as he grew in **GRACE**, he desired to preach the gospel. He became an evangelist, and hundreds and hundreds were brought to a saving knowledge of the Lord Jesus Christ through his ministry.

The **GRACE** of God is sufficient for the vilest, and He can take the wickedest of men and make them monuments of His **GRACE**. He did this with Saul of Tarsus at the very time he was breathing out threatenings and slaughter against the disciples of the Lord. He did it with Berry the hangs man. He will do it for hundreds more in response to our cries.

You will notice that when Ananias came into that house, he called the one-time enemy of the gospel, "Brother Saul." He recognized that in those three days a blessed work had been wrought and that he had been brought into relationship with the Father and with the Lord Jesus Christ. Was not this enough? No, there was something further, and for this purpose, the Lord had sent him to that house. The Lord Jesus had sent him to that house to put his hands upon this newly saved brother that he might receive his sight and be filled with the Holy Ghost. You say, "But it does not say that he spoke in tongues."

We know that Paul did speak in tongues; that he spoke in tongues more than all the Corinthians. In those early days, they were so near the time of that first Pentecostal outpouring that they would never have been satisfied with anyone receiving the Baptism unless they received it according to the original pattern given on the Day of Pentecost.

When Peter was relating what took place in the house of Cornelius at Caesarea, he said, “And as I began to speak, the Holy Ghost fell on them, as on us at the beginning.” Later, speaking of this incident, he said, “God, which knoweth the hearts, bear them witness, giving them the Holy Ghost, even as He did unto us; and put no difference between them and us, purifying their hearts by faith.” And we know from the account of what took place at Cornelius’ household that when the Holy Ghost fell “they heard them speak with tongues and magnify God.”

Many people think that God does make a difference between us and those at the beginning. But they have no Scripture for this. When anyone receives the gift of the Holy Ghost, there will assuredly be no difference between his experience today and that which was given on the Day of Pentecost. And I cannot believe that when Saul was filled with the Holy Ghost, the Lord made any difference in the experience that He gave Him from the experience that He had given to Peter and the rest a short while before.

It was about sixteen years ago that a man came to me and said, “Wigglesworth, do you know what is happening in Sunderland? People are being baptized in the Holy Ghost the same way as the disciples were on the Day of Pentecost.” I said, “I would like to go.” I immediately took the train and went to Sunderland.

I went to the meetings and said, “I want to hear these tongues.” I was told, “When you receive the Baptism in the Holy Ghost, you will speak in tongues.” I said, “I have the Baptism in the Holy Ghost.” One man said, “Brother when I received the Baptism I spoke in tongues.” I said, “Let’s hear you.” He could not speak in tongues to order; he could only speak as the Spirit gave him utterance and so my curiosity was not satisfied.

I saw these people were very earnest and I became quite hungry. I was anxious to see this new manifestation of the Spirit, and I would be questioning all the time and spoiling a lot of the meetings. One man said to me, “I am a missionary, and I have come here to seek the Baptism in the Holy Ghost, I am waiting on the Lord, but you have come in and are spoiling everything with your questions." I began to argue with him, and our love became so hot that when we walked home, he walked on one side of the road and the other.

That night there was to be a tarrying meeting, and I purposed to go. I changed my clothes and left my key in the clothes I had taken off. As we came from the meeting in the middle of the night, I found I did not have my key upon me, and this missionary brother said, "You will have to come and sleep with me." But do you think we went to bed that night? Oh, no, we spent the night in prayer. We received a precious shower from above. The breakfast bell rang, but that was nothing to me. For four days I wanted nothing but Cod. If you only knew the unspeakably wonderful blessing of being filled with the Third Person of the Trinity, you would set aside everything else to tarry for this infilling.

I was about to leave Sunderland. This revival was taking place in the vestry of an Episcopal church. I went to the Vicarage that day to say goodbye, and I said to Sister Boddy, the vicar's wife, "I am going away, but I have not received the tongues yet." She said, "It isn't tongues you need, but the Baptism." I said, "I have the Baptism, Sister, but I would like to have you lay hands on me before I leave." She laid her hands on me and then had to go out of the room. The fire fell. It was a wonderful time as I was there with God alone.

It seemed as though God bathed me in power. I was given a wonderful vision. I was conscious of the cleansing of the precious blood and cried out, "Clean! Clean! Clean!" I was filled with the joy of the consciousness of the cleansing. I saw the Lord Jesus Christ. I saw the empty cross, and I saw Him exalted at the right hand of God the Father. As I was extolling, magnifying, and praising Him, I was speaking in tongues as the Spirit of God gave me utterance. I knew now that I had received the real Baptism in the Holy Ghost.

And so Saul was filled with the Holy Ghost and in the later chapters of the Acts of the Apostles we see the result of this infilling. Oh, what a difference it makes. When I got home, my wife said to me, "So you think you have received the Baptism of the Holy Ghost. Why I am as much baptized in the Holy Ghost as you are." We had sat on the platform together for twenty years, but that night she said, "Tonight you will go by yourself."

I said, "All right." As I went up to the platform that night the Lord gave me the first few verses of the sixty-first chapter of Isaiah. "The Spirit of the Lord God is upon me; because the Lord hath anointed me to preach good tidings unto the meek: He hath sent me to bind up the broken-hearted, to proclaim liberty to the captives, and the opening of the prison to them that are bound."

My wife went back to one of the furthermost seats in the hall, and she said to herself, "I will watch it." I preached that night on the subject the Lord had given me, and I told what the Lord had done for me. I told the people that I was going to have God in my life and I would gladly suffer a thousand deaths rather than forfeit this wonderful infilling that had come to me.

My wife was very restless, just as if she were sitting on a red-hot poker. She was moved in a new way and said, "That is not my Smith that is preaching. Lord, you have done something for him." As soon as I had finished, the secretary of the mission got up and said, "Brethren, I want what the leader of our mission has got."

He tried to sit down but missed his seat and fell on the floor. There were soon fourteen of them on the floor, my wife included. We did not know what to do, but the Holy Ghost got hold of the situation, and the fire fell. A revival started, and the crowds came. It was only the beginning of the flood-tide of blessing. We had touched the reservoir of the Lord's life and power. Since that time the Lord has taken me to many different lands, and I have witnessed many blessed outpourings of God's Holy Spirit.

The **GRACE** of God that was given to the persecuting Saul is available for you. The same Holy Ghost infilling he received is likewise available. Do not rest satisfied with any lesser experience than the Baptism that the disciples received on the Day of

Pentecost, then move on to a life of continuous receiving of more and more of the blessed Spirit of God.

Righteousness

It is written of our blessed Lord, "Thou hast loved righteousness, and hated iniquity; therefore God, even thy God, hath anointed thee with the oil of gladness above thy fellows." It is the purpose of God that we are indwelt by the Spirit of His Son. We should likewise love righteousness and hate iniquity.

I see that there is a place for us in Christ Jesus where we are no longer under condemnation but where the heavens are always open to us. I see that God has a realm of divine life opening up to us where there are boundless possibilities, where there is limitless power, where there are untold resources, where we have victory over all the power of the devil. I believe that, as we are filled with the desire to press on into this life of true holiness, desiring only the glory of God, there is nothing that can hinder our true advancement.

Peter commences his second epistle with these words, "Simon Peter, a servant and an apostle of Jesus Christ, to them that have obtained like precious faith with us through the righteousness of God and our Saviour Jesus Christ." It is through faith that we realize that we have a blessed and glorious union with our risen Lord. When He was on earth, Jesus told us, "I am in the Father and the Father in me."

"The Father that dwelleth in Me, He doeth the works." And He prayed to His Father, not only for His disciples but for those who should believe on Him through their word; "That they all may be one; as Thou, Father, art in Me, and I in Thee, that they also may be one in us: that the world may believe that Thou hast sent Me." Oh what inheritance is ours when the very nature, the very righteousness, the very power of the Father and the Son are made real in us.

That is God's purpose, and as we by faith lay hold on the purpose we shall be ever conscious of the fact that greater is He that is in us than he that is in the world. The purpose of all Scripture is to move us on to this wonderful and blessed elevation of faith where our constant experience is the manifestation of God's life and power through us.

Peter goes on writing to these who have obtained like precious faith, saying, "**GRACE** and peace be multiplied unto you through the knowledge of God, and Jesus our Lord." We can have the multiplication of this **GRACE** and peace only as we live in the realm of faith. Abraham attained to the place where he became a friend of God, on no other line than that of believing God. He believed God, and God counted that to him for righteousness. Righteousness was imputed to him on no other ground than that he believed God. Can this be true of anybody else?

Yes, every person in the whole wide world who is saved by faith is blessed with faithful Abraham. The promise which came to him because he believed God was that in Him all the families of the earth should be blessed. When we believe God, there is no knowing where the blessing of our faith will end.

Some are tied up because, when they are prayed for, the thing that then= are expecting does not cone off the same night. They say they believe, but you can see that they are really in turmoil of unbelief. Abraham believed in God. You can hear him saying to Sarah, "Sarah, there is no life in you, and there is nothing in me, but God has promised us a son, and I believe God." And that kind of faith is a joy to our Father in heaven.

One day I was having a meeting in Bury, in Lancashire, England. A young woman was present who came from a place called Ramsbottom, to be healed of goiter. Before she came, she said, "I am going to be healed of this goiter, mother." After one meeting she came forward and was prayed for. The next meeting she got up and testified that she had been wonderfully healed, and she said, "I shall be so happy to go and tell mother that I have been wonderfully healed."

She went to her home and testified how wonderfully she had been healed, and the next year when we had the convention she came again. To the natural view, it looked as though the goiter was just as big as ever; but that young woman believed God, and she was soon on her feet giving her testimony, and saying, "I was here last year, and the Lord wonderfully healed me. I want to tell you that this has been the best year of my life." She seemed to be greatly blessed in that meeting, and she went home to testify more strongly than ever that the Lord had healed her. She believed God.

The third year she was at the meeting again, and some people who looked at her said, "How big that goiter has become." But when the time came for testimony, she was up on her feet and testified, "Two years ago the Lord graciously healed me of goiter. Oh, I had most wonderful healing. It is grand to be healed by the power of God." That day someone remonstrated with her and said, "People will think there is something the matter with you.

Why don't you look in the glass? You will see your goiter is bigger than ever." That good woman went to the Lord about it and said, "Lord, you so wonderfully healed me two years ago. Won't you show all the people that you healed me?" She went to sleep peacefully that night still believing God, and when she came down the next day, there was not a trace or a mark of that goiter.

God's word is from everlasting to everlasting. His word cannot fail. God's word is true and when we rest in the fact of its truth what mighty results we can get. Faith never looks in the glass. Faith has a glass into which it can look. It is the glass of the perfect law of liberty.

"Whoso looketh into the perfect law of liberty, and continueth therein, he being not a forgetful hearer, but a doer of the work, this man shall be blessed in his deed." To the man who looks into this perfect law of God, all darkness is removed, and he sees his completeness in Christ. There is no darkness in faith. There is only darkness in nature. Darkness only exists when the natural is put in the place of the divine.

Not only is **GRACE** multiplied to us through knowledge of God and of Jesus Christ, but peace also. As we know our God and Jesus Christ whom He has sent, we will have peace multiplied to us even in the multiplied fires of ten thousand Nebuchadnezzar. It will be multiplied to us even though we are put into the den of lions, and we will live with joy amid the whole thing. What was the difference between Daniel and the king that night when Daniel was put into the den of lions?

Daniel knew, but the king was experimenting. The king came around the next morning and cried, "Oh Daniel, servant of the living God, is thy God, whom thou Servest continually, able to deliver thee from the lions?" Daniel answered, "My God bath sent His angel, and bath shut the lions' mouths." The thing was done. It was done when Daniel prayed with his windows open toward heaven. All our victories are won before we go into the fight. Prayer links us on to our lovely God, our abounding God, our multiplying God. Oh, I love Him! He is so wonderful!

You will note, as you read these first two verses of the first chapter of the second epistle of Peter, that this **GRACE** and peace is multiplied through the knowledge of God, but that first, our faith comes through the righteousness of God. Note that righteousness comes first and knowledge afterwards. It cannot be otherwise. If you expect any revelation of God apart from holiness you will have only a mixture. Holiness opens the door to all the treasures of God.

He must first bring us to the place where we, like our Lord, love righteousness and hate iniquity before He opens up to us these good treasures. When we regard iniquity in our hearts, the Lord will not hear us, and it is only as we are made righteous and pure and holy through the precious blood of God's Son that we can enter into this life of holiness and righteousness in the Son. It is the righteousness of our Lord Himself made real in us as our faith stays in Him.

After I was baptized with the Holy Ghost, the Lord gave me a blessed revelation. I saw Adam and Eve turned out of the garden for their disobedience and unable to partake of the tree of life, for the cherubim with a flaming sword kept them away from this tree. When I was baptized, I saw that I had begun to eat of this tree of life and I saw that the flaming sword was all round about. It was there to keep the devil away.

Oh, what privileges are ours when we are born of God. How marvelously He keeps us so that the wicked one touches us not. I see a place in God where Satan dare not come. We are hidden in God. And He invites us all to come and share this wonderful hidden place where our lives are hid with Christ in God, where we dwell in the secret place of the Most High and abide under the shadow of the Almighty. God has this place for you in this blessed realm of **GRACE**.

Peter goes on to say, "According to as His divine power bath given unto us all things that pertain unto life and godliness, through the knowledge of Him that hath called us to glory and virtue." God is calling us to this realm of glory and virtue where, as we feed on His exceeding great and precious promises; we are made partakers of the divine nature.

Faith is the substance of things hoped for right here in this life. It is right here that God would have us partake of His divine nature. It is nothing less than the life of the Lord Himself imparted and flowing into our whole beings so that our very body is quickened, so that every tissue and every drop of blood and our bones and joints and marrow receive this divine life. I believe that the Lord wants this divine life to flow right into our natural bodies, this law of the spirit of life in Christ Jesus that makes us free from the law of sin and death. God wants to estabish our faith so that we shall lay hold on this divine life, this divine nature of the Son of God so that our spirit and soul and body will be sanctified wholly and preserved unto the corning of the Lord Jesus Christ.

When that woman was healed of the issue of blood, Jesus perceived that power had gone out of Him. The woman's faith laid hold, and this power was imparted, and immediately the woman's being was surcharged with life, and her weakness departed. The impartation of this power produces everything you need, but it comes only as our faith moves out for its impartation. Faith is the victory. If thou canst believe, it is thine.

I suffered for many years from piles, until my whole body was thoroughly weak; the blood used to gush from me. One day I got desperate, and I took a bottle of oil and anointed myself. I said to the Lord, “Do what you want to, quickly.” I was healed at that very moment. God wants us to have an activity of faith that dares to believe God. There is what seems like faith, and appearance of faith, but real faith believes God right to the end.

What was the difference between Zacharias and Mary? The angel came to Zacharias and told him, “Thy wife Elizabeth shall bear thee a son.” Zacharias was there in the holy place, but he began to question this message, saying, “I am an old man, my wife is well stricken in years.” Gabriel rebuked him for his unbelief and told him, “Thou shalt be dumb, and not able to speak, until the day that these things shall be performed, because thou believest not my words.” But note the contrast when the angel came to Mary.

She said, “Behold the handmaid of the Lord; be it unto me according to thy word.” And Elizabeth greeted Mary with the words, “Blessed is she that believed: for there shall be a performance of those things which were told her from the Lord.” God would have us to lay hold on His word in like manner. He would have us to come with the boldness of faith declaring, “You have promised it, Lord. Now do it.” God rejoices when we manifest a faith that holds Him to His word. Can we get there?

The Lord has called us to this glory and virtue; and, as our faith lays hold on Him, we shall see this in manifestation. I remember one day I was holding an open-air meeting. My uncle came to that meeting and said, “Aunt Mary would like to see Smith before she dies.” I went to see her, and she was assuredly dying. I said, “Lord, can’t you do something?” All I did was this, to stretch out my hands and lay them on her. It seemed as though there was an immediate impartation of the glory and virtue of the Lord. Aunt

Mary cried, "It is going all over my body." And that day she was made perfectly whole.

One day I was preaching, and a man brought a boy who was done up in bandages. The boy was in irons, and it was impossible for him to walk, and it was difficult for them to get him to the platform. They passed him over about six seats. The power of the Lord was present to heal, and it entered right into the child as I placed my hands on him. The child cried, "Daddy, it is going all over me." They stripped the boy and found nothing imperfect in him.

The Lord would have us to be walking epistles of His word. Jesus is the Word and is the power in us, and he desires to work in and through us His own good pleasure. We must believe that He is in us. There are boundless possibilities for us if we dare to act in God and dare to believe that the wonderful virtue of our living Christ shall be made manifest through us as we lay our hands on the sick in His name.

The exceeding great and precious promises of the Word are given to us that we might be partakers of the divine nature. I feel the Holy Ghost is grieved with us because, when we know these things, we do not do greater exploits for God. Does not the Holy Ghost show us wide-open doors of opportunity? Shall we not let God take us on to greater things? Shall we not believe God to take us on to greater manifestations of His power? His call for us is to forget the things that are behind and reach forth unto the things which are before and to press toward the mark for the prize of the high calling of God in Christ Jesus.

Rising into the heavenlies

Published in the Pentecostal Evangel, May 30, 1925.

Whenever, in the history of the world, there has been a divine revelation, God coming forth in some manifestation of His Spirit, there have been antagonism and opposition to the same with the persecution of those who received such manifestations or revelations. In the old dispensation, as well as in the new, when the Spirit of God has been moving mightily, there has been trouble and difficulty.

Why is this? It is because there are some things very much against the revelation of God and the operation of the Spirit of God. First, there is the flesh, the natural man, because, “The carnal mind is enmity against God.” The very fact that men throughout the world, as a rule, are opposed to the working of God, is evidence of the truth of this statement of Scripture.

Out of this enmity of the mind of the natural man against God grows the opposition of the world, which is the mass of these antagonistic individuals. Our Lord Jesus Christ has made it unmistakably plain to all His followers for all time that the world is contrary to Him and His kingdom. He said concerning His disciples, “I have given them thy word; and THE WORLD HATH HATED THEM, because they are not of the world, even as I am not of the world.”

The devil and all his evil hosts are also arrayed against all manifestations of God. The devil is “the prince of this world;” and he is “the spirit that now worketh in the children of disobedience.” All these are opposed to God and His working, but they can never defeat the purposes of God.

So far as the human eye can see, God's cause is often in the minority; but viewed by those who have spiritual eyesight. “They that be with us are more than they that be with them.” So, as Elisha said to his servant, “Fear not.” Wickedness may increase and abound; but when the Lord raises His banner over the saint, it is victory, though the saint may seem to be in the minority.

So we read in the first verse that these saints were “scattered abroad,” meaning that they did not have much liberty to meet together, but were driven from place to place. In the days of John Knox of Scotland, the people who served God had to be in very close quarters because the Roman church set out to destroy them.

They were in the minority from the human viewpoint, but they swept through to victory, and the Roman power was defeated in Scotland. Cry to God that it may not rise again, for it has always meant bloodshed to the saints of God and opposition to the working of the Holy Ghost.

The Holy Ghost wants us to understand our privileges—"elect according to the foreknowledge of God the Father, through sanctification of the Spirit." This work of the sanctification of the Spirit does not refer to cleansing from sin. It refers to a higher order of redemptive work.

The blood of Jesus is all-powerful for cleansing. But when sin is gone and when we are clean and when we know we have the Word of God in us, and when the power of the Spirit is bringing everything to a place where we triumph over all evil, then comes a revelation through the Spirit. It lifts you on to higher ground and unveils the fulness of the life of Christ within us in such a way that we are led on till we are "FILLED unto all the FULNESS of God."

This is the sanctification of the Spirit. It is the great work for which the Spirit is given. This is the purpose for which God has called you; but whether you haye accepted your election, whether you proved yourself worthy of your election, whether you have allowed this Spirit to sanctify you thus, I do not know; but if you yield yourself to God and let His Holy Spirit have His way in your spirit to lead you into the will of God, as it is revealed in the Word of God, He will not fail to "do exceeding abundantly above all that we ask or think."

This word "elect" is a very precious word to me. It shows me that, before the world was, God planned to bring us into such glorious triumph and victory in Christ that "unto him (shall) be the glory in the church by Christ Jesus throughout all ages, world without end. Amen." Feed upon these words.

Let them sink into your heart—God has purposed to do for those in the church something which will redound to the glory of His Name unto the endless ages. This is the most solid ground for faith—that salvation is to be "to the praise of the glory of His **GRACE**." God has predetermined, has planned, has made full provision to accomplish this wondrous work in all who will not "frustrate the **GRACE** of God."

Some people pervert this blessed truth; they say, "Oh, well, you see, we are elected; we are all right." I know manv who believe in that kind of election. They say they are elected to be saved, and they believe others are elected to be damned. It is not true. Everybody is elected to be saved; whether they come into it or not is another thing.

This perverted view of this precious truth makes souls indifferent to its great purpose, the "sanctification of the Spirit." This is one of the ways in which Satan opposes the work of God in the world. He perverts it, making it appear to mean something that it does not mean; so that souls are kept from pressing on into the glorious purpose of God for which salvation was planned. That would be poor salvation which did not deliver man from the thing which causes all the sorrow and trouble in this world—SIN.

Notice again, this sanctification of the Spirit is "unto obedience and sprinkling of the blood of Jesus Christ." There is no sanctification if it is not sanctification unto obedience. There would be no trouble with any of us if we would all come definitely to the place where we understand and accept that Word of our Lord Jesus when He said, "For their sakes, I sanctify myself, that they also might be sanctified through the truth.

Sanctify them through thy truth; thy word is the truth." When you come into the election of the sanctification of the Spirit, you will be obedient to everything revealed in that Word; and in the measure that you are not obedient, you have not come into the sanctification of the Spirit.

A little thing spoils many good things. People say, "Mrs. So-and-So is very good, but—" "Oh, you know that young man is progressing tremendously, but—" There are no "buts" in the sanctification of the Spirit. "But" and "if" are gone, and it is "shall" and "I will" all the way through. Beloved, if there are any "buts" in your attitude toward the Word of Truth, it indicates that there is something unyielded to the Spirit. I do pray God that we may be willing to yield ourselves to the sanctification of the Spirit, that we may enter into the mind of God regarding this election, in actual possession of it.

Perhaps to encourage you, it will be helpful to show you what election is; because there is no difficulty in proving whether you are elected or not. Why are you interested in this book? Is it because you have a desire for more of God? If so, it is God who has given you that desire; and God is drawing you unto Himself.

If you have truly received Jesus as your Lord and Savior, it has been because the Father drew you to Him; for He said, "No man can come to me, except the Father which hath sent me draw him." And we may be sure that God will not go back on what He has begun to do; for our Lord, Jesus added to the above, "And I will raise him up at the last day." Also, the apostle Paul says, in Philippians 1:6, "Being confident of this very thing, that he which hath begun a good work in you will perform it until the day of Jesus Christ."

When I think of my case, I recall that in my childhood I was strangely moved upon by the Spirit. At the age of eight years, I was definitely saved; and at nine, I felt the Spirit come upon me just as when I spoke in tongues. You may say, "When I was in sin, I was troubled." Thank God for it; for it was His Spirit that troubled you.

It is a most blessed thought that we have a God of love, of compassion, and of **GRACE**, who willed not the death of one sinner. God has made it possible for all men to be saved, by causing Jesus, His well beloved Son, to die for the sins of the whole world. It is true that He took our sins; it is true that He paid the price for the whole world; it is true that He gave Himself a ransom for many; it is true, beloved, it is true. And you say, "For whom?"

"Whosoever will let him take the water of life freely." What about the others? It would have to be a refusal of the Blood of Jesus; it would have to be a refusal to have Christ reign over them; that's it. It is "Whosoever will," on the one side, and "Whosoever won't" on the other side; and there are people in the world who "won't." What is up with them? "The god of this world hath blinded the minds of them that believed not, lest the light of the glorious gospel of Christ, who is the image of God, should shine unto them."

Through sanctification of the Spirit, according to this election, you will get to a place where you are not disturbed. There is a peace in the sanctification of the Spirit because it is a place of revelation—of heavenly places into which you are brought. It is a place where God comes and makes Himself known unto you, and when You are face to face with God, you get a peace that passes all understanding, and which lifts you from state to state of inexpressible wonderment. Oh, it is wonderful!

"Blessed be the God and Father of our Lord Jesus Christ, which according to His abundant mercy, hath begotten us again unto a lively hope by the resurrection of Jesus Christ from the dead." This sanctification of the Spirit brings us into a definite line with this wonderful "lively hope" of the glory of God.

A lively hope is exactly the opposite of something dead. A lively hope means movement. A lively hope means looking into what we hope for. A lively hope means pressing into that which is promised. A lively hope means leaving behind you other things. A lively hope means keeping the vision. A lively hope sees Jesus coming. And you live in this lively hope.

You are not trying to make yourself feel that you are believing. But this lively hope keeps you waiting, and ready, and filled with the joy of expectation of the coming of the King. Praise the Lord! If the thought of the coming of the King is not such a lively hope to you, you need to search whether you have ever truly enthroned Him as King over your own life. God has this in mind for you. There is real joy in expectation of His coming, and there will be infinitely greater joy in the realization.

I trust that you will be so reconciled to God that not one thing will interfere with your having this lively hope. If you have any love for the world, this hope cannot be a lively hope to you; for His coming will mean the overthrow of the world. If there is in you the pride of life, this hope cannot be to you a lively hope; for every high thing will be brought low in that day.

Salvation is a very much misunderstood subject. That which comes to you in a moment of time, by believing, is only the beginning. Salvation is so wonderful, and so mighty, so tremendous, that it goes on and on from one degree to another until there shall be nothing in us from which we need to be delivered. Either in spirit, or soul, or mind, or body. Everything is ready so far as God is concerned, and is waiting for man to get ready to receive it.

Sin began in the soul of man, and salvation must be wrought out there before there can be deliverance from the consequences of sin. In the meantime, if we rest our faith in the power of God, we will be "kept by the power of God through faith unto salvation ready to be revealed in the last time."

You have no idea what God wants to do for you through trials and temptations. They do two things for us: Where there is anything wrong in us which we are not recognizing, they bring it to the surface, that we may see our need of God's salvation in this respect. But why are the most faithful also of God's children tried and tempted?

It is that their very faithfulness and loyalty and the purity of their faith may be MADE MANIFEST, and "found unto praise and honor and glory at the appearing of Jesus Christ." Gold has to he tried with fire, and it is made more precious thereby. Your faith,

Peter says, "is MUCH MORE PRECIOUS than gold that perishes."

One day I went to a certain place, and a gentleman there said to me, "Would you like to see the purification of gold?" I replied, "Yes." So he got some gold and put it into a crucible, and put a blast of heat under it. First, it became blood red and then changed and changed. Then this man took an instrument and passed it over the gold. It drew off something, which was foreign to the gold. He did this several times until every bit of that foreign substance was taken away. Then he said to me, "Look!" And there we both saw our faces in the gold! It was wonderful!

My brother, the trial of your faith is much more precious than of gold that perishes. As you are tested in the fire, the Master is bringing the dross to the surface, that He may take it away, all that hinders His image being seen in you—taking away all the dross from your life, all that is not enduring, all that is not precious in His sight.

It is lovely to know that, in times of misunderstanding, times when you are in the right and yet are treated as though you were in the wrong, God is meeting you, blessing you, and accomplishing something which will not only glorify His name but be to your "praise and honor and glory at the appearing of Jesus Christ." So do not chafe or fret; let the fire burn; it will do you good.

"Whom having not seen, ye love." Oh, how sweet! There is no voice so gentle, so soft, and so full of tenderness to me, as His; and no touch. Is it possible to love Him when we have not seen Him? God will make it possible; and, "though now ye see him not, yet believing," He will enable you to "rejoice with joy unspeakable and full of glory," Rejoice! We have something to rejoice over. Oh, what a salvation God has provided for us in all our worthlessness and nothingness and helplessness!

I entreat you from the Lord to be so reconciled to Him that there will be no division between you and Him. Will you give Him preeminence in all things? Shall He not have His rightful place, and decide for you the way and plan of your life? Beloved, when you allow Him to decide for you when you want nothing but His blessed will, when He is in very deed Lord and sovereign of all, you will have a foretaste of heaven all the time. The Lord bless you with **GRACE** to leave all and say, "I will follow Thee, Lord Jesus."

From the author Dr. Michael H Yeager's

I labored more abundantly yet not I, but the GRACE of God which was with me

Here is an amazing set of Scriptures. They give us deep insight into the spiritual truths regarding the grace of God. Paul the apostle who was mightily used of the Lord, and yet he declares it was not him, but the grace of God at work within him.

1 Corinthians 15:8 And last of all he was seen of me also, as of one born out of due time. 9 For I am the least of the apostles, that am not meet to be called an apostle, because I persecuted the church of God. 10 But by the grace of God I am what I am: and his grace which was bestowed upon me was not in vain; but I labored more abundantly than they all: yet not I, but the grace of God which was with me.

Paul, the apostle, said: by the **GRACE** of God, I am what I am. Grace is the divine enablement of God at work in the human heart that has humbled itself and surrendered to the will of the father. Paul said that he recognized that he did not even deserve to be an apostle. May God grant to us this revelation of divine recognition of unworthiness?

Yes, we are unworthy even to be saved. Many very shallow ministers of the gospel would have you to believe otherwise. Jesus ministered in the time when many Pharisees, scribes, Sadducees were filled with the insanity of pride. Jesus by the spirit tried to shock them into the truth. He made this true but amazing statement: My Father could raise up sons and daughters of God out of the racks themselves. Yes, God will make us worthy, but it is his grace in operation within a yielded and surrendered heart.

Isaiah 57:15 For thus saith the high and lofty One that inhabiteth eternity, whose name is Holy; I dwell in the high and holy place, with him also that is of a contrite and humble spirit, to revive the spirit of the humble, and to revive the heart of the contrite ones.

Watch out for people who think they deserved better. That's pride. Pride is the absolute opposite of the divine nature of God. Contention only comes by pride. A believer full of pride will say how dare you to treat me that way. If you slap a proud person, they will turn right around and slap you back. I am not talking about pacifism. A believer full of pride will say how dare you talk to me that way. How dare you treat me like that? Out of that pride will come every evil work. What is true spirituality? Look at Jesus!

1 Peter 2: 19 For this is thankworthy, if a man for conscience toward God endure grief, suffering wrongfully. 20 For what glory is it, if, when ye be buffeted for your faults, ye shall take it patiently? but if, when ye do well, and suffer for it, ye take it patiently, this is acceptable with God. 21 For even hereunto were ye called: because Christ also suffered for us, leaving us an example, that ye should follow his steps: 22 who did no sin, neither was guile found in his mouth: 23 who, when he was reviled, reviled not again; when he suffered, he threatened not; but committed himself to him that judgeth righteously: 24 who his own self bare our sins in his own body on the tree, that we, being dead to sins, should live unto righteousness: by whose stripes ye were healed.

True spirituality is that when you're reviled, you do not revile. When people do you wrong, you do not do them wrong. When people attack you, you do not attack them. Pastor Mike, do you ever attack back when you were attacked? It's not about me. It just reveals to me that I'm not as humble or spiritual as I think I am.

See, true humility is becoming utterly dependent upon God. You're dependent and nobody but Jesus. How does **GRACE** come? It comes by faith in what God has said. Did you know that? It comes by faith and humility. It takes faith to acknowledge you're a nobody. You're nothing, and he's everything. See, people are teaching a faith that takes from God instead of a faith that surrenders to God. See, there is a faith that takes from God. But Pastor Mike do you not take from God? Yes, I take from God what I need to do, the will of God. I strive to use faith to bring me into obedience with the will of the Father.

So I take God-given faith, and I say, okay, there's God's will, and there are the oppositions in front of me that are contrary to God's will. But I submit myself to God, and I declare by grace that I'm going to do God's will. I take the **GRACE**, the divine inability that comes from God to do the will of God. I've had a lot of experiences, and I'm not bragging. It's only because I know I'm nothing. I know I'm nothing. I know that I am nothing and less than nothing without Jesus Christ.

God's grace hit me as I was hanging 250 feet in the air from an 18-inch radio tower. I was about 56 years old and 20 pounds overweight.

So here in January 2013 our lights went out on our radial tower. We got to have the lights on because of the FAA the FCC. We have a radio station that God gave us, and I have to have those lights on at night. Now, this is a 250-foot high tower that is only approximately 18 inches wide on its three sides. The last time I climbed that tower had been about ten years previous to this. I paid for it for the next two weeks. I walked around like a gorilla; my arms and my legs were all bunched up. Every part of my body was stiff, and it hurt for the next two weeks. So here I was in my late 50s and didn't really want to climb the tower. Plus I was 20 pounds overweight.

But I put down my flesh and headed down to the transmitter building and the radio tower. One of the young men from my congregation said he could easily climate for me. You know how young men are boastful and proud. I'll do it; I'll do it he told me. Man, I did not want to do it. I said to this young man who was probably in his 20s are you sure you can get the job done? Oh yeah, pastor. I can get up there and do it. I'm not picking on him because it's easy to say you can do something and find out that you really do not have what it takes to do it.

He got up about 50 feet, and my son Daniel was there with me and others. This young man began to tremble like a leaf in the wind as he was about 50 feet up the tower. I thought, oh, we're in trouble. It's only 18 inches wide. He had to go up 250 feet. So he kept climbing up, and he got the first set of light. Finally, he was up there. But before we knew what he was doing, he began to climb back down. He told me that he could not find the problem. I told him: you cannot be up there for three minutes and determine you cannot find the problem. To make a long story short, he went back up for a couple more minutes and came back down telling me he could not do it.

We quit for that day, but I knew in my heart that we had to get this job done. About three days later another young buck climbed up the tower, and he got up there to the middle light. He was up there for about maybe five minutes. When he got up there, he yelled down and said that he was hyperventilating and that he couldn't breathe. The middle light is about 175 feet up. So young man came back down. He volunteered to go back up, and I told him, if you go up there this time, don't you come back down to you fix the problems with the light. I said we do not want to get a fine from the FCC or the FAA. Well, to make a long story short he went back up to the middle lights, and turned right around and came down.

At that moment I knew that I knew in my heart that I was going to have to climb this radial tower. I just knew it in my heart. But here's the problem. How many know when God heals you, the devil's going to come back to you. So I had broken my foot one time, and my ankle was trying to act up on me. I felt like I could not walk on it. I had ripped my knee cap off one time from a snowmobile accident, and my knee cap felt like he was giving out on me. I also had broken my back one time as a young man, but God healed me. But lately, my back, my kneecap, and my ankle had been giving me much pain.

So the devil says to me, oh, you can't climb that tower. Your ankle is giving out, your knees cap is being messed up and besides that your back is hurting you to the point where it’s almost unbearable.

But guess what, Paul said, when **I am weak, then I'm strong**. That's when the **GRACE** of God comes in because now I really need help. So I strapped all the equipment on and began to climb the tower. I'm praying all the way up the tower, and man, my legs trying to cramp up with Charley horses. My ankle doesn’t want to support my weight. My kneecap is trying to pop out. My back feels like it’s going to snap in half. But when I am weak as a look to Christ then am I strong.

The whole time the devil was whispering you're dead. You're stupid. You're going to get stuck up there. You’re going to fall. I simply told the devil to shut up. God has not given me a spirit of fear but of power love and a sound mind. I was not depending upon myself, but I was depending upon God to get me up there and get me back down safely. To make a long story short, I get up there and find out that we had major electrical problems. The electric wires were ripped away from the tower. I'm up on that tower but I needed more wire.

The Sun was setting. I don't have a flashlight. The wind is picking up trying to blow me off the tower. It feels like I'm freezing to death. I'm up there for over three hours. I have a utility knife with a razor blade. I have to cut the electric tape, and I am almost cutting my hand with the razor blade trying to put everything together. I had sent the guys to the church to get the wire, but it turns out somebody had stalled it. I told them to get an extension cord and that I would cut the ends off to use it to replace the wire that was no good.

Thank God Brother Jim had enough brains to encourage me to take the role of twine with me up the tower. Honest to God, I'm up there 175 feet working on the lighting for the tower with pain hitting me in every part of my body plus I'm freezing, and the wind is trying to blow me off of this tower. A 50-year-old out of shape and overweight man and an 18-inch tower 175 feet in the air with another 75 feet to go.

Now, while I am up there the whole time I am crying out for help from God. I'm confessing my stupidity in my desperate need for him. Then something happened that has happened to me more times than I can count in the last 40 years. The divine **GRACE** of God hits me. I mean there is a divine infusion of the Holy Ghost strength and joy. I started laughing. I'm not lying to you. It was like out of my belly came this invisible strength, and I'm up to, I could have stayed up there all night long. The **GRACE** of God hits me. I'm up there, and I started laughing, and I'm enjoying myself even though my legs are still cramping, my hands are freezing, my back is hurting.

My hands were so cold, and I can hardly open them, but I've got the peace that passes understanding, and joy unspeakable and full of glory. Finally after hours even into the dark hanging 250 feet up in the air, I got the job done. I came down the tower very slowly, and my body was already hurting from this climb. By the next morning, I should have been like a crippled man. Listen, honest to God; I got up on Thursday morning and not only was I not one bit sore, but every single symptom was gone instantly. God's grace in manifestation within my mortal body.

My Mom's Hip Miraculously Healed

I was visiting my parent's home in Wisconsin. One day when I came home, my mother asked me to help her get her hip back into place where it belonged. For some reason her right hip would pop out of place which was extremely painful and difficult for her. When this happened she would lay on the floor and grab onto something heavy and solid like the china hutch or the dining room table leg. Next, she would have one of us four boys grab her right ankle and pull with all our might with a heavy jerk until her hip would go back into place. She was just a little lady, so when we pulled her leg it would pull her whole body off the floor.

I told my mother I would help her. She laid down on her back on the dining room floor and grabbed the dining room table leg. I knelt down on my knees and took a hold of her right ankle with both hands. She was waiting for me to jerk her leg with a powerful pull but Instead of pulling like I normally would, I whispered: "In the name of Jesus Christ of Nazareth I command this hip to go back into place."

The minute I whispered this a wonderful miracle transpired. Her leg instantly shot straight out. She was very surprised asked with a shocked voice, "Michael, what did you just do to me?" I told her what I had done. Then I shared the reality of Jesus with her. As far as I know until she went home to be with the Lord, for the next 25 years she never had another problem with that hip popping out of its socket.

And these signs shall follow them that believe; In my name shall they cast out devils; they shall speak with new tongues; They shall take up serpents; and if they drink any deadly thing, it shall

not hurt them; they shall lay hands on the sick, and they shall recover (Mark 16:17-18).

God did not do this for Mike Yeager, but he did it because he was wanting to speak to my moms heart. He was wanting to tell my mom: I'm real, I'm here, your son did not do this, I did this!

God Heals Antagonistic Mafia Man's Eyes!

I have a house where I take in and keep single men. Some of these men come from rough backgrounds. I had one such gentleman that I was renting to who was quite large and intimidating. I would try to share Christ with him whenever the opportunity arrived, but he was so liberal in his thinking that it did not seem to be having any impact upon him. Everything I believe that is wrong, he proclaimed was right. And everything that I believe is right, he would argue against.

He informed me that in his past he had worked for the Mafia, and at one time he was what they called a THUMPER! I asked him what he meant by a thump-err? He said that he had never physically murdered anyone, but that they would send him to rough up people, you know thump them! I have no doubt at all that what he told me was true.

One day as I was at the house where I keep these men, I saw him standing in the main front room. He seemed quite upset and distressed. I asked him what was wrong. He informed me that he had just come from the doctors because he had been having terrible problems with his eyes. After the Doctor, had conducted all of the test they came back with a very disturbing report. They informed him that he had an eye disease (long medical term) that was going to cause him to go blind.

At that moment, the spirit of God rose with in me, and I proclaimed boldly that in the name of Jesus Christ he was not going to go blind. I told him: close your eyes! He said what? I said: close your eyes! He shut his eyes, and I took my two thumbs and laid them forcefully over his two eyelids. I declared: in the name of Jesus Christ you lying spirit of infirmity, come out of these eyes right now! Be healed in Jesus name! I then removed my thumbs from his eyelids, he looked at me with questioning eyes. I said to him: it's done! He said what? I said it is done. You are healed in the name of Jesus. He said: really? I said: yes Christ has made you whole. It seemed for a minute that tears formed in his eyes as I turned around and walked away.

Approximately a week later he showed up at our thrift store that we manage. He walked into the store asking for Pastor Mike. They informed him that I was not there. Tears were rolling down his face, and they asked him what they could do for him. He told them with great joy and excitement that he had gone back to the doctors, and that his eyes were completely healed. He started hugging the people that where they're running the store. This large ex-Mafia thump-er gave his heart to Jesus Christ that day, and became a part of the church I pastor.

There have been times where I was preaching, and the Reality of God was so real it literally felt like there was a hand on my shoulder. I'm telling you I could literally feel a and on my shoulder, even slightly squeezing it as I was preaching the word of God. I believe it was God speaking to me saying: you're going in the right direction, your preaching the truth. Why would we think that God cannot do these things? He spoke everything into existence with in six days. Surely the Lord God of heaven and earth can manifest himself with physical signs and wonders to speak to us.

BEWARE FALSE PROPHETS

There are false prophets that tell people peace, peace, when in all reality there is nothing but coming destruction and judgment because of sin. It is like a man telling you that everything is going to be okay, when it in all reality is not going to be okay. False preachers are telling people all the time that they are right with God, and that God loves them no matter what they do. They put these poor souls into a very dangerous and precarious position because instead of seeking the Lord, these people who have been told that everything is okay, simply believe this lie. If somebody would've told them the truth, they could've been crying out to God for his mercy and his forgiveness.

A false prophet will keep you out of the will of God, by letting you believe that you can do whatever you want, live however you want, act however you want, and the blood of Jesus Christ covers all of your sins, even the ones that you are living in and committing. They will tell you that you are okay the way you are.

Do not listen to the words of the prophets who prophesy to you ...They speak a vision of their own heart, Not from the mouth of the Lord. They continually say to those who despise Me, 'The Lord has said, 'You shall have PEACE'; And to everyone who walks according to the dictates of his own heart, they say, 'No evil shall come upon you. - Jeremiah 23:16-17

CHAPTER EIGHT

The Word of God is a stimulant to our faith.

The Lord would have us all come into a new place of **GRACE**, that all may see us as new creatures in Christ Jesus, all the old things of the flesh done away and all things become new and all things of God.

Note the word "behold" at the beginning of our text. What does it mean? It means that the Holy Spirit is arousing our attention. He has something special to say. He wants us to pay attention to the fact that our loving Father in heaven has bestowed such **GRACE** upon us that believe, that He calls us sons. He wants us, in likeness, in character, in spirit, in longings, in acts, to be made like unto His own beloved Son in whom He was well pleased. He purposes that we should be conformed to the image of His Son, that He might be the firstborn among many brethren.

You can reach this altitude only by faith. No man can keep himself. The old nature is too difficult to manage. You have been ashamed of it many times. However, God can change you. He will operate upon you by His power and will make you an entirely new creation if you will only believe. Then you can have this testimony: "I am kept by the power of God." The Almighty will stretch His covering over you, and you will know what it is to be able to do all things through Christ who strengtheneth you. All things are possible to him that believeth.

Christ says to us, "Learn of Me; for I am meek and lowly in heart: and ye shall find rest unto your souls." The world has no rest. It is full of trouble. But in Christ, there is a peace that passeth understanding, and from Him, there is an inward flow of divine power that changes your nature until you live, move, and act in the power of God. The Scripture says, "Therefore the world knoweth us not, because it knew Him not."

I will give you an illustration of this. I have lived in one house for sixty years. I have preached from my doorstep, and all the people in our neighborhood know me. They know me when they need someone to pray for them, when they are in trouble, or when they are in any special need.

But when they call their friends, do they call me? No! Why? They would say, "He is sure to want a prayer meeting, but we want to finish up with a dance." Wherever Jesus came, sin was revealed, and men did not as sin revealed. But it is a sin that separates from God forever.

You are in a good place when you become sensitive to the least sin and weep before God, repenting over the least thing in which you have grieved Him. You may have spoken unkindly; you realize that it was not like the Lord, and your conscience has taken you to prayer. It is a wonderful thing to have a keen conscience.

It is when we are close to God that our hearts are revealed to us; it is then we learn to loathe ourselves, and the Holy Spirit turns us to Christ. We take Him to be our righteousness and our holiness. God intends us to live in purity. He has said, "Blessed are the pure in heart: for they shall see God." And the pure in heart can see Him all the time in everything.

"Beloved, now are we the sons of God, and it doth not yet appear what we shall be: but we know that, when He shall appear, we shall be like Him; for we shall see Him as He is. And every man that hath this hope in him purifieth himself, even as He is pure." That is God's standard. Don't accept a lower one. Our Lord, who died for us, became poor that we might be made rich, that we might be made pure, that we may be made holy. What an offering! He suffered for us; He died for us.

He was buried, but rose again, and is now living for us how we should love Him! What a privilege to know that you may be a son of God now! How simple it is. It is written, "As many as received Him, to them gave He the power to become the sons of God, even to them that believe on His name." When we believe, we receive Him. When we receive Him, anything may take place, for all power is given unto Him.

Paul wrote to the Corinthians, "In everything ye are enriched by Him, in all utterance, and all knowledge. Come behind in no gift; waiting for the coming of our Lord Jesus Christ." God wants us to be enriched with utterance for Him so that everywhere we go we are joyous witnesses of the goodness of the Lord. Wherever I am, whether traveling by train or ship, I preach to the people. It is God's plan for me. On board ship, the captain hears, the sailors hear, and the stewards hear. "Oh," they say, "we have another on board!" The world thinks there is something wrong with you if you are full of zeal for God.

One time, on board ship, a young man came to me and asked me to take part in a sweepstake. I said to him, "I am preaching on Sunday. Will you come if I do?" He said, "No!" Later there was entertainment. I said I would take part. It was the strangest thing for me. I said I would sing.

I saw men dressed as clergymen entertaining the people with foolishness. I was troubled. I cried out to God. Then came my turn, just before the dance. A young woman came to take my book and accompany me. She was only half dressed. She said, "I can't play that!" I said, "Never worry." Then I sang, "If I could only tell you how I love Him, I am sure that you would make Him yours today!" There was no dance. A number began to weep, and six young men gave their hearts to God in my cabin.

No man that lives in sin has power. Sin makes a man weak. Sin dethrones, but purity strengthens. The temptation it self is not sin but giving into it is. The devil is a liar, and he will try to take away your peace. But we must always live in the Word of God and on that scripture which tells us, "There is therefore now no condemnation to them that are in Christ Jesus."

If Christ condemns you not, who is he that can condemn you? Do not condemn yourself. If there is anything wrong, confess it out and then come to the blood of Jesus Christ. "If we confess our sins, He is faithful and just to forgive us our sins, and to cleanse us from all unrighteousness. If we walk in the light, as He is in the light, we have fellowship one with another, and the blood of Jesus Christ His Son cleanseth us from all sin."

You can come into a new experience in God, with all fear gone. You can live in a new realm—among the sons of God with power.

"If our heart condemns us not, then have we confidence toward God. And whatsoever we ask, we receive of Him, because we keep His commandments, and do those things which are pleasing in His sight."

Not long ago I received a wire asking me if I would go to Liverpool. There was a woman with cancer and gallstones, and she was very much discouraged. If I know God is sending me, my faith rises. The woman said, "I have no hope." I said, "Well, I have not come from Bradford to go home with a bad report." God said to me, "Establish her in the fact of the new birth."

When she had the assurance that her sin was gone and she was born again, she said, "That's everything to me. The cancer is nothing now. I have got Jesus." The battle was won. God delivered her from her sin, from her sickness, and she was free, up and dressed, and happy in Jesus. When God speaks, it is as a nail in a sure place.

Will you believe, and will you receive Him? Life and immortality are ours in the gospel. This is our inheritance through the blood of Jesus—life for evermore!

A Straightened place

Gen 32:24: And Jacob was left alone, and there wrestled a man with him until the breaking of the day. As we look back over our spiritual career, we shall always see there has been a good deal of our day, and that the end of our day was the beginning of God day. **Can two walk together, except they are agreed?**

Flesh and blood cannot inherit the kingdom of God, neither doth corruption inherit incorruption, and we cannot enter the deep things of God until we are free from our ideas and ways. Jacob! The name means supplanter, and when Jacob came to the end of his way God had a way.

How slow we are to see that there is a better day. Beloved, the glory is never as wonderful as when God has His plan, and we are helpless and throw down our sword and give up our authority to another. Jacob was a great worker, and he would go through any hardship if he could have his way.

In many ways, he had his way, and in ignorance how gloriously God preserved him from calamity. There is a good, and there is a better, but God has a best, a higher standard for us than we have yet attained. It is a better thing if it is God's plan and not ours. Jacob and his mother had a plan to secure the birthright and the blessing, and his father agreed to his going to Padan-aram, but God planned the ladder and the angels. The land whereon thou liest, to thee, will I give it I am with thee and will keep thee in all places whither thou goest, and will bring thee again into this land; for I will not leave thee until I have done that which I have spoken to thee of.

What a good thing for the lad, amid the changes, God obtained the right place. The planning for the birthright had not been a nice thing, but here at Bethel, he found God was with him. Many things may happen in our lives, but when the veil is lifted, and we see the glory of God, His tender compassion over us all the time, to be where God is, how wonderful it is.

Bethel was the place where the ladder was set up twenty-one years before. Twenty-one years of wandering and fighting and struggling. Listen to his conversation with his wives: Your father hath deceived me and changed my wages ten times, but God suffered him not to hurt me. To his father-in-law: Except the God of my father had been with me, thou hadst sent me away empty. God hath seen my affliction and the labor of my hands.

Jacob had been out in the bitter frost at night watching the flocks. He was a thrifty man, a worker, a planner, a supplanter. We see the whole thing around us in the world today supplanters. There may be a measure of blessing, but God is not first in their lives. We are out judging them, but there is a better way, better than our best. God's way. God first! **There is a way that seemeth right unto a man, but the end thereof are the ways of death.**

But there is a way that God establishes, and I want us to keep that way before us this morning" the way that God establishes. In our natural planning and way, we may have many blessings, of a kind; but oh, beloved, the trials the hardships, the barrenness, the things missed which God could not give us! I realize this morning by the Holy Ghost; I realize by the anointing of the Spirit that there is a freshness, a glow, planning in God where you can know that God is with you all the time. Can we know that God is with us all the time? Yes! Yes! Yes! I tell you there is a place to reach where all that God has for us can flow through us to a needy world all the time.

For as the heavens are higher than the earth, so are My ways higher than your ways, and My thoughts than your thoughts. Verse 24: And Jacob was left alone, and there wrestled a man with him until the breaking of the day. Oh, to be left alone! Alone with God! In the context, we read that several things had gone on. His wives had gone on, his children had gone on, and all had gone on. His sheep and oxen had gone on, his camels and asses had gone on, all had gone on. He was alone.

You will often find you are alone. Whether you like it or not, your wives will go on; your children will go on, your cattle will go on. Jacob was left alone. His wife could not make atonement for him, his children could not make atonement for him, and his money was useless to help him. And Jacob was left alone, and there wrestled a man with him until the breaking of the day.

What made Jacob come to that place of loneliness, weakness, and knowledge of himself? The memory of the **GRACE** with which God had met him twenty-one years before, when he saw the ladder and the angels. He had heard the voice of God: Behold I am with thee and will keep thee, and will bring thee again into this land; for I will not leave thee until I have done that which I have spoken to thee of.

He remembered Gods mercy and **GRACE**. Here he was returning to meet Esau. His brother had become very rich, he was a chief, he had been blessed abundantly in the things of this world, and he had authority and power to bind all Jacob had and to take vengeance upon him. Jacob knew this. He also knew that there was only one way of deliverance.

What was it? The mind of God. No one can deliver me but God. God had met him twenty-one years before when he went out to empty. He had come back with wives and children and goods, but he was lean in soul and impoverished in spirit. Jacob said to himself, If I do not get a blessing from God I can never meet Esau, and he made up his mind he would not go on until he knew that he had favor with God.

Jacob was left alone, and unless we get alone with God, we shall surely perish. God interposes where strife is at an end; the way of revelation is plain, and the Holy Ghosts plan is so clear, that we have to say it was God after all Jacob was left alone. He knelt alone. The picture is so real to me.

Alone! Alone! Alone! He began to think. He thought about the ladder and the angels. I think as he began to pray his tongue would cleave to the roof of his straitened place, which revealed the face of God's mouth. Jacob had to get rid of a lot of things. It had all been Jacob! Jacob! Jacob! He got alone with God, and he knew it if you get alone with God, what a place of revelation! Alone with God! Jacob was left alone, alone with God. We stay too long with our relations, our camels and our sheep. Jacob was left alone. It would be an afternoon.

So hour after hour passed. He began to feel the presence of God. But God was getting disappointed with Jacob. If ever God is disappointed with you when you tarry in his presence, it will be because you are not white-hot. If you do not get hotter, and hotter, and hotter, you disappoint God. If God is with you and you know it, be in earnest.

Pray! Pray! Pray! Lay hold! Hold fast the confidence and the rejoicing of the hope firm unto the end. If you do not, you disappoint God. Jacob was that way. God said: you are not real enough; you are not hot enough; you are too ordinary; you are no good to me unless you are filled with zeal, white hot! He said, Let me go, for the day breaketh. Jacob knew if God went without blessing him, Esau could not be met. If you are left alone with God and you cannot get to a place of victory, it is a terrible time. You must never let go, whenever you are seeking â fresh revelation, light on the path, some particular need, never let go.

Victory is ours if we are in earnest enough. All must pass on, nothing less will please God. Let me go, the day breaketh! He was wrestling with equal strength. Nothing is obtained that way. You must always master that which you are wrestling with. If darkness covers you if it is the fresh revelation you need, or your mind to be relieved, always get the victory.

God says you are not in earnest enough. Oh, you say, the Word does not say that. But it was Gods mind. In wrestling, the strength is in the neck, chest, and thigh; the thigh is the strength of all. So, God touched his thigh. That strength is gone, defeat is sure. What did Jacob do? He hung on. God means to have a people severed by the power of His power, so hold fast; He will never leave go. And if we do leave go, we shall fall short. Jacob said I will not let Thee go, except Thou bless me. And God blessed him.

Verse 28: Thy name shall be called no more Jacob, but Israel. Now a new order is beginning, sons of God. How wonderful the change of Jacob to Israel! Israel! Victory all the time, God building all the time, God enough all the time. Power over Esau, power over the world, and power over the cattle.

The cattle are nothing to him now. All are in subjection as he comes out of the great night of trial. The sun rises upon him. Oh, that God may take us on, the sun rising, God supplanting all! What after that? Read how God blessed and honored him. Esau meets him. No fighting now. What a blessed state of **GRACE**! They kissed each other. **When a man's ways please the Lord, he maketh his enemies to be at peace with him.** What about all these cattle, Jacob? Oh, it's a present.

Oh, I have plenty; I don't want your cattle. What a joy it is to see your face again! What a wonderful change! Who wrought it? God. Verse 25: When he saw that he prevailed not against Him. Could he hold God? Can you hold God? It is irreverent to say oh, yes, you can. Sincerity can hold Him, dependence can hold Him, and weakness can hold Him. When you are weak, then are you strong. I tell you what cannot hold Him. Self-righteousness cannot hold Him; pride cannot hold Him, the assumption cannot hold Him, high-mindedness cannot hold Him; thinking you are something when you are nothing, puffed up in your imagination.

Nothing but sincerity! You can hold Him in the closet, in the prayer meeting, everywhere. If any man hears my voice and open the door I will come in and will sup with him, and he with me. Can you hold Him? There may be a thought, sometimes, that He has left you. Oh, no! He does not leave Jacob, Israel. What changed his name? The wrestling?

What changed his name? The holding on, the clinging, the brokenness of spirit? If you do not help me I am no good, no good for the worlds needs. I am no longer salt. Jacob obtained the blessing on two lines: the favor of God, and a yieldedness of will. Gods Spirit was working in him to bring him to a place of helplessness; God co-working to bring him to Bethel, the place of victory.

Jacob remembered Bethel, and through all the mischievous conditions he had kept his vow. When we make vows and keep them, how God helps us, we must call upon God and give Him an account of the promise. Verse 30: And Jacob called the name of the place Peniel, for I have seen God face to face, and my life is preserved. How did he know? Do you know when God blesseth you when you have victory? But twenty years afterwards the vision of the ladder and the angels! How did he know?

We must have a perfect knowledge of what God has for us. He knew that he had the favor of God and that no man could hurt him. Let us in all our seeking see we have the favor of God, walking day by day beneath open heaven. Keeping His commandments, walking in the Spirit, tender in our hearts, lovable, appreciated by God; if so, we shall be appreciated by others, and our ministry will be a blessing to those who hear. God bless you. God bless you for Jesus sake.

Substance of things hoped for

Published in the Pentecostal Evangel, October 25, 1924.

Read Hebrews 11. This is a wonderful passage; all the Word of God is wonderful. It is not only wonderful, but it has the power to change conditions. Any natural condition can be changed by the Word of God, which is a supernatural power. In the Word of God is the breath, the nature, and the power of the living God, and His power works in every person who dares to believe His Word.

There is life through the power of it, and as we receive the Word in faith, we receive the nature of God Himself. It is as we lay hold of God's promises in simple faith that we become partakers of the divine nature. As we receive the Word of God, we come right into touch with a living force, a power which changes nature into **GRACE**, a power that makes dead things live, a power which is of God, which will be manifested in our flesh.

This power has come forth with its glory to transform us by divine act into sons of God, to make us like unto THE Son of God, by the Spirit of God who moves us on from **GRACE** to **GRACE** and from glory to glory as our faith rests in this living Word.

It is important that we have a foundation truth, something greater than ourselves, on which to rest. In Hebrews 12 we read, "Looking unto Jesus, the author, and finisher of our faith." Jesus is our life, and He is the power of our life. We see in the 5th chapter of Acts that as soon as Peter was let out of prison the word of God came, "Go speak... all the words of this life." There is only one Book that has life. In this Word, we find Him who came that we might have life and have it more abundantly, and by faith, this life is imparted to us.

When we come into this life by divine faith (and we must realize that it is by **GRACE** we are saved through faith and that it is not of ourselves, but is the gift of God), we become partakers of this life. This Word is greater than anything else. There is no darkness at all in it.

Anyone who dwells in this Word is able under all circumstances to say that he is willing to come to the light that his deeds may be made manifest. But outside of this Word is darkness, and the manifestations of darkness will never come to light because their deeds are evil. But the moment we are saved by the power of the Word of God we love the light, the truth. The inexpressible divine power, force, passion, and fire that we receive is of God. Drink, my beloved, drink deeply of this Source of life.

Faith is the substance of things hoped for. Someone said to me one day, "I would not believe in anything I could not handle and see," Everything you can handle and see is temporary and will perish with the using. But the things not seen are eternal and will not fade away.

Are you dealing with tangible things or with the eternal things, the things that are facts that are made real to faith? Thank God that through the knowledge of the truth of the Son of God I have within me a greater power, a mightier working, an inward impact of life, of power, of vision and of truth more real than anyone can know who lives in the realm of the tangible. God manifests Himself to the person who dares to believe.

But there is something more beautiful than that. As we receive divine life in the new birth, we receive a nature that delights in doing the will of God. As we believe the Word of God a well of water springs up within our heart. Spring is always better than a pump. But I know that a spring is apt to be outclassed when we get the Baptism of the Holy Ghost.

It was a spring to the woman at the well, but with the person who has the Holy Ghost, it is flowing rivers. Have you these flowing rivers? To be filled with the Holy Ghost is to be filled with the Executive of the Godhead, who brings to us all the Father has, and all the Son desires; and we should be so in the Spirit that God can cause us to move with His authority and reign by His divine ability.

I thank God He baptizes with the Holy Ghost. I know He did it for me because they heard me speak in tongues and then I heard myself. That was a scriptural work, and I don't want anything else, because I must be the epistle of God. There must be emanating through my body a whole epistle of the life, of the power, and the resurrection of my Lord Jesus, There are wonderful things happening through this divine union with God Himself.

"God... hath in these last days spoken unto us by his Son, whom he hath appointed heir of all things, by whom also he made the worlds." By this divine Person, this Word, this Son, God made all things. Notice that it says that He made the worlds by this Person and made them out of the things that were not there. Everything we see was made by this divine Son.

I want you to see that as you receive the Son of God, and as Christ dwells in your heart by faith, there is a divine force, the power of limitless possibilities, within you, and that as a result of this incoming Christ God wants to do great things through you. By faith, if we receive and accept His Son, God brings us into son ship, and not only into son ship but into joint-heirship, into sharing with Him all that the Son possesses.

I am more and more convinced every day I live that very few who are saved by the **GRACE** of God have a right conception of how great is their authority over darkness, demons, death, and every power of the enemy. It is a real joy when we realize our inheritance on this line.

I was speaking like this one day, and someone said, "I have never heard anything like this before. How many months did it take you to get up that sermon?" I said, "My brother, God pressed my wife from time to time to get me to preach, and I promised her I would preach. I used to labor hard for a week to get something up, then give out the text and sit down and say, 'I am done.'

Oh, brother, I have given up getting things up. They all come down. And the sermons that come down stop down, then go back, because the Word of God says His word shall not return unto Him void. But if you get anything up, it will not stop up very long, and when it goes down, it takes you down with it."

The sons of God are made manifest in this present earth to destroy the power of the devil. To be saved by the power of God is to be brought from the realm of the ordinary into the extraordinary, from the natural into the divine.

Do you remember the day when the Lord laid His hands on you? You say, "I could not do anything but praise the Lord." Well, that was only the beginning. Where are you today? The divine plan is that you increase until you receive the measureless fullness of God. You do not have to say, "I tell you it was wonderful when I was baptized with the Holy Ghost." If you have to look back to the past to make me know you are baptized, then you are backslidden. If the beginning was good, it ought to be better day by day, until everybody is fully convinced that you are filled with the might of God in the Spirit.

Filled with all the fullness of God! "Be not drunk with wine wherein is excess, but be filled with the Spirit." I don't want anything else than being full, and fuller, and fuller, until I am overflowing like a great big vat. Do you realize that if you have been created anew and begotten again by the Word of God that there is within you the word of power and the same light and life as the Son of God Himself had?

God wants to flow through you with measureless power of divine utterance and **GRACE** till your whole body is a flame of fire. God intends each soul in Pentecost to be a live wire. Not a monument, but a movement. So many people have been baptized with the Holy Ghost; there was a movement but they have become monuments, and you cannot move them. God wake us out of sleep lest we should become indifferent to the glorious truth and the breath of the almighty power of God. We must be the light and salt of the earth, with the whole armor of God upon us. It would be a serious thing if the enemies were about and we had to go back and get our sandals.

It would be a serious thing if we had on no breastplate. How can we be furnished with the armor? Take it by faith. Jump in, stop in, and never come out, for this is a baptism to be lost in, where you only know one thing, and that is the desire of God at all times. The Baptism in the Spirit should be an ever-increasing endowment of power, an ever-increasing enlargement of **GRACE**. Oh Father, grant unto us a real look into the glorious liberty Thou hast designed for the children of God who are delivered from this present world, separated, sanctified, and made meet for Thy use, whom Thou hast designed to be filled with all Thy fullness.

Nothing has hurt me so much as this, to see so-called believers have so much unbelief in them that it is hard to move them. There is no difficulty in praying for a sinner to be healed. But with the "believer," when you touch him he comes back and says, "You did not pray for my legs."

I say you are healed all over if you believe. Everything is possible to them that believe. God will not fail His Word whatever you are. Suppose that all the people in the world did not believe, that would make no difference to God's Word; it would be the same. You cannot alter God's Word. It is from everlasting to everlasting, and they who believe in it shall be like Mount Zion which cannot be moved.

I was preaching on faith one time, and there was in the audience a man who said three times, "I won't believe." I kept right on preaching because that made no difference to me. I am prepared for a fight any day, the fight of faith. We must keep the faith which has been committed unto us.

I went on preaching, and the man shouted out, "I won't believe." As he passed out of the door, he cried out again, "I won't believe." Next day a message came saying there was a man in the meeting the night before who said out loud three times. "I won't believe," and as soon as he got outside the Spirit said to him, "Because thou wouldst not believe thou shalt be dumb."

It was the same Spirit that came to Zacharias and said, "Thou shalt be dumb, and not able to speak, until the day that these things shall be performed, because thou believest not my words." I believe in hell. Who is in hell? The unbeliever. If you want to go to hell, all you need to do is to disbelieve the Word of God. The unbelievers are there.

Thank God they are there for they are no good for any society. I said to the leader of that meeting, "You go and see this man and find out if these things are so." He went to the house, and the first to greet him was the man's wife. He said, "Is it true that your husband three times in the meeting declared that he would not believe, and now he cannot speak?" She burst into tears and said, "Go and see."

He went into the room and saw the man's mouth in a terrible state. The man got a piece of paper and wrote, "I had an opportunity to believe. I refused to believe, and now I cannot believe, and I cannot speak." The greatest sin in the world is to disbelieve God's Word. We are not of those who draw back, but we are of those who believe, for God's Word is a living Word, and it always acts.

One day a stylishly dressed lady came to our meeting and on up to the platform. Under her arm, going down underneath her dress, was a concealed crutch that nobody could see, She had been helpless in one leg for twenty years, had heard of what God was doing, and wanted to be prayed for. As soon as we prayed for her, she exclaimed, "What have you done with my leg?" Three times she said it, and then we saw that the crutch was loose and hanging and that she was standing straight up. The lady that was interpreting for me said to her, "We have done nothing with your leg.

If anything has been done, it is God who has done it." She answered, "I have been lame and used a crutch for twenty years, but my leg is perfect now." We did not suggest that she get down at the altar and thank God; she fell down among the others and cried for mercy. I find when God touches us it is a divine touch, life, power, and it thrills and quickens the body so that people know it is God and conviction comes, and they cry for mercy. Praise God for anything that brings people to the throne of **GRACE**.

God heals by the power of His Word. But the most important thing is, Are you saved, do you know the Lord, are you prepared to meet God? You may be an invalid as long as you live, but you may be saved by the power of God. You may have a strong, healthy body but may go straight to hell because you know nothing of the **GRACE** of God and salvation.

Thank God I was saved in a moment, the moment I believed, and God will do the same for you. God means by this divine power within you to make you follow after the mind of the Spirit by the Word of God, till you are entirely changed by the power of it. You might come on this platform and say, "Wigglesworth, is there anything you can look up to God and ask Him for in your body?"

I will say now that I have a body in perfect condition and have nothing to ask for, and I am 65. It was not always so. This body was a frail, helpless body, but God fulfilled His Word to me according to Isaiah and Matthew—Himself took my infirmities and my diseases, my sicknesses, and by His stripes, I am healed. It is fine to go up and down and not know you have a body. He took our infirmities; He bore our sickness. He came to heal our broken-heartedness.

Jesus would have us to come forth in the divine likeness, in resurrection force, in the power of the Spirit, to walk in faith and understand His Word, what He meant when He said He would give us power over all the power of the enemy. He will subdue all things until everything comes into perfect harmony with His will. Is He reigning over your affections, desires, will? If so, when He reigns you will be subject to His reigning power. He will be an authority over the whole situation. When He reigns, everything must be subservient to His divine plan and will for us.

See what the Word of God says: "No man can say that Jesus is the Lord but by the Holy Ghost." "Lord!" Bless God forever. Oh, for Him to be Lord and Master! for Him to rule and control! For Him to be filling your whole body with the plan of truth! Because you are in Christ Jesus all things are subject to Him. It is lovely, and God wants to make it so to you. When you get there, you will find divine power continually working. I absolutely believe that no man comes into the place of revelation and activity of the gifts of the Spirit but by this fulfilled promise of Jesus that He will baptize us in the Holy Ghost.

I was taken to see a beautiful nine-year-old boy who was lying on a bed. The mother and father were distracted because he had been lying there for seven months. They had to lift and feed him; he was like a statue with flashing eyes. As soon as I entered the place the Lord revealed to me the cause of the trouble, so I said to the mother, "The Lord shows me there is something wrong with his stomach." She said, "Oh no, we have had two physicians, and they say it is paralysis of the mind." I said, "God reveals to me it is his stomach." "Oh no, it isn't.

These physicians ought to know; they have X-rayed him." The gentleman who brought me there said to the mother, "You have sent for this man, you have been the means of his coming, now don't you stand out against him. This man knows what he has got to do." But Dr. Jesus knows more than that. He knows everything. You do not need to ring the bell for doctors.

All you have to do is ring your bell for Jesus, and He will come down. You should never turn to human things because divine things are so much better and just at your call. Who shall interfere with the divine mind of the Spirit which has all revelation, who understands the whole condition of life, for the Word of God declares He knoweth all things, is well acquainted with the manifestation of thy body, for everything is naked and open before Him with whom we have to do. Having the mind of the Spirit, we understand what the will of God is.

I prayed over this boy and laid my hands on his stomach. He became sick and vomited a worm thirteen inches long, and was perfectly restored. Who knows? God knows. When shall we come into the knowledge of God? When we cease from our mind and allow ourselves to become clothed with the mind and authority of the mighty God.

The Spirit of God would have us understand there is nothing that can interfere with our coming into perfect blessing except unbelief. Unbelief is a terrible hindrance. As soon as we are willing to allow the Holy Ghost to have His way, we will find great things will happen all the time. But oh how much of our human reason we have to get rid of, how much human planning we have to become divorced from. What would happen right now if everybody believed God? I love the thought that God the Holy Ghost wants to emphasize the truth that if we will only yield ourselves to the divine plan, He is right there to bring forth, the mystery of truth.

How many of us believe the Word? It is easy to quote it, but it is more important to have it than to quote it. It is very easy for me to quote, "Now are we the sons of God," but it is more important for me to know whether I am a son of God. When the Son was on the earth, He was recognized by the people who heard Him. Never man spake like Him.

His word was with power, and that word came to pass. Sometimes you have quoted, "Greater is he that is in you than he that is in the world," and you could tell just where to find it. But brother, is it so? Can demons remain in your presence? You have to be greater than demons, Can disease lodge in the body that you touch? You have to be greater than the disease. Can anything in the world stand against you and hold its place if it is a fact that greater is He that is in you than He that is in the world? Dare we stand on the line with the Word of God and face the facts of the difficulties before us?

I can never forget the face of a man that came to me one time: His clothes hung from him, his whole frame was shriveled, his eyes were glaring and glassy, his jaw bones stuck out, his whole being was a manifestation of death. He said to me, "Can you help me?" Could I help him? Just as we believe the Word of God can we help anybody, but we must be sure we are on the Word of God.

If we are on the Word of God, it must take place. As I looked at him, I thought I had never seen anybody alive that looked like him. I said, "What is it?" He answered with a breath voice, "I had cancer on my chest. I was operated on and in removing cancer they removed my swallower; so now I can breathe but cannot swallow."

He pulled out a tube about nine inches long with a cup at the top and an opening at the bottom to go into a hole. He showed me that he pressed one part of that into his stomach and poured the liquid into the top, and for three months had been keeping himself alive that way. It was a living death. Could I help him?

See what the Word of God says: **"Whosoever... shall not doubt in his heart, but shall believe that those things which he saith shall come to pass; he shall have whatsoever he saith."** God wants to move us on scriptural lines. On those lines, I said, "You shall have a good supper tonight." "But," he said, "I cannot swallow." I said, "You shall have a good supper tonight." "But I cannot swallow." "You shall have a good supper; go and eat."

When he got home, he told his wife that the preacher said he could have a good supper that night. He said, "If you will get something ready I'll see if I can swallow." His wife got a good supper ready, and he took a mouthful. He had had mouthfuls before, but they would not go down. But the Word of God said "whatsoever," and this mouthful went down, and more and more went down until he was full up.

Then what happened? He went to bed with the joy of the knowledge that he could again swallow, and he wakened the next morning with that same joy. He looked for a hole in his stomach, but God had shut that up when he opened the other.

Faith is the substance of things hoped for. Faith is the Word. You were begotten of the Word, the Word is in you, the life of the Son is in you, and God wants you to believe.

The GRACE of longsuffering the counterpart of "gifts of healing."

The Latter Rain Evangel, April 1923.

From "Salvation of God Is All-Inclusive."

This morning we will move on to the "gifts of healing." "To another, faith by the same Spirit; to another the gifts of healing by the same Spirit." [1Co 12.9]

There is no use expecting to understand the gifts and to understand the epistles unless you have the Holy Ghost. All the epistles are written to baptized people, and not to the unregenerated. They are written to those who have grown into maturity as a manifestation of the Christ of God. Do not jump into the epistles before you have come in at the gate of the baptism of the Spirit. I believe that this teaching God is helping me to bring to you will move on you to become restless and discontented on every line till God has finished with you.

If we want to know the mind of God through the epistles, there is nothing else to bring the truth but the revelation of the Spirit himself. He gives the utterance: He opens the door. Don't live in a poverty state when we are all around, in and out, up and down, pressed out beyond measure [2Co 1.8] with the rarest gems of the latest word from God.

"Ask, and it shall be given you; seek, and ye shall find; knock, and it shall be opened unto you. For everyone that asketh receiveth; and he that seeketh findeth; and to him that knocketh it shall be opened." [Mt 7.7-8]

There is the authority of God's word. And remember, the authority of God's word is Jesus. These are the utterances by the Spirit of Jesus to us this morning.

I come to you with a great inward desire to wake you up to your great possibilities. Your responsibilities will be great, but not as great as your possibilities. You will always find that God is over-abundance on every line he touches for you, and he wants you to come into mind and thought with him so that you are not straightened in yourselves. Be enlarged in God!

[Tongues and interpretation. "It is that which God hath chosen for us, which is mightier than we. It is that which is bottomless, higher than the heights, more lovely than all beside. And God in a measure presses you out to believe all things that you may endure ail things, and lay hold of eternal life through the power of the Spirit."]

The "gifts of healings" are wonderful gifts. There is a difference between having a gift of healing, and "gifts of healings." God wants us not to come behind in anything. I like this word, "gifts of healing." To have the accomplishment of these gifts, I must bring myself to a conformity to the mind and will of God in purpose. It would be impossible to have "gifts of healing" unless you possessed that blessed fruit of "longsuffering." You will find these gifts run parallel with that which will bring them into operation without a leak.

But how will it be possible to minister the gifts of healing, considering the peculiarities there are in the Assemblies and the many evil powers of Satan which confront us and possess bodies? The man who will go through with God and exercise the gifts of healing will have to be a man of longsuffering; always have a word of comfort. If the one who is in distress and helpless doesn't see eye to eye in everything and doesn't get all he wants, longsuffering will bear and forbear. Longsuffering is a **GRACE** Jesus lived in and moved in. He was filled with compassion, and God will never be able to move us to the help of the needy one until we reach that place.

Sometimes you might think by the way I went about praying for the sick that I was unloving and rough; but oh friends, you have no idea what I see behind the sickness and the afflicted. I am not dealing with the person; I am dealing with the satanic forces that are binding the afflicted. As far as the person goes, my heart is full of love and compassion for all, but I fail to see how you will ever reach a place where God will be able definitely to use you until you get angry at the devil.

One day a pet dog followed a lady out of her house and ran all around her feet. She said to the dog, "I cannot have you with me today." The dog wagged its tail and made a great fuss. "Go home, pet," she said, but it didn't go. At last, she shouted roughly, "Go home!" and off it went. Some people play with the devil like that. "Poor thing!" The devil can stand ail the comfort anybody in the world could give. Cast him out! You are not dealing with the person; you are dealing with the devil.

If you say, with authority, "Come out, you demons, in the name of the Lord!" They must come out. You will always be right when you dare to treat sickness as the devil's work, and you will always be near the mark when you treat it as sin. Let Pentecostal people wake up to see that getting sick is caused by some misconduct; there is some neglect, something wrong somewhere, a weak place where Satan has had a chance to get in. And if we wake up to the real facts of it, we will be ashamed to say that we are sick because people will know we have been sinning.

Gifts of healings are so varied in all lines you will find the gift of discernment often operated in connection in addition to that. And the manifestations of the Spirit are given to us that we may profit withal. [1Co 12.7] You must never treat a cancer case as anything else than a living, evil spirit which is always destroying the body. It is one of the worst kinds I know. Not that the devil has anything good; every disease of the devil is bad, either to a greater or less degree, but this form of the disease is one that you must cast out.

Among the first people, I met in Victoria Hall was a woman who had cancer in the breast. As soon as the cancer was cursed, it stopped bleeding because it was dead. The next thing that happened the body cast it off because the natural body has no room for dead matter. When it came out, it was like a big ball with thousands of fibers. All these fibers had spread out into the flesh, but the moment the evil power was destroyed they had no power.

Jesus gave us the power to bind and power to loose; we must bind the evil powers and loose the afflicted and set them free. There are many cases where Satan has control of the mind, and those under the satanic influence are not all in asylums.

I will tell you what freedom is: No person in this place who enjoys the fullness of the Spirit with a clear knowledge of redemption should know that he has a body. You ought to be able to eat and sleep, digest your food, and not be conscious of your body; a living epistle of God's thought and mind, walking up and down the world without pain. That is redemption. To be fully in the will of God, the perfection of redemption, we should not have a pain of any kind.

I have had some experience along this line. When I was weak and helpless, and friends were looking for me to die, it was in that straitened place that I saw the fullness of redemption. I read and re-read the 91st Psalm and claimed long life: "With long life will I satisfy him." What else? "And show him my salvation." [Ps 91.16]

This is greater than long life. The salvation of God is deliverance from everything, and here I am. At 25 or 30 they were looking for me to die; now at 63, I feel young. So there is something more in this truth that I am preaching than mere words. God hath not designed us for anything else than to be first fruits, sons of God with power over all the power of the enemy, [Lk 10.19] living in the world but not of it. [Jn 17.16]

We have to be careful in casting out demons, who shall give the command. A man may say "Come out," but unless it is in the Spirit of God, our words are vain. The devil always had a good time with me in the middle of the night and tried to give me a bad time. I had a real conflict with evil powers, and the only deliverance I got was when I bound them in the name of the Lord.

I remember taking a man who was demon-possessed out for a walk one day. We were going through a thickly crowded place, and this man became obstreperous. I squared him up, and the devil came out of him, but I wasn't careful, and these demons fastened themselves on me right on the street there, so that I couldn't move. Sometimes when I am ministering on the platform, and the powers of the devil attack me, the people think I am casting demons out of them, but I am casting them out of myself.

The people couldn't understand when I cast that evil spirit out of that man on the street, but I understood. The man who had that difficulty is now preaching and is one of the finest men we have. But it required someone to bind the strong man. [Mk 3.27] You must be sure of your ground, and sure it is a mightier power than you that is destroying the devil. Take your position from the first epistle of John and say, "Greater is he that is in me than he that is in the world." [1Jn 4.4] If you think it is you, you make a great mistake. It is your being filled with him; he acts in place of you; your thought, your mouth, your all becoming exercised by the Spirit of God.

At L----- in Norway, we had a place seating 1,500 people. When we reached there, it was packed, and hundreds were unable to get in. The policemen were standing there, and I thought the first thing I would do would be to preach to the people outside and then go in. I addressed the policemen and said, "You see this condition. I have come with a message to help everybody, and it hurts me very much to find as many people outside as in; I want the promise of you police officials that you will give us the marketplace tomorrow. Will you do it?" They put up their hands that they would.

It was a beautiful day in April, and there was a big stand in the woods about 10 feet high in the great park, where thousands of people gathered. After preaching, we had some wonderful cases of healing. One man came 100 miles, bringing his food with him. He hadn't passed anything through his stomach for over a month for there was great cancer there. He was healed in the meeting, and opening up his lunch began eating before all the people.

Then there was a young woman who came with a stiff hand. I cursed the spirit of infirmity, and it was instantly cast out, and the arm was free. She waved it over her head and said, "My father is the chief of police. I have been bound since I was a girl." At the close of the meeting, Satan laid out two people with fits. That was my day! I jumped down to where they were and in the name of Jesus delivered them. People said, "Oh isn't he rough," but when they saw those afflicted stand up and praise God, that was a time of rejoicing.

Oh, we must wake up, stretch ourselves out to believe God! Before God could bring me to this place, he had to break me a thousand times. I have wept, I have groaned, I have travailed night after night till God broke me. Until God has mowed you down, you will never have this longsuffering for others.

When I was at Cardiff, the Lord healed a woman right in the meeting. She was afflicted with ulceration, and while they were singing she fell full length and cried in such a way, I felt something must be done. I knelt down alongside the woman, laid my hands on her body, and instantly the powers of the devil were destroyed, and she was delivered from ulceration; rose up and joined in the singing.

We have been seeing wonderful miracles in these last days, and they are only a little of what we are going to see. When I say "going to see" I do not want to throw something out ten years to come, nor even two years. I believe we are in the "going," right on the threshold of wonderful things.

You must not think that these gifts fall upon you like ripe cherries. You pay the price for everything you get from God. There is nothing worth having that you do not have to pay for, either temporally or spiritually. I remember when I was at Antwerp and Brussels. The power of God was very mighty upon me there. Coming through to London I called on some friends at C-----. To show you the leading of the Lord, these friends said, "Oh, God sent you here. How much we need you!"

They sent a wire to a place where there was a young man 26 years old, who had been in bed 18 years. His body was so much bigger than an ordinary body, because of inactivity, and his legs were like a child's; instead of bone, there was gristle. He had never been able to dress. When they got the wire, the father dressed him, and he was sitting in a chair. I felt it was one of the opportunities of my life.

I said to this young man, "What is the greatest desire of your heart?" "Oh," he said, "that I might be filled with the Holy Ghost!" I put my hands upon him and said, "Receive, receive ye the Holy Ghost." Instantly he became drunk with the Spirit and fell off the chair like a big bag of potatoes. I saw what God could do with a helpless cripple. First, his head began shaking terrifically; then his back began moving very fast, and then his legs, just like being in a battery.

Then he spoke clearly in tongues, and we wept and praised the Lord. His legs were still as they had been, by all appearances, and this is where I missed it. These "missing's" sometimes are God's opportunities for teaching you important lessons. He will teach you through your weaknesses that which is not faith. It was not faith for me to look at that body, but human. The man who will work the works of God must never look at conditions, but at Jesus in whom everything is complete.

I looked at the boy, and there was no help. I turned to the Lord and said, "Lord, tell me what to do," and he did. He said, "Command him to walk, in my name." This is where I missed it. I looked at his conditions, and I got the father to help lift him up to see if his legs had strength. We did our best, but he and I together could not move him. Then the Lord showed me my mistake, and I said, "God, please forgive me."

I got right down and repented, and said to the Lord, "Please tell me again." God is so good, and he will never leaves us to ourselves. Again he said to me, "Command him in my name to walk." So I shouted, "Arise and walk in the name of Jesus." Did he do it? No, I declare, he never walked: He was lifted up by the power of God in a moment, and he ran. The door was wide open; he ran out across the road into a field where he ran up and down and came back. Oh, it was a miracle!

There are miracles to be performed, and these miracles will be accomplished by us when we understand the perfect plan of his spiritual **GRACE**s which has come down to us. These things will come to us when we come to a place of brokenness, of surrender, of wholehearted yieldedness, where we decrease but where God has come to increase; and where we dwell and live in him.

Will you allow him to he the choice of your thoughts? Submit to him, the God of all **GRACE**. [1Pe 5.10] You may be well-furnished with faith for every good work, [2Ti 3.17] that the mind of the Lord may have free course in you, run and be glorified. [2Th 3.1] The heathen shall know, [Ek 37.28] the uttermost parts of the earth shall be filled with the glory of the Lord as the waters cover the deep. [Ha 2.14]

From the author Dr. Michael H Yeager's

*BRAGGING about the GRACE of God

Look what Paul said, but by the **GRACE** of God, I am what I am, and His **GRACE**, which was upon me was not in vain, but I labored more abundantly than they all. Paul, are you bragging about yourself? No, He was BRAGGING about the **GRACE** of God. He said I did more than all of the other apostles together. **How?** How come God used Paul in a more significant way than all the other apostles? And then he clarifies with asking a question. Should we sin that **GRACE** May abound, heaven forbid? **What?** What are you saying? Paul, the apostle, was saying: listen because I knew in my heart I needed God more than they knew. The **GRACE** of God worked in me, and I did more. I labored more abundantly. Why was God's grace operating in Paul in a much stronger way than in the other apostles? Because he was so dependent upon God.

God, I need you. I'm not talking about having a self-pity party. Oh, God, I cannot do this without you, Jesus. I know I'm going to mess up. I know I'm going to fail. I know I'm going to fall short on God. You told me to do this. I know you told me to do this because I not want to do it. See when your flesh does not want to do something, you know, it's God. It takes **GRACE** to give financially the way that God tells you to. You can humble yourself and let that **GRACE** work, or you can decide in your heart I'm not doing it.

Sunday morning I was standing in the back of the sanctuary where Marks and Natalia two-year-old little boy was having the time of his life. He is running around and acting goofy. He did not care what anybody thought about him. He's was enjoying the time of his life. Enjoy your walk with God. People, you know, I enjoy my walk with God. I don't have a reputation to hold on to. Yes, we need to walk with integrity.

But I do not care what people think about me because before I was saved, all they did was mock me and make of me. I could hardly hear with my bad ears. My speech impediment was so bad that you could not really understand what I was saying. So before I was born again, I was free from what people thought about me. I knew what they thought about me. Because they mocked me my whole life until I gave my heart to Jesus at 19 years old.

The **GRACE** of God flows into the humble. The **GRACE** of God flows like a mighty River. And you know who the humble our, the humble are them who say, Lord, I just want your will. God is able to make all **GRACE** abound towards those who cry out from the depth of their hearts, I just want you will Father. And God promises you will always have all sufficiency in all things that you may abound to every good work.

Grace produces good works

I know many people who misquote what **GRACE is**. They do not read Ephesians one and two correctly. I love the book of Ephesians. As a young Christian, it was the very first epistle that I memorized by heart. To this day I can quote it from beginning to end. Ephesians chapter 1 talks about what is the exceeding greatness of his power to us who believe. According to the working of his mighty power which you wrought in Christ when he raised him from the dead and set him at his own right hand in the heavenly places, far above all principality and power and might and dominion and every name that is named not only in this world but also in that which is to come.

After the apostle Paul finishes up chapter 1, we leap into chapter 2. This is where Paul begins to reveal the beautiful truths about the **GRACE** of God. The **GRACE** of God saves us because of faith in Christ Jesus. Where faith is not in operation; you'll discover that grace is not working. The divine enablement of the Lord can only happen where people are having trust, confidence, reliance, dependence upon God.

Paul, the apostle, reveals by the spirit of God that we are God's workmanship created in Christ Jesus and to good works. God has before ordained that we should walk in these good works. The true **GRACE** of God gives you the ability to run through a troop, to leap over a wall, to overcome temptations, test, trials, and every devil. When you with your whole heart to God, say I surrender. You do not want me to do this, so I surrender to you, Lord. At that very moment, God gives me the victory over the demonic world. The **GRACE** of God flows to the lowest point. So the more humble you are, the more divine grace you will experience. The more yielded you are to the will of God, the greater the **GRACE** will be manifested in you.

GOD Said: You Better Not Lie, or You'll Die to!

A number of years ago I picked up a book by a well-known author. This book had come highly recommended by one of my favorite preachers at that time. The topic was about angelic visitations. This was something I was interested in, because of my many experiences with the supernatural. I began to read this book, and noticed immediately that there were experiences he said he had, which did not seem to line up with the Scriptures. I did not want to judge his heart, but we do have the responsibility to examine everything considering God's Word. If it does not line up with the word of God, then we must reject it, no matter who wrote it.

As I was pondering the stories in this book, the Spirit of the Lord spoke to my heart very strongly. It was as if He was standing right there next to me, speaking audibly. What He spoke to me was rather shocking! The Lord told me that the writer of this book would be dead in three months from a heart attack. I asked the Lord why He was telling me this. He said the stories in the man's book were exaggerated, and judgment was coming. The Lord warned me that day that if I were ever to do the same thing, judgment would come to me. I did not realize that the Lord would have me to be writing books, many of them filled with my own personal experiences. Now I understand why he spoke this to me, telling me that I better not exaggerate my experiences.

When the Spirit of the Lord spoke this to me, I turned and told my wife. I held the book up and said, in a very quiet whispering, trembling, wavering voice, "Honey, the man who wrote this book will be dead in three months from a heart attack." Plus, I told her why the Lord told me this. I wish I had been wrong. Exactly 3 months later, the man died from a heart attack. God can speak to us through the positive and the negative circumstances of life. We had better take heed to what he is saying.

Many Preachers are filled with wisdom when they are in the pulpit, but are used of the devil in everyday living.

I had a well-known lady who spoke here one time at a women's conference. I invited her, because I had listened to some of her messages someone gave me, and they were powerful and wonderful. When she spoke at our conference, her messages were marvelous, filled with wisdom and revelation. Now after one of the meetings, all of the speakers, including myself and my wife went out to eat. Something extremely shocking and disheartening happened as we were sitting there around the table eating and listening to her speak.

As this lady began to open her mouth at the table what came out of her mouth was terrible. I never heard such garbage, gossip and complaining come out of one person's mouth in such a short period. In the pulpit as she ministered the word of God, truth and revelation came forth, but in her private life what came out of her mouth was terrible.

I ran into another similar situation a number of years ago, there was a young man that the Lord had me help, giving him the opportunity to speak for the first time in his life in the pulpit. I knew by the spirit of the Lord when I met him that he was called to preach and teach the word of God, even though I had never heard him. From the very moment, he began to speak, everybody knew the spirit of the Lord was calling him to preach.

There was only one major issue that I could see that would destroy every endeavor that he would ever strive to accomplish for Christ, it was the fact that he was extremely critical and faultfinding of everybody he knew. I constantly encouraged him not to be finding fault with others, to no avail. Even those he called his closest friends, and even relatives, behind their backs he would be constantly finding fault and speak negatively about them. Every time he would say something negative about a person, I would try to come back with something positive. Now this was a generational curse that was passed on from his mother, from his grandmother, and who knows how many other generations.

This young man had no concept of respecting those in authority because he had been raised from a child by those who had no respect for authority. For two years, (I still continue to pray for him to this day) I prayed daily for him, and his family members that they would be delivered from this satanic attitude. While my wife and I were gone to Israel, that spirit rose in him, and he began to speak to the congregation evil and slanderous words about myself and my family.

When we arrived back from our journey overseas, people who had been with us for many years were now gone. I'm not speaking evil of this person, just the fact that we need to walk tenderly and softly before the Lord. We will be judged by the same judgment that we judge others with. We need to deal with these generational curses that are so deeply rooted in our mind and our heart, that without Christ we will never be delivered and set free from.

Ephesians 4:29 Let no corrupt communication proceed out of your mouth, but that which is good to the use of edifying, that it may minister grace unto the hearers.

James 4:11 Speak not evil one of another, brethren. He that speaketh evil of his brother, and judgeth his brother, speaketh evil of the law, and judgeth the law: but if thou judge the law, thou art not a doer of the law, but a judge.12 There is one lawgiver, who is able to save and to destroy: who art thou that judgest another?

GOD Said: Come Back to Jamaica

I am absolutely amazed at the different ways in which God will speak to his people. There is one time that God even spoke to me through a TV commercial. This is kind of a strange experience that I had in 1983. First let me start this story by saying that we do not have a TV in our house. My wife and I just simply decided that we did not need one, or want one.

I was ministering at a local church when I mentioned the fact that we did not have a TV in our house, and did not want one or need one. Several days later there was a knock at our house door, and here it was one of the older sisters from that meeting in which I had been ministering. She seemed so excited and happy. She said: the other night you stated that you did not have a TV, praise the Lord I had a brand-new black-and-white TV set at my house that I have never used, and I want to give it to you.

Bless this older sister heart, she must have misunderstood what I was saying at the meeting. I did not want to offend her, so I put a smile on my face, and accepted her gift. It sat in its box for a while in the living room, in a corner, on the floor. One day as I walked past it, a thought came to my silly head that said: just plug it in for a moment, it won't hurt anything. I gave into this thought, taking it out of its box, and plugging it in. The reception wasn't very good at all, allowing me only to pick up 2 to 3 channels that were kind of foggy, so this TV just sat there, never really being used. One afternoon as I was busy working in the house, it came into my heart to turn on the TV, and Immediately there appeared on the screen a commercial that said: C**ome back to Jamaica!**

As I watched this commercial something strange happened in my heart. I was so moved in my heart that I started weeping for the souls that were in Jamaica. I had never even thought about Jamaica, or prayed for Jamaica, or ever had a burden for Jamaica. Here I was now literally weeping over Jamaica. People who really do not have good understand of how God works would have immediately bought an airline ticket, jumped on a plane, and gone to Jamaica. It's important that we get before the Lord to find out exactly what he is saying before we run off and respond to these visitations.

I went before the Lord with a very seriously attitude and began to pray over Jamaica, knowing the Lord was speaking to me through this commercial. Yes, God can talk to you through a secular commercial. I did not sense in my heart that the Lord wanted me to go there now. (Eventually I did make a trip to Jamaica) Now every time I would see this commercial whether at my house, in a store, or somewhere else, I would literally begin to cry for Jamaica. From the moment, I saw this commercial about Jamaica, I began to stand in the gap, interceding and pray for its people, for the nation, and for what God was wanting to do there. I knew the Lord was doing, or about to do something wonderful in Jamaica. Approximately three months went by with this burden in my heart, when one day this burden suddenly lifted off for me.

A short time later I received a newsletter from a well-known evangelist who had just come back from Jamaica, reporting that a tremendous move of God had taken place while he was there. The Lord spoke to my heart and said this to me: I placed a burden upon your heart for Jamaica in order that you would pray and intercede, to stand in the gap to prepare the way for these meetings. He also revealed to me that I was not the only one he had given this burden to. That there were many others during this time who were also praying for Jamaica. Those who had made the commercial about coming back to Jamaica had no idea that God would use this commercial to create a burden for the precious souls of that land.

CHAPTER NINE

The Words of This Life

Bible Reading-Acts 5:1-20.

Notice this expression that the Lord gives of the Gospel message - "the words of this life." It is the most wonderful life possible - the life of faith in the Son of God. This is the life where God is all the time. He is round about, and He is within.

It is the life of many revelations and of many manifestations of God's Holy Spirit, a life in which the Lord is continually seen, known, felt and heard. It is a life without death, for "we have passed from death unto life." The very life of God has come within us. Where that life is within in its fullness, the disease cannot exist. It would take me a month to tell out what there is in this wonderful life. Everyone can go in and possess and be possessed by this life.

It is possible for you to be within the vicinity of this life and yet miss it. It is possible for you to be in a place where God is pouring out His Spirit and yet miss the blessing that God is so willing to bestow. It all comes through shortness of revelation and through a misunderstanding of the infinite **GRACE** of God, and of the "God of all **GRACE**," who is willing to give to all who will reach out the hand of faith. This life that He freely bestows is a gift. Some think they have to earn it and they miss the whole thing. Oh, for a simple faith to receive all that God so lavishly offers. You can never be ordinary from the day you receive this life from above. You become extraordinary, filled with the extraordinary power of our extraordinary God.

Ananias and Sapphira were in this thing and yet they missed it. They thought that possibly the thing might fail. So they wanted to have a reserve for themselves in case it did turn out to be a failure. They were in the wonderful revival that God gave to the early church and yet they missed it. There are many people like them today who make vows to God in times of a great crisis in their lives.

But they fail to keep their vows, and in the end, they become spiritually bankrupt. Blessed is the man who will swear to his own hurt and change not; who keeps the vow he has made to God; who is willing to lay his all at God's feet. The man who does this never becomes a lean soul. God has promised to "make fat his bones." There is no dry place for such a man; he is always fat and flourishing, and he becomes stronger and stronger. It pays to trust God with all and to make no reservation.

I wish I could make you see how great a God we have. Ananias and Sapphira were doubting God and were questioning whether this work that He had begun would go through. They wanted to get some glory for selling their property, but because of their lack of faith, they kept back part of the price in reserve in case the work of God should fail.

Many are doubting whether this Pentecostal revival will go through. Do you think this Pentecostal work will stop? Never. For fifteen years I have been in constant revival, and I am sure that it will never stop. When George Stephenson made his first engine, he took his sister Mary to see it. She looked at it and said to her brother, "George, it'll never go." He said to her, "Get in, Mary." She said again, "It'll never go." He said to her, "We'll see, you get in." Mary, at last, got in-the whistle blew, there were a puff and a rattle, and the engine started. Then Mary cried out, "George, it'll never stop! It'll never stop!"

People are looking on at this Pentecostal revival, and they are very critical, and they are saying, "It'll never go;" but when they are induced to come into the work, they one and all say, "It'll never stop." This revival of God is sweeping on and on, and there is no stopping the current of life, of love, of inspiration, and power.

(Interpretation; It is the living Word who has brought this. It is the Lamb in the midst, the same yesterday, today and forever.)

God has brought unlimited resources for everyone. Do not doubt. Hear with the ear of faith. God is in the midst. See that it is God who bath set forth that which you see and hear today.

I want you to see that in the early church, controlled by the power of the Holy Ghost; it was not possible for a lie to exist. The moment it came into the church, there was instant death. And as the power of the Holy Ghost increases in these days of the Latter Rain, it will be impossible for any man to remain in our midst with a lying spirit. God will purify the church; the Word of God will be in such power in healing and other spiritual manifestations, that great fear will be upon all those who see the same.

It seems to the natural mind a small thing for Ananias and Sapphira to want to have a little to fail back on; but I want to tell you that you can please God, and you can get things from God, the only ova the line of a living faith. God never fails. God never can fail.

When I was in Bergen, Norway, there came to the meeting a young woman who was employed at the hospital as a nurse. Big cancer had developed on her nose, and the nose was enlarged and had become black and greatly inflamed. She came out for prayer, and I said to her, "What is your condition?" She said, "I dare not touch my nose; it gives me so much pain."

I said to all the people, "I want you to look at this nurse and notice her terrible condition. I believe that our God is merciful and that He is faithful, and that He will bring to naught this condition that the devil has brought about. I am going to curse this disease in the all-powerful name of Jesus. The pain will go. I believe God will give us an exhibition of His **GRACE** and I will ask this young woman to come to the meeting tomorrow night and declare what God has done for her."

Oh, the awfulness of sin! Oh, the awfulness of the power of sin! Oh, the awfulness of the consequences of the fall! When I see cancer, I always know it is an evil spirit. I can never believe it is otherwise. The same with tumors. Can this be the work of God? God help me to show you that this is the work of the devil, and to show you the way out.

I do not condemn people that sin. I don't scold people. I know what is back of the sin. I know that Satan is always going about as a roaring lion, seeking whom he may devour. I always remember the patience and love of the Lord Jesus Christ when they brought to Him a woman that they had taken in adultery, telling Him that they had caught her in the very act.

He simply stooped down and wrote on the ground. Then He quietly said, "He that is without sin among you, let him cast the first stone." I have never seen a man without sin. "All have sinned and come short of the glory of God." But I read in this blessed Gospel message that God bath laid upon Jesus the iniquity of us all; so, when I see an evil condition, I feel that I must stand in my office and rebuke the condition.

I laid my hands on the nose of that suffering nurse and cursed the evil power that was causing her so much distress. The next night the place was packed, and the people were jammed together so that it seemed that there was not room for one more to come into that house. Oh, how God's rain fell upon us. How good God is, so full of **GRACE** and so full of love. I saw the nurse in the audience, and I asked her to come forward. She came and showed everyone what God had done. He had perfectly healed her. Oh, I tell you He is just the same, Jesus. He is just the same today. All things are possible if you dare to trust God.

When the power of God came so mightily upon the early church, even in the death of Ananias and Sapphira, great fear came upon all the people. And when we are in the presence of God, when God is working mightily in our midst, there comes a great fear, a reverence, holiness of life, a purity that fears to displease God. We read that no man durst join them, but God added to the church such as should be saved. I would rather have God add to our Pentecostal church than have all the town join it. God added daily to His church.

The next thing that happened was that people became so assured that God was working that they knew that anything would be possible, and they brought their sick into the streets and laid them on beds and couches, that at least the shadow of Peter passing by might overshadow them. Multitudes of sick people and those oppressed with evil spirits were brought to the apostles, and God healed them every one. I do not believe that it was the shadow of Peter that healed, but the power of God was mightily present, and the faith of the people was so aroused that they joined with one heart to believe God. God will always meet people on the line of faith.

God's tide is rising all over the earth. I had been preaching at Stavanger in Norway, and was very tired and wanted a few hours rest. I went to my next appointment, arriving at about 9:30 in the morning. My first meeting was to be at night. I said to my interpreter, "After we have had something to eat, let us go down to the fjords." We spent three or four hours down by the sea and at about 4:30 returned.

We found the end of the street, which has a narrow entrance, just filled with autos, wagons, etc., containing invalids and sick people of every kind. I went up to the house and was told that the house was full of sick people. It reminded me of the scene described in the fifth chapter of Acts. I began praying for the people in the street, and God began to heal the people. How wonderfully He healed those people, who were in the house. We sat down for lunch, and the telephone bell rang, and someone at the other end was saying, "What shall we do? The town hall is already full; the police cannot control things."

In that little Norwegian town, the people were jammed together, and oh, how the power of God fell upon us. A cry went up from every one, "Isn't this the revival?"

Revival is coming. The breath of the Almighty is coming. The breath of God shows up every defect, and as it comes flowing in like a river, everybody will need a fresh anointing, a fresh cleansing of the blood. You can depend upon it that that breath is upon us.

At one time I was at a meeting in Ireland. There were many sick carried to that meeting, and helpless ones were helped there. There were many people in that place who were seeking for the Baptism of the Holy Ghost. Some of them had been seeking for years. There were sinners there who were under mighty conviction. There came a moment when the breath of God swept through the meeting.

In about ten minutes every sinner in the place was saved. Everyone who had been seeking the Holy Spirit was baptized, and every sick one was healed. God is a reality, and His power can never fail. As our faith reaches out, God will meet us and the same rain will fall. It is the same blood that cleanseth, the same power, the same Holy Ghost, and the same Jesus made real through the power of the Holy Ghost! What would happen if we should believe God?

Right now the precious blood of the Lord Jesus Christ is efficacious to cleanse your heart and bring this life, this wonderful life of God, within you. The blood will make you every whit whole if you dare believe. The Bible is full of entreaty for you to come and partake and receive the **GRACE**, the power, the strength, the righteousness, and the full redemption of Jesus Christ. He never fails to hear when we believe.

At one place where I was, a lame man was brought to me who had been in bed for two years, with no hope of recovery. He was brought thirty miles to the meeting, and he came up on crutches to be prayed for. His boy was also afflicted in the knees, and they had four crutches between the two of them. The man's face was filled with torture.

There is healing virtue in the Lord, and He never fails to heal when we believe. In the name of Jesus-that name so full of virtue-I put my hand down that leg that was so diseased. The man threw down his crutches, and all were astonished as they saw him walking up and down without aid. The little boy called out to his father, "Papa, me; papa, me, me, me!" The little boy who was withered in both knees needed healing. The same Jesus was there to bring a real deliverance for the little captive. He was completely healed.

These were legs that were touched. If God will stretch out His mighty power to loose afflicted legs, what mercy will He extend to that soul of yours that must exist forever? Hear the Lord say, "The Spirit of the Lord is upon me, because be hath anointed me to preach the gospel to the poor; he hath sent me to heal the broken hearted, to preach deliverance to the captive, and recovering of sight to the blind, to set at liberty them that are bruised."

He invites you, "Come unto me, all ye that labor and are heavy laden, and I will give you rest." God is willing in His great mercy to touch thy limbs with His mighty vital power, and if He is willing to do this, how much more anxious is He to deliver thee from the power of Satan and to make thee a child of the King. How much more necessary it is for you to be healed of your soul sickness than of your bodily ailments. And God is willing to give the double cure.

I was passing through the city of London one time, and Mr. Mundell, the secretary of the Pentecostal Missionary Union, learned that I was there. He arranged for me to meet him at a certain place at 3:30 p. m. I was to meet a certain boy whose father and mother lived in the city of Salisbury. They had sent this young man to London to take care of their business. He had been a leader in Sunday school work, but he had been betrayed and had fallen. Sin is awful, and the wages of sin is death. But there is another side-the gift of God is eternal life.

This young man was in great distress; he had contracted a horrible disease and feared to tell anyone. There was nothing but death ahead for him. When the father and mother got to know of his condition they suffered inexpressible grief.

When we got to the house, Brother Mundell suggested, that we get down to prayer. I said, "God does not say so, we are not going to pray yet. I want to quote scripture, `Fools, because of their transgression, and because of their iniquities, are afflicted: their soul abhorreth all manner of meat; and they draw near unto the gates of death."' The young man cried out, "I am that fool." He broke down and told us the story of his fall. Oh, if men would only repent, and confess their sins, how God would stretch out His hand to heal and to save. The moment that young man repented, a great abscess burst, and God sent virtue into his life, giving him a mighty deliverance.

God is gracious and not willing that any should perish. How many are willing to make a clean breast of their sins? I tell you that the moment you do this, God will open heaven. It is an easy thing for Him to save your soul and heal your disease if you will but come and shelter today in the secret place of the Most High. He will satisfy you with long life and show you His salvation. In His presence there is the fullness of joy, at His right hand, there are pleasures forevermore. There is full redemption for all through the precious blood of the Son of God.

Use and misuse of the gift of prophecy

Preached at the Union Pentecostal Meeting, 2 November 1922. This morning I believe the Lord will impress us with the necessity of understanding the gifts of the Spirit: Why and when and where we should manifest them. I have been trying to impress upon you the importance of being filled with the Holy Ghost, but I do not want you to think that you can understand or use gifts apart from the Giver. I know that the Holy Ghost has nine gifts to minister, and I know that Jesus has gifts, and you will never find that the gifts of the Holy Ghost and the gifts of Jesus clash. They are perfectly in order.

In the fourth chapter of Ephesians, we read that Jesus went up on high and received gifts for men, [Ep 4.8] and the most remarkable of all is that he received gifts for the rebellious. Paul knew that, because God had been ministering to him gifts, and yet he was the most rebellious of all. When you look at that calling and see the remarkableness of his life and see how he persecuted the church, [1Co 15.9] and then in his examination of his personality, his weakness, he calls himself the chief of sinners. [1Ti 1.15]

And in that revelation, realizing how God had been gracious to him, he writes here, “even the rebellious also.” [Ps 68.18] So all the people in this place, without exception, are eligible for the gifts. It is not what you were or is; it is what God will do for you, and you must see that by the power of God all things are possible. [Mk 10.27] He wants every person in this place to know that he is not and never will be pleased with a fig tree that bears nothing but leaves. Jesus was disappointed in it. [Mk 11.13]

Never think that gifts can ever be of any source whatever; only on the lines, they have to be exercised, wrought out by the power of God. You must never allow yourself to be led into any trap to use a gift. If you do, you will surely have trouble in your life. You must understand that all the gifts are to be made manifest only for the glory of Jesus. Everything that you have come heir to since you came into the fact of salvation, everything from that day, without exception, has been and must continue to be for the glory of God.

If it is not, you will find yourself amongst the wood and the hay and the stubble. [1Co 3.12-13] There is nothing going to be of any importance to your life or any other lives, only that which is gold and silver, and precious stones; something that cannot be destroyed by fire. God would have us this morning to have an inward revelation that we have been delivered from the corruption of the world. That the powers of Christ may rest upon us, that the glory of God may be seen. That we may be inwardly and outwardly always bearing about in our body the dying of the Lord, that the life of the Lord should always be eminently manifested to the glory of God.

[Tongues and interpretation. "The Lord of glory came from the heights thereof to dispense of his **GRACE**s in the world, in the church; to establish and bring forth a ministry of power that should permeate the earth, and bring to naught the things that are.]

One of the reasons why Jesus came was to make in the world new orders in the Spirit. We must this morning see our vocation in the Spirit. We must under all circumstances understand that God has something far over that day when we first saw the light. You must see that he took your sins only for one purpose: That you might be channels for the covenant of promise.

The fourth of Ephesians is very distinct on this line: That Jesus went up on high, and he made prophets, apostles, evangelists, and teachers, [Ep 4.11] and it was for "the perfecting of the saints," [Ep 4.12] of which you will see the need. God has nothing in his ministry for us on any lines; the only perfection. God is a cleanser. All the mighty movings of God are always to purge you, perfect you, make you holy, make you see that he can dwell in you mightily, and move in you by the Spirit gloriously. We have to be insulators, as it were, of the mighty power, the saving power in the world. There is such a thing as a preserving power; God wants us to be a preserving power in the world, that sin may have no place where we are; God controlling everything we touch.

Did you hear me say that you must not expect gifts until after you have received the Holy Ghost? Gifts are the property of the Holy

Ghost, and they do not clash, as I said, with the gifts of Jesus. If you are filled with the Holy Ghost, he will drive you, from day to day and hour to hour, to the truth. Jesus is the way, the truth, and the life, [Jn 14.6] and the word of God is the power of the Christ and the life of Christ.

It will be no comparison. However, you are filled with the Spirit. However you are filled with joy, whatever peace you have, and whatever conditions are in your life, to your leaving out the word of God. If you do, you will leak out and become weak; your peace will fade, and your joy will leak out. The word of God brings one into a place of fact. We must be in a place where we know what we know, and the baptized believer knows what he doesn't know. He has forgotten a lot that he used to know, and that is a blessing.

Now, beloved, we dealt with the word of wisdom, and we must clearly understand the power of the Holy Ghost within the body. Paul says, "I would not have you ignorant, brethren, of spiritual gifts." [1Co 12.1] We must examine ourselves and see if we are in this faith, for I reckon that all the spiritual revelations of God are on the lines of faith, and you cannot have faith without you have the word, for the word of God is faith. If you turn to Hebrews 12.2, you will find that Jesus is the author and finisher of our faith; [He 12.2] so if you have Jesus, you have faith. You will have the Giver within you. And as you let the word of God move in your life, you will find you are living in the real place of the personality of Jesus Christ.

In the first place, the Holy Ghost must make within you ministrations, in the second it must be in operation, and the third essential is the manifestation. If you are afraid of manifestation you haven't come into operation, and if you are afraid of operation, it is because you never had ministrations.

The same Spirit will bring you these three effects, and when they are in your heart and life, you will find God takes you and moves upon you just as he did upon Moses and Aaron, and Samuel and the prophets. The difference between the dispensation of the Jews and the dispensation of **GRACE** to the gentiles is this: In the days of the prophets the Holy Ghost was upon them from time to time.

The Spirit of the Lord was upon Samuel from time to time; the Spirit of the Lord came upon Moses, upon Samson; it came upon Ezekiel and the prophets. These operations were types of the greater dispensation of things to come. Remember this is an important matter because if you hear the word of God and do not take heed, you will come into the line where God uses the gentiles to perfect the Jews.

Without us, the Jews cannot be made perfect. So we are living in a great day; we are in the dispensation of the **GRACE** of God, with the fullness of the revelation of the inward power, personality, and presence of the Holy Ghost. And so we are in a greater day in every way than the Jews were. Not that the day isn't coming for the Jews; it is, but we are in a greater day than the Jews have had heretofore.

God has an appointment with every baptized soul, and his appointment is that we are in the earth for the specialty of witnessing and bringing out the glories of the cross. No baptized soul who is going on with God can ever again enter into worldly things as long as he lives. And God will strip him of all superfluities and foolishness. If you are not stripped of worldliness there becomes a mixture in the church instead of a perfect place in God. Mixtures are a!ways bad; that is why there was to be no mixture in the priest's garment; it had to be pure linen and pure wool. [Dt 22.11]

I find that the world is becoming worse and worse on these lines because she is full of mixtures. When you go shopping, you never know whether you will get a pure article or adulteration. The Spirit of God is no mixture. If, after you have received the Holy Ghost you go back into carnal lines, the people will know it. The man who is going on with God can tell it in a minute. You cannot deceive him. Language is not Spirit, and noise is not Spirit, and you cannot get it that way. The power of God is presence. Moses said, "Except thy presence goes with me. I will go not hence." [Ex 33.15]

If the gifts of the Spirit are not in the church, you can call it what you like; it is a back-letter church. You can be baptized in the water a thousand times; it will not make the Spirit move. You will have to have something better than water baptism. You will have to have a fire. You will have to have the inward presence of God.

Where the Holy Ghost comes, the gifts are manifest, unless the church has backslidden, and Ichabod [1Sa 4.21] is over the door. Oh, you can backslide, and there is not a **GRACE** that you cannot forfeit! "Let him that thinketh he standeth take heed lest he falls." [1Co 10.12] There is only one way for every one of us to keep faithful, and that is down in humiliation, the brokenness of spirit, living victoriously over the natural, and having the light of life in our being.

I have had people say to me, "You know I once had the gifts of healings and me haven't them now." I never believed it, whatever they say, for the simple reason that when the gift is manifested, that is the permanent gift; it is always there. But I would go so far as to say you may be so filled with the Holy Ghost that a gift may be manifested because of the fullness of the presence of God in your body.

If you lived in the place where the power of God was upon you, that the virtue of Christ passed through you, and if you haven't that fullness now, it is because you have passed out of the depths of God. Do not say you do not know how it happened. You always know. A stranger can never enter into your heart. "The heart knoweth its own bitterness," [Pr 14.10] but a stranger can never enter into its recesses.

I warn you that if you want to continue to have the power of God manifested through you, you have to live in the Spirit continually; not occasionally, not once a day, but always. Oh beloved, at any cost, pay any price to live in it, for it is worth the world. I would rather speak five minutes under the unction of the Holy Ghost than to have a thousand dollars given to me. I thank God we may live in the Spirit and walk in the Spirit, and be continually filled with the Spirit. Then the gifts of healings will be manifested on these lines, and you will find that when God gets you to that place, he will make you definite.

For instance, I was speaking in a meeting in a place, and as I sat in that meeting, I saw a man there in a state of terrible pain. I said, "Brethren, you must allow me to deliver this man so he can enjoy the services." He came on the platform. It is a wonderful thing when the Spirit of God comes upon you, and you are not touching a person in fear, not experimenting, but are in a place where you know. I told the people this man would be healed the moment I laid my hands upon him, and upon the pledge of God's truth to me, I rebuked the thing, and he was perfectly free to all the people's amazement.

Here is another instance: I just received a letter from Springfield, Missouri, about a man for whom I prayed. His mouth was filled with cancer, and he was in pain all the time. I said to the people, "This man will be delivered of this cancer and be made free within a few days. From the moment I put my hand upon his mouth, he will have no more pain." The moment I did that, instantly the pain lifted. Now I have this letter: "You will be interested to know about the man with cancer. One day he spits out half of cancer and the next day the balance. He lost about a quart of blood and is weakened as a result, but God has surely undertaken."

Now gifts of healings, miracles, are identical with what God's word says. It is not what we think; it is not how we feel; it is what God's word says. Dare you believe it? Jesus speaking expressly to the 70 who went out and came back saying what wonderful things had happened, said, "Behold, I give unto you power to tread on serpents and scorpions, and over all the power of the enemy, and nothing shall by any means hurt you." [Lk 10.19]

But let me say this: No man will go forward with God if he gets proud. To keep in touch with God, he must continue humble. You will never find that God can use a proud man. His word says,

"Show me thy salvation; the humble shall hear thereof and be glad," [Ps 34.2] and you will find that God is preparing the hearts of the humble to receive his word. "The rich are sent empty away"—the people who feel they can manage without God, but "the hungry he fills with good things." [Lk 1.53]

And so God would not have us under any circumstances to think that we are in the place of blessing when we are not in the place of humiliation and humbleness. It cannot be. Jesus, our blessed Lord, was the meekest, the most lovely, and the most beautiful in character. You never find him like this: "Stand aside now. I am a man who has the gifts!" You never find that in Jesus, but he was so moved with compassion that he could raise the widow's son. [Lk 7.11-17] We will not have had compassion except by the inward power of God moving us. Everybody can be humble. It costs nothing except your pride and ugly self to be put out of the way.

Now, what is a miracle? It is where the power of the Spirit of God comes to absolute helplessness, where no human aid can reach, but where God alone comes and performs the supernatural; when God comes and the body is made whole in a minute—not in an hour or a week, but in a minute—that is a miracle.

I was going into a big meeting in London one day, and a man who stood in the doorway said to me, "Don't you know me?" I said, "No, I do not recognize you just at this moment." "Don't you know my daughter?" he said. "No." "Nor my wife?" They all stood there. "No, I seem to have lost recollection of you." "Well," he said, "I am Smith from Brighton." Then I recognized them.

"Now," he said, "look at her," turning to his daughter, a beautiful young woman. They brought her to me stretched out in a carriage where she had been for years and years, helpless; had to be lifted about, and in a moment, as soon as God's touch came upon her, from the crown of her head to the sole of her foot, [Is 1.6] there wasn't a weakness. She was perfect and had been walking ever since. No man can do those things. There has never been a man living who could do it; only the man Christ Jesus, and if we wish to be used in that way we shall have to have him, know him, and understand him, for he is the Holy One.

The ministry of healing became so mighty in Australia that in some places I had to give up a day to minister to the sick, beginning at 9 and continuing until 4 o'clock to get through, praying with nearly 700 people. There is a chance for a lifetime. You talk about opportunity; I would not take the world's worth for the opportunity, and we ought to buy up our opportunities. You never will know what you have until you experiment upon what you have in faith. Every man that has ever done anything for God was amazed to find God respond the first time he ventured out in faith.

I say all these things to you to move you into a living faith in God; for what will it profit me without some of you are turned into flames of fire? What will it profit me if I turn from these meetings and you have only heard my voice and seen me? God would never have John and Peter and James to move up and down the world and leave people where they found them.

They were to make disciples of all nations, [Mt 28.19] and in the name of Jesus I am here, as it were, to make disciples; to create within you a deeper thirst and a longing for deeper things of God. If this is not my object, I ought not to be here. We have a higher calling, a nobler calling than to be fascinated with things of ourselves. It is not the fascination of ourselves; it is the inward fire that burns by the power of God, that attracts.

A very important gift is the gift of prophecy. I reckon no man can work miracles without he has gentleness, and no man can ever be a prophetic utterance for God without he is good. You will find that those gifts are in perfect conjunction with the **GRACE**s. First, the word of wisdom: You will find love controls the word of wisdom, and you will find the word of knowledge is controlled by joy; faith coincides exactly with peace, and you will never have faith if you have not peace. Peace comes from an unmovable, established position on the word of God. Now you could not have gifts of healings without you knew something about longsuffering, and you could not have the gift of miracles without you knew something about gentleness, nor prophecy without you knew something about goodness.

We must never despise prophecy, [1Th 5.20] but I will tell you what you must do. You must always judge it, [1Th 5.21] and you will find that a person who refuses to have his prophecy judged is wrong inwardly, and his expressions are wrong outwardly. I know people think discernment is a wonderful gift. This is real to the people who have discernment.

I will tell you what would be a fine thing: If those who think they have discerning of spirits displayed it upon themselves, they would get such a revelation of themselves in 12 months, they would not be harsh or critical of others. God does not want us to be harsh or critical of others. He means us to be filled with the Spirit.

Prophecy causes more trouble than anything else in the world. If you turn to the Old Testament, you will find prophetic utterances. Prophetic utterances beginning in the flesh and ending in the flesh are wrong. People do it because they like to be heard, and it destroys confidence. There are men who believe they have the power to go up and down and make prophets. It is unscriptural, and I can prove it to a very ordinary man. The man who would make a man a prophet is in a bad way, and the man who is willing to be made a prophet is in a worse way. No man can save you; no man can baptize you in the Spirit; no man can give a gift.

Turn to Ephesians 4.8: "Wherefore he saith, When he ascended up on high, he led captivity captive, and gave gifts unto men." [Ep 4.8] Who is he that ascended up on high but Jesus? "He gave some apostles; and some, prophets; and some, evangelists; and some, pastors and teachers." [Ep 4.11] No man has ever had the power to give these offices. The most you can do is to lay hands on a person to receive the Holy Ghost, which is a perfectly scriptural thing to do. I have seen hundreds receive the Holy Ghost while I have had my hands upon them, but was it I? No, but you may have the power of God so upon you and through you and in you, until from you will flow the healing virtue as from the body of Jesus, and when you touch people, they will be healed.

I have touched people who were dying, and they have been instantly healed from head to foot. I remember one night going into a house where a woman lay dying. Her husband came to me and said his wife would like to say just a word before she passed away. I went in and took hold of her hand, and she said, "Sam, I am healed. The virtue from Smith is going all over me." She was perfectly healed in that touch.

And I believe too that if you are filled with the Holy Ghost you will create a desire for the Spirit, an inward thirst for God, and with the laying on of hands, the gift of the Spirit will be moving in that man. You do not bestow the gift, but the power of God works through you, and remember there is never a baptism of the Holy Ghost but what God is there.

It is the promise of the Father. You never have a baptism of the Holy Ghost without Jesus is there, for he baptizes; you never have the baptism of the Holy Ghost without the Holy Ghost comes in, so you have the trinity there. Every touch of God that I get makes me to see how I need more of him all the time. I hope no one in this meeting will ever be so foolish as to allow any person to make you anything, but that you will all be willing to let God make you something.

Is prophecy real? It is just as real as anything else. When you have prophecy be sure it is the Spirit of God that gives it, and when it is given be sure it is nothing personal. There are foolish and ridiculous things taking place in some parts. I think a man ought to have the choice of his wife, but when prophecy goes forth that you are to have a wife of their choosing, you are on dangerous ground. When prophecy goes forth that you are to have a certain house on a certain street, you know that is carnal. All these things make our position one of ridicule and a laughingstock in the eyes of the people. God save us from foolishness and ignorance. How will he save us? When we are humble enough to be taught.

The deceptiveness of the devil is shown in prophecy tremendously. When prophetic utterances from the Lord go forth they are of great blessing to everybody, but where is the mistake? It often lies in people going up to the one who has given the message and saying, “Oh, I got so blessed through that prophecy. It was wonderful. We must have it written down,” and you spoil the people who give the prophecy.

It is a very serious thing because prophecy is a gift, and the seriousness of the thing is to use a gift without the power of God upon you. They begin to say, “Thus saith the Lord,” and go on forever. Now listen: If the prophecy is not given in the unction of the Spirit, it will be damnation. It is blessed when the clear prophecy comes through, because a person may have prophecy who knows very little of the word of God and yet have perfect prophetic utterance.

If you turn to the seventh chapter of the Acts of the Apostles and read the prophecy that Stephen utters, it is most sublime. As he prophesied under the power of the Spirit, the power of the devil came upon those people; they couldn’t stand it. It meant his death, but it was in the power of the Spirit. There is something about the prophecy that makes you know it is God.

Here is a man in the assembly who starts in to pray. He has prayed many times in the assembly, and you have been blessed, but suddenly you catch fire, and you feel the inspiration as the Spirit prays through him, and you know when God has finished and when he begins his prayer. The lesson to learn in Pentecost is when to finish, for it is a serious thing to go on after the Lord has finished. You begin in the Spirit and end in the flesh. The same thing is true of prophecy; they begin in the Spirit and end in the flesh.

Then there are some foolish people in the world who, when they know someone has the gift of prophecy, go around to his house and try to find out something by prophecy. That is as bad as going to a medium. Do you think you can get a prophetic message on those lines? Now listen: Wisdom is justified by her children, [Lk

7.35] and if you do not keep in wisdom, nobody wants anything to do with you, so do not work along those lines. If you want to know the mind of God, get it in the book; you do not need a prophet to tell you. God is his interpreter.

I was saved when I was a boy eight years old, and I have never lost the witness. I never went to school, and so I had no chance to learn to read. When I got married, my wife taught me both to read and write, though she could never teach me to spell, I do the best I can. I so love the word of God. I do not remember spending any time but with the word. Papers and books have no fascination for me. The word of God is my meat and my drink. I get a fresh breath from heaven every time I read it. It is full of prophetic utterances that make my soul rejoice.

The Way of faith

Published in the Pentecostal Evangel, June 15, 1935.

In Romans 4:16 we read, "It is of faith, that it might be by **GRACE**," meaning that we can open the door and God will come in. What will happen if we open the door by faith? God is greater than our thoughts. He puts it to us, "Exceeding abundantly above all that we ask or think." When we ask a lot, God says "more."

Are we ready for the "more"? And then the "much more"? We may be, or we may miss it. We may be so endued by the Spirit of the Lord in the morning that it shall be a tonic for the whole day. God can so thrill us with new life that nothing ordinary or small will satisfy us after that. There is a great place for us in God where we won't be satisfied with small things.

We won't have any satisfaction unless the fire falls, and whenever we pray we will have the assurance that what we have prayed for is going to follow the moment we open our mouth. Oh this praying in the Spirit! This great plan of God for us! In a moment we can go right in. In where? Into His will. Then all things will be well.

You can't get anything asleep these days. The world is always awake, and we should always be awake to what God has for us. Awake to take! Awake to hold it after we get it! How much can you take? We know that God is more willing to give than we are to receive. How shall we dare to be asleep when the Spirit commands us to take everything on the table. It is the greatest banquet that ever was and ever will be—the table where all you take only leaves more behind. A fullness that cannot be exhausted! How many are prepared for a lot?

"And Jesus entered into Jerusalem, and into the temple: and when he had looked round about upon all things, and now the eventide was come, he went out unto Bethany with the twelve. And on the morrow, when they were come from Bethany, he was hungry: and seeing a fig tree afar off having leaves, he came, if haply he might find anything thereon: and when he came to it, he found nothing but leaves; for the time of figs was not yet. And Jesus answered and said, No man eat fruit of thee hereafter forever. And his disciples heard it." Mark 11:11-14.

Jesus was sent from God to meet the world's need. Jesus lived to minister life by the words He spoke. He said to Philip, "He that hath seen me hath seen the Father… the words that I speak unto you, I speak not of myself: but the Father that dwelleth in me." I am persuaded that if we are filled with His words of life and the Holy Ghost, and Christ is made manifest in our mortal flesh, then the Holy Ghost can move us with His life, His words, till as He was, so are we in the world. We are receiving our life from God, and it is always kept in tremendous activity, working in our whole nature as we live in perfect contact with God.

Jesus spoke, and everything He said must come to pass. That is a great plan. When we are filled only with the Holy Spirit, and we won't allow the Word of God to be detracted by what we hear or by what we read, then comes the inspiration, then the life, then the activity, then the glory! Oh to live in it! To live in it is to be moved by it. To live in it is to be moved so that we will have God's life, God's personality in the human body.

By the **GRACE** of God I want to impart the Word, and bring you into a place where you will dare to act upon the plan of the Word, to so breathe life by the power of the Word that it is impossible for you to go on under any circumstances without His provision. The most difficult things that come to us are to our advantage from God's side.

When we come to the place of impossibilities, it is the grandest place for us to see the possibilities of God. Put this right in your mind and never forget it. You will never be of any importance to God till you venture in the impossible. God wants people on the daring line. I do not mean foolish daring. "Be filled with the Spirit," and when we are filled with the Spirit, we are not so much concerned about the secondary thing. It is the first with God.

Everything of evil, everything unclean, everything Satanic in any way is an objectionable thing to God, and we are to live above it, destroy it, not to allow it to have any place. Jesus didn't let the devil answer back. We must reach the place where we will not allow anything to interfere with the plan of God.

Jesus and His disciples came to the tree. It looked beautiful. It had the appearance of the fruit, but when He came to it, He found nothing but leaves. He was very disappointed. Looking at the tree, He spoke to it: Here is shown forth His destructive power.

"No man eat the fruit of thee hereafter forever." The next day they were passing by the same way, and the disciples saw the tree "dried up from the roots." They said to Jesus, "Behold, the fig tree which thou cursedst is withered away." And Jesus said, "Have faith in God."

There isn't a person that has ever seen a tree dried from the root. Trees always show the first signs of death right at the top. But the Master had spoken. The Master dealt with a natural thing to reveal to these disciples a supernatural plan. If He spoke, it would have to obey. And, God, the Holy Ghost, wants us to understand clearly that we are the mouthpiece of God and are here for His divine plan. We may allow the natural mind to dethrone that, but in the measure we do, we won't come into the treasure which God has for us. The Word of God must have first place. It must not have a second place. In any measure that we doubt the Word of God, from that moment we have ceased to thrive spiritually and actively. The Word of God is not only to be looked at and read but received as the Word of God to become life right within our life. "Thy word have I hid in my heart that I might not sin against thee."

"I give unto you power… over all the power of the enemy." Luke 10:19. There it is. We can accept or reject it. I accept and believe it. It is a word beyond all human calculation: "Have faith in God." These disciples were in the Master's school.

They were the men who were to turn the world upside down. As we receive the Word we will never be the same; if we dare to act as the Word goes forth and not be afraid, then God will honor us. "The Lord of hosts is with us; the God of Jacob is our refuge." Jacob was the weakest of all, in any way you like to take it. He is the God of Jacob, and He is our God. So we may likewise have our names changed to Israel.

As the Lord Jesus injected this wonderful word, "Have faith in God," into the disciples, He began to show how it was to be. Looking around about Him He saw the mountains, and He began to bring a practical application. Truth means nothing unless it moves us. We can have our minds filled a thousand times, but it must get into our hearts if there are to be any results. All inspiration is in the heart. All compassion is in the heart.

Looking at the mountains, He said, "Shall not doubt in his heart." That is the barometer. You know exactly where you are. The man knows when he prays. If his heart is right how it leaps. No man is any good for God and never makes progress in God who does not hate sin. You are never safe. But there is a place in God where you can love righteousness and where you can hate iniquity till the Word of God is a light in your bosom, quickening every fiber of your body, thrilling your whole nature. The pure in heart see God. Believe in the heart! What a word! If I believe in my heart God says I can begin to speak, and "whatsoever" I say shall come to pass.

Here is an act of believing in the heart. I was called to Halifax, England, to pray for a lady missionary. I found it an urgent call. I could see faith was absent, and I could see there was death: Death is a terrible thing, and God wants to keep us alive. I know it is appointed unto man once to die, but I believe in a rapturous death. I said to the woman, "How are you?" She said, "I have faith," in a very weak tone of voice. "Faith? Why are you dying? Brother Walshaw, is she dying?" "Yes." "Nurse, is she dying?" "Yes." To a friend standing by, "Is she dying?" "Yes."

Now I believe there is something in a heart that is against defeat, and this is the faith which God hath given to us. I said to her, "In the name of Jesus, now believe and you'll live." She said, "I believe," and God sent life from her head to her feet. They dressed her, and she lived.

"Have faith." It isn't saying you have faith. It is he that believeth in his heart. It is a grasping of the eternal God. Faith is God in the human vessel. "This is the victory that overcometh the world, even our faith." 1 John 5:4. He that believeth overcomes the world. "Faith cometh by hearing, and hearing by the Word of God." He that believeth in his heart!

Can you imagine anything easier than that? He that believeth in his heart! What is the process? Death! No one can live who believes in his heart. He dies to everything worldly. He that loves the world is not of God. You can measure the whole thing up, and examine yourself to see if you have faith. Faith is life. Faith enables you to lay hold of that which is and get it out of the way for God to bring in something that is not.

Just before I left home, I was in Norway. A woman wrote to me from England saying she had been operated on for cancer three years before, but that it was now coming back. She was living in constant dread of the whole thing as the operation was so painful. Would it be possible to see me when I returned to England? I wrote that I would be passing through London on the 20th of June last year. If she would like to meet me at the hotel, I would pray for her. She replied that she would be going to London to be there to meet me. When I met this woman, I saw she was in great pain, and I have great sympathy for people who have tried to get relief and have failed. If you preachers lose your compassion you can stop preaching, for it won't be any good.

You will only be successful as a preacher as you let your heart become filled with the compassion of Jesus. As soon as I saw her, I entered into the state of her mind. I saw how distressed she was. She came to me in a mournful spirit, and her whole face was downcast. I said to her, "There are two things going to happen today. One is that you are to know that you are saved." "Oh, if I could only know I was saved," she said. "There is another thing. You have to go out of this hotel without pain, without a trace of cancer."

Then I began with the Word. Oh, this wonderful Word! We do not have to go up to bring Him down; neither do we have to go down to bring Him up. "The word is nigh thee, even in thy mouth, and in thy heart: that is, the word of faith, which we preach." Romans 10:8. I said, "Believe that He took your sins when He died at the cross.

Believe that when He was buried, it was for you. Believe that when He arose, it was for you. And now at God's right hand, He is sitting for you. If you can believe in your heart and confess with your mouth, you shall be saved." She looked at me saying, "Oh, it is going all through my body. I know I am saved now. If He comes today, I'll go how I have dreaded, the thought of His coming all my life! But if He comes today, I know I shall be ready."

The first thing was finished. Now for the second. I laid my hands upon her in the name of Jesus, believing in my heart that I could say what I wanted and it should be done. I said, "In the name of

Jesus, I cast this out." She jumped up. "Two things have happened," she said. "I am saved, and now the cancer is gone."

Faith will stand amid the wrecks of time,
Faith unto eternal glories climb;
Only count the promise true,
And the Lord will stand by you—
Faith will win the victory every time!

So many people have nervous trouble. I'll tell you how to get rid of your nervous trouble. I have something in my bag, one dose of which will cure you. "I am the Lord that healeth thee." How this wonderful Word of God changes the situation. "Perfect love casteth out fear." "There is no fear in love."

I have tested that so often, casting out the whole condition of fear and the whole situation has been changed. We have a big God; only He has to be absolutely and only trusted. The people who do believe God are strong, and "he that hath clean hands shall be stronger and stronger."

At the close of a certain meeting, a man said to me, "You have helped everybody but me. I wish you would help me." "What's the trouble with you?" "I cannot sleep because of nervous trouble. My wife says she has not known me to have a full night's sleep for three years. I am just shattered." Anybody could tell he was.

I put my hands upon him and said, "Brother I believe in my heart. Go home and sleep in the name of Jesus." "I can't sleep." "Go home and sleep in the name of Jesus." "I can't sleep." The lights were being put out, and I took the man by the coat collar and said, "Don't talk to me any more." That was sufficient. He went after that. When he got home his mother and wife said to him, "What has happened?" "Nothing. He helped everybody but me." "Surely he said something to you." "He told me to come home and sleep in the name of Jesus, but you know I can't sleep in anything."

His wife urged him to do what I had said, and he had scarcely got his head on the pillow before the Lord put him to sleep. The next morning he was still asleep. The next morning he was still asleep. She began to make a noise in the bedroom to awaken him, but he did not waken. Sunday morning he was still asleep. She did what every good wife would do. She decided to make a good Sunday dinner and then awaken him. After the dinner was prepared, she went up to him and put her hand on his shoulder and shook him, saying, “Are you never going to wake up?” From that night that man never had any more nervousness.

A man came to me for whom I prayed. Then I asked, “Are you sure you are perfectly healed?” “Well,” he said, “there is just a little pain in my shoulder.” “Do you know what that is?” I asked him. “That is unbelief. Were you saved before you believed or after?” “After.” “You will be healed after.” “It is all right now,” he said, It was all right before, but he hadn’t believed.

The Word of God is for us. It is by faith that it might be by **GRACE**.

From the author Dr. Michael H Yeager's

THE QUICKENING OF GRACE

Jesus said: ***my words are spirit and they are life. It is the spirit that quickened, the flesh profits nothing.***

Remember that the 1st Adam was a living soul, and the 2nd Adam is a quickening spirit. The quickening of the Holy Ghost is when the word of God is made alive by the spirit of God. It is when the reality of Christ becomes more real to you than the natural world around us. Actually, to a great extent this is what faith is, when God and his word becomes more real to you than the natural surroundings you find yourself in. Now I do not need to have a quickening to raise my hands, or to obey the everyday instructions of God's word.

James 1:22 But be ye doers of the word, and not hearers only, deceiving your own selves.

There is a natural aspect of just doing what the bible says to do. When I 1st got born again I had never been around anyone who raised their hands, or who danced before the Lord, or anyone who shouted, or who laid on their face before the Lord. I simply read it in the Bible, and when I saw it in the Bible, I began to do that which I read.

1 Timothy 2:8 I will therefore that men pray everywhere, lifting up holy hands, without wrath and doubting.

These Scripture that had impacted my lifestyle were not quickened to me by the spirit, I just simply did what I read. Here's a good example: God commands us to forgive, and therefore we do it by faith. The Bible says if you do not forgive, you will not be forgiven. As we study Grace we begin to understand it is the quickened by the spirit in order to do the basic things God's word instructs us to do.

Actually, as we do these simple basic things, the spirit of God will begin to quicken us to do many other amazing things. I believe that every supernatural act that God has us perform is a supernatural quickening by his Holy Spirit. These quickening s can happen so quickly, so unexpectedly, that it will surprise you when it happens. You could have read a verse from the Bible for many years, then all of a sudden one day as you are reading it, it literally jumps right out of the Bible into your heart. Faith becomes alive in you, and now your excited, and full of joy and peace. **This is what we call a quickening of the Holy Spirit.**

Hebrews 4:12 For the word of God is quick, and powerful, and sharper than any twoedged sword, piercing even to the dividing asunder of soul and spirit, and of the joints and marrow, and is a discerner of the thoughts and intents of the heart.

The Holy Ghost will take the word and breathe life into it, causing the letter of the word to be turned into spirit. For the Holy Spirit to do this, we must be in complete agreement with the Bible. You do not need to understand the Scriptures to agree with them. Simply boldly declared to yourself, I agree with the Bible, no matter what it says. Every dream, vision, supernatural experience is a quickening of the Holy Ghost. This quickening is revealed to us in the book of Romans when God spoke to the heart of Abraham.

Romans 4:17 (As it is written, I have made thee a father of many nations,) before him whom he believed, even God, who

quickeneth the dead, and calleth those things which be not as though they were.

A falling Lamp Pole would have killed my son!

This actually happened to my son Michael a number of years ago. If you ever visit our facilities, you will see in our parking lot several real tall metal street lights. We installed these street lights over 25 years ago. Now, one day Michael, my oldest son was out in the parking lot with his back to one of these heavy steel street lights. He was just standing there minding his own business looking across the parking lot, when unexpected there was a Divine quickening in Michaels heart to take a step over to his right side. He told me: dad I wasn't even thinking, just in my heart I knew I had to step over to the right-hand side. Now at that very moment when he moved to his right side, something came whizzing past him very close to his left shoulder and arm. Then there was a loud crash of something hitting the ground.

Here in less than a second after Michael had moved that tall, heavy and large steel street light, fell over. It slammed down right next to him on to the parking lot. If he would not have moved exactly at that moment when he did, he would' have been slammed in the head by that heavy falling steel lamp. In all probability, it would have killed him instantly on the spot. Thank God for the quickening of the Holy Spirit, and Michael's quick response to that quickening. Many people die early deaths because they do not hearken to the moving of the spirit. Just a matter of inches and seconds made all the difference in the world between life and death for my son Michael. I am convinced that when we get to Heaven we will talk to many of Gods people who will tell us that they died early deaths because they did not listen or respond to this quickening. When God puts a quickening in our hearts, we need to respond immediately, without thinking.

When I wrote Living in the Realm of the Miraculous

Back in 2011, I was ministering in a church in Wild-wood, New Jersey. In this meeting, I began to share a number of my amazing experiences that I have had with the Lord since 1975. After the service, pastor Rob told me that people really love to hear the stories. At that moment, it was dropped into my heart to go back to the hotel, and begin to write down all of the miracles that God had done in my life. Within two hours the Holy Spirit had brought back to my mind over 120 stories. I simply gave each story a title, with a brief description of the story at that time.

When my wife and I arrived back home in Pennsylvania, the Lord spoke to my heart, leading me to write a book about these experiences. This was so quickened to me by the spirit of God that literally within 2 1/2 weeks I wrote a 200-page book. Of course, this did not include the editing and the printing of this book. As far as I know, there is no one in my family lineage who has ever even written a book, or even accomplished very much in the natural.

My accomplishments are all by the quickening, energizing, power of the Holy Ghost, quickening the word in my heart. God by his spirit has so quickened me, that up to this moment I have memorized 10 books of the New Testament, and thousands of other Scriptures. Now, God is not a respecter of people, and he wants to manifest himself in the supernatural in a powerful way in all of our lives.

Ephesians 3:20Now unto him that is able to do exceeding abundantly above all that we ask or think, according to the power that worketh in us,

Oh, brothers and sisters if only we could take a hold of this reality, that God by his quickening can empower us in ways we have not yet imagined. That God by his quickening spirit will lead and guide us in every affair of life. Now to what degree God

Quickens us is determined by the amount of the word of God we have hid in our hearts.

Romans 8:11 But if the Spirit of him that raised up Jesus from the dead dwell in you, he that raised up Christ from the dead shall also quicken your mortal bodies by his Spirit that dwelleth in you.

The spirit of God can quicken our mortal flesh to dance, or shout, sing, speak, or run. The spirit of God will enable you to preach and proclaim the truth in the way that you never could in the flesh! There are so many wonderful examples of this from Genesis to Revelation. It tells us in the old covenant about the time that the prophet Elijah being quickened by the Holy Ghost, out ran the King and his horses.

God calls us, he quickens us and enables by His word and Spirit. When God told Joshua and the Israelite's to go into the land of Canaan, he also quickened them by his word, and enable them to overcome all of the enemies. If you study the Scriptures very closely you'll also discover that David overcame the lion and the bear, Goliath and the other obstacles in his life because God quickened him by his Spirit. I am convinced that God quickened the heart of David to confront Goliath, and enabled him to overcome this giant.

Proverbs 3:5 Trust in the Lord with all thine heart; and lean not unto thine own understanding.6 In all thy ways acknowledge him, and he shall direct thy paths.

When God quickens us, we need to learn how to submit, and to operate tin that quickening.

James 4:7Submit yourselves therefore to God. Resist the devil, and he will flee from you.

*W*ho exactly is it that the devil does not have to flee from? From those who will not submit to God. Have I disobeyed the voice of God today? I am convinced that the more sensitive I become to God, and obey Him, the more God can quicken my heart, my flesh, and my mind!

God Gave Him a Brand-new liver

One day I walked into a man's room who I did not know. The Holy Spirit drew me to this particular room as I was walking down the hospital hallway. I asked the man who was lying in the bed what his problem was. He told me that his liver was completely shot, and that he was dying. I perceived in my heart that it was because of alcoholism. I told him that I would like to pray for him, and asked if that was possible. He agreed to my request. I laid my hands on him, commanding in the name of Jesus Christ for the spirit of infirmity to come out. And then I spoke into him a brand-new liver, in the name of Jesus Christ of Nazareth! I do not speak loud. I do not have to because I know my Authority in Christ, when I am submitted to the authority of Christ! I do not pray real long prayers, or even dozens of scriptures. The Word is already in my heart!

Now believe me when I tell you that if I wanted to pray real long prayers in those situations I easily could. I could stand over the person and quote whole books of the Bible by memory. When you are moving in the realm of faith none of these things are really necessary. Many times I think people are simply trying to work up faith. If you study the life of Jesus and his ministry he never spent a long time praying or speaking over people. The long hours of prayer, and speaking the word was done in private, when he was up on the mountain, or alone in the wilderness. When I was done praying I simply said goodbye, and out the door I went. I went to go see another sick person who was in the hospital. It was three years later when I found out what happened on that particular day.

One day one of the members of my congregation was down on the streets of Gettysburg witnessing to those he met. He ran into this particular gentleman who was dying because of a bad liver. This particular man said: I know who your pastor is! The parishioner asked: how do you know my pastor? He said: three years ago I was dying with a bad liver, and your pastor walked in to my hospital room. He laid his hands on me, commanding me to be healed, and to have a brand-new liver, and God did give me a brand-new liver!

In order to discover whether or not the circumstances that we find our self in is of God we need to see if it contradicts the divine nature and character of God. For instance, if a man or a woman is married, God is not going to send them another mate. It is absolutely unbelievable the bizarre things I hear people say. Many times God gets blamed for things which is not of his doing at all. I have known quite a number of people who have claimed that certain events they experienced were of the Lord when they simply were not. Most of these people will not change their minds even though you show them within God's word they are wrong.

Proverbs 16:18 Pride goeth before destruction, and an haughty spirit before a fall.

God Gave Me Grace to Beat a Chess Champion

This is about a friend of mine who was an agnostic, if not a total atheist. This friend of mine was a local champion chess player where I grew up. Before I was born again he could easily beat me at almost every game of chess. I had not played chess with him since I had left for the Navy back in 1973. Now, here it was 1975, and he was filled with more pride than ever, believing that he had advanced a long way in the game of chess. He had made it an absolute priority in his life to be the best. Well after I was born again, I kept trying to tell this arrogant friend of mine about Jesus Christ. He simply did not want to hear anything about the Lord. Now he was really biting at the bit to play chess with me again in order to make me look like a fool. He had to realize that something supernatural had happened in my life in the last three years because the terrible speech impediment that I had my whole life was not completely gone. When I had been baptized in the Holy Ghost, my speech impediment was completely healed. I could speak just as clear and precise as anyone. Yet this supernatural evidence of God moving in my life did not seem to touch him in the least.

For a brief period after I was discharged from the Navy I spent a short period of time back in Wisconsin. I could tell that he desperately wanted to play a game of chess with me, I am sure he wanted to play me just so that he could rub my nose in the fact that he was a chess champion, and I a dummy. He was convinced that he could easily beat me at this game like he had done so many times in the past. I truly perceived in my heart that God wanted me to play him, so I agreed to play him one game of chess. What I am about to tell you, is the absolute truth.

As I looked down at that board with all the chess pieces laid out before me, I felt in my heart that God was about to do something amazing and supernatural. I am telling you that the spirit of the Lord quickened me, taking over this chess game. I began to move pieces across the board by the leading of the Holy Ghost not even thinking about my moves.

This chess champion literally began to laugh at the dumb moves that I was making. He literally began to mock me as I began to lose piece after piece to him. When it looked like the game was utterly lost to him and that he had one me easily, out of the blue, and unexpectedly I put his King in checkmate. Neither him or I could believe what just took place. He was so frustrated and upset because he knew that I had played the game in such an unconventional and foolish way that there's no way I could win.

During the time that I was playing I was speaking about Jesus as much as possible. He had no choice but to listen to me because of the game in front of us. He insisted that it was simply luck that I had won, and that I needed to play him again. Yes, I told him let's play another game. Once again, we set all the pieces up, and I made the first move. It was almost an exact repeat of the first game in the seemingly stupid moves I was making. He laughed and mock me as I made stupid move after stupid move. Then to our utter and complete surprise, once again he found his King in checkmate. He could barely contain himself because of his total frustration and anger at me winning this game with making so many stupid moves.

At that moment, He became like a gambler who could not stop gambling until he won his money back. What I am sharing with you is the absolute truth, with no exaggeration whatsoever. The spirit of the living God was directing my every move in this chess game. I was not leaning to the understanding of my mind. It was like I was watching God pick up these pieces with my right hand, and move them around the board. I won five games, eight games, 11 games, a total of 13 games straight in a row. After 13 games of winning this chess champion, I finally quit because I knew he was about to lose his mind. From that day to now, over 40 years have passed and he has never played me another game of chest. He declared that I had won these games because I was so stupid. That I did not know the normal way to play chess.

God had used this circumstance to reveal himself in a wonderful way to this man who was antagonistic towards the gospel. God was using this circumstance to touch his heart, to let him know that he was not playing mike Yeager!

1 Corinthians 1:27 But God hath chosen the foolish things of the world to confound the wise; and God hath chosen the weak things of the world to confound the things which are mighty;

CHAPTER TEN

Way to Overcome: Believe!

1 John 5. The greatest weakness in the world is unbelief. The greatest power is the faith that works by love. Love, mercy, and **GRACE** are bound eternally to faith. There is no fear in love and no question as to being caught up when Jesus comes. The world is filled with fear, torment, remorse, and brokenness, but faith and love are sure to overcome. "Who is he that overcomes the world, but he that believes that Jesus is the Son of God?" (1 John 5:5). God hath established the earth and humanity on the lines of faith. As you come into line, fear is cast out, the Word of God comes into operation, and you find bedrock. The way to overcome is to believe Jesus is the Son of God. The commandments are wrapped up in it.

When there is fidelity between you and God and the love of God is so real that you feel you could do anything for Jesus, all the promises are yea and amen to those who believe. Your life is centered there. You are always overcoming what is in the world.

Who keeps the commandments? The born of God. "Ye are of God, little children, and have overcome them: because greater is he that is in you, than he that is in the world" (1 John 4:4). They that believe, love. When did He love us? When we were in the mire. What did He say? Thy sins are forgiven thee. Why did He say it? Because He loved us. What for?

That He might bring many sons into glory. His object? That we might be with Him forever. All the pathway is an education for this high vocation and calling. This hidden mystery of love to us, the undeserving! For our sins the double blessing. "…whatsoever is born of God overcomes the world: and this is the victory…even our faith" (1 John 5:4). He who believes – to believe is to overcome. On the way to Emmaus Jesus, beginning from Moses and all the prophets, interpreted to them in all the Scriptures the things concerning Himself (Luke 24:27).

He is the root! In Him is life. When we receive Christ, we receive God and the promises (Galatians 3:29), that we might receive the promise of the Spirit through faith. I am heir to all the promises because I believe. Great heirship! I overcome it because I believe the truth. The truth makes me free.

TONGUES AND INTERPRETATION: "It is God who exalts, God who makes rich. The Lord in His mighty arms bears thee up – it is the Lord that encompasses round about thee. When I am weak, then I am strong."

No wavering! This is the principle. He who believes is definite, and because Jesus is in it, it will come to pass. He is the same yesterday, today, and forever (Hebrews 13:8). They that are poor in spirit are heirs to all. There is no limit to the power, for God is rich to all who call upon Him. Not the will of the flesh, but God (John 1:13). Put in your claim for your children, your families, your co-workers, that many sons may be brought to glory (Hebrews 2:10), for it is all on the principle of faith.

There is nothing in my life or ambition equal to my salvation, a spiritual revelation from heaven according to the power of God, and it does not matter how many flashlights Satan sends through the human mind; roll all on the blood. Who overcomes? He who believes Jesus is the Son (1 John 5:5). God calls in the person with no credentials; it's the order of faith, He who believes overcomes – will be caught up.

The Holy Ghost gives revelation all along the line. He that is not against us is for us, and some of the godliest have not touched Pentecost yet. We must have a good heart especially to the household of faith. "...If any man loves the world, the love of the Father is not in him" (1 John 2:15). The root principle of all truth in the human heart is Christ, and when grafted deeply there are a thousand lives you may win. Jesus is the way, the truth, and the life (John 14:6), the secret to every hard problem in the world.

You can't do it! Joseph could not! Everything depends on the principles in your heart. If God dwells in us the principle is light; it comprehends darkness. If thine eye is single, thy whole body shall be full of light, breaking through the hardest thing. "Herein is our love made perfect, that we may have boldness in the Day of Judgment: because as he is, so are we in this world (1 John 4:17) – for faith has full capacity. When a man is pure, and it is easy to detect darkness, he that hath this hope purifies himself (1 John 3:3).

TONGUES AND INTERPRETATION: "God confirms in us faith that we may be refined in the world, having neither spot nor blemish nor any such thing. It is all on the line of faith, he that hath faith overcomes – it is the Lord Who purifies and bringeth where the fire burns up all the dross, and anoints with fresh oil; see to it that ye keep pure. God is separating us for Himself.

"...**I will give you a mouth and wisdom, which all your adversaries will not be able to gainsay nor resist" (Luke 21:15).** The Holy Spirit will tell you at the moment what you shall say. The world will not understand you, and you will find as you go on with God that you do not under-stand fully. We cannot comprehend what we are saved to, or from. None can express the joy of God's indwelling. The Holy Spirit can say through you the need of the moment. The world knows us not because it knew Him not.

“Who is he that overcomes the world, but he that believes Jesus is the Son of God?” (1 John 5:5). A place of confidence in God, a place of prayer, a place of knowledge, that we have what we ask because we keep His commandments and do the things that are pleasing in His sight. Enoch before his translation had the testimony; he had been well-pleasing unto God. We overcome by believing.

First Published in Flames of Fire p. 2 March 1917

Living in the spiritual realm of GRACE

And we must see that God is all the time loosing us by the Spirit. When God gets us loose, we are ready for any association. No matter what ship I travel on people is always saved on that ship. And if I go on a railroad journey, I am sure there is someone saved before I get through. It isn’t possible for me to live without getting people ready for dying. I believe we have to live in a new spiritual realm of **GRACE** where all our mind, our walk, and everything is in the Holy Ghost. Beloved, the Spirit alone can do this. You can never reach these attainments under any circumstances in the flesh: “Ye are not in the flesh but the Spirit.” [Ro 8.9] May God help us to see our destined position.

I say, and I will never draw it back till God shows me differently, that the child of God ought to thirst for the word. The child of God should know nothing else but the word, and he should know nothing amongst men save Jesus. He can never know God through a newspaper and very little through books. You will find that books will disturb your mind and cause all kinds of ruptures in your ordinary communion. God has shown me that I dare not trust any book but the word of God.

I have never read a book, but the bible and I am as satisfied as possible. It is the only book, and it is the only food for the believer. **"Man shall not live by bread alone, but by every word that proceedeth out of the mouth of God." [Mt 4.4]** And we are of his substance. We are his life. There is something in humanity that God has made for all his divine attributes, that man can receive of God and walk up and down insulated through and through by this God-indwelling presence. Ah, it is lovely! And it is all because of the word of knowledge, by the same Spirit that gave the word of wisdom.

The next word also is a great word, especially among Pentecostal people who seem to be hungry for it more than anything else now, the **"word of faith by the same Spirit." [1Co 12.9]** You will find that coupled right along with this, is peace. And it could not be otherwise. You cannot find any man who has a living faith which is in trouble. You will never accomplish anything on any line except when you are in peace.

It may be a blessing for you to know that if ever I have trouble and my peace is destroyed on any line, I always know it is satanic; it is never God under any circumstances. If I am not at peace, there is something wrong somewhere, and I must get to know what it is because they that keep their minds stayed upon God shall be kept in continual peace. [Is 26.3]

When I find where the leakage is I shall be able to put my hand upon it and say, "That is healed." Beloved, God wants to take us into that solid peace. It will make a difference in our prayers; it will make a difference in our reading and our conversation when we are at peace with God and with one another. All the blasts of hell's furnace whenever they come, cannot touch you.

For those who pass from death unto life, there is perfect peace, and yet we cannot have peace unless we have faith. God wants all his people so built on this groundwork of faith that everybody that sees you will be impressed; they will be moved. You will never move the world if you are in trouble, but show the world that there is a peace that brings joy; that there is a joy that brings a song; that lifts you up, and it will lift all that gather round you.

The children of God must see clearly that they do not belong to this world. **"Ye are not of the world." [Jn 15.19] "If you love the world, the love of the Father is not in you." [1Jn 2.15]** Therefore you must be delivered from the world, be strengthened by the power of God, and be new creatures every day. Let us get down to this solid place of faith because there is something in it for us all. Faith can so rest in God's plan and thought that whatever is going on in the world will make no difference. If your house was on fire and you were really at peace with God and resting in faith, you could laugh.

One of our workers said to me at Christmastime, "Wigglesworth, I never was so near the end of my purse in all my life. To which I replied, "Thank God, you are just at the opening of God's treasures." If you get hold of the true principles of God, there is no person in this place can ever be poor. Even in believer's deepest poverty, he is made rich.

When he has nothing at all, he has more to give than he ever had before, making many rich because he has reached a place of poverty. When you possess nothing, it is just the time when you possess all things. That is a seeming contradiction, but there are many apparent contradictions in the word of God to the mind who has not looked into the perfect law of liberty. [Jm 1.25]

But the child of God who goes in the perfect law of liberty sees that there is no binding; it is all liberty. You will never have liberty unless you have peace and you will never have peace unless you have faith. There are three things which always work correctly, and they are on those lines. You can never have feeling make a fact, but you can have faith make a fact that will bring feeling.

Beloved, God has a plan for these days, and when he comes in, no flesh can stand against him. Faith always works a faith. It always brings peace; it is always in the clear light of God perfecting and being perfected. There are two things we must know; every principle of this 12th chapter of Corinthians is based upon gifts.

When I speak about "gifts," I speak about the gifts which are brought into the human heart and abide there, for "the gifts and calling of God are without repentance." [Ro 11.29] Just like the Holy Ghost, when he comes in he never leaves. He may be grieved, and he may be quenched to such an extent that it may seem all was dormant, but it will always be because the life is not in submission. When the life is submissive to God's power, taking hold of that body, that body never loses its unction but goes on further and further to know more of the mind and will of God.

The difference between a gift within you and a gift administered through you because of the Holy Ghost unction is that one always takes you into a place beyond where you were before you received the gift. For instance, all men have faith who are saved; saving faith. But the "gift of faith" is much different. That faith always abides.

That is the reason why we may take for granted the security of the believer because we are not saved by works; **[Ep 2.8] we are saved by faith.** And your position in Christ is according to where you are on the lines of faith. As I said the other day, no man in the place is any better than his faith. If his faith is perfected he is being perfected in every way.

If he sees Jesus even though his faith is imperfect, the same perfection in Jesus will be perfected in him. If he sees Jesus in all his divine glories, attributes, and gifts, he will find that he will come into the divine position where Jesus exchanges his robe for his. If he can believe it, it is true. If you have no limitations, God has a plan to lift you into all his divine plan.

God has no place for anybody who is not thirsty. You are unusable. The Holy Ghost has no movement in you. But the word of God which we receive when we are born again by the incorruptible word: As that word abides, and you don't interfere with it but nurture it, you will find it has the power to make a perfect Christ in you because it is the seed of God.

There is a great fullness in being a child of God. As God was in the heavens, seeing Jesus in the water, having come down there with John—just as he came to the place where they were, there was perfect surrender, then God burst through the heavens, saying: "This is my beloved Son in whom I am well pleased." [Mt 3.17] What was it that pleased him? That which will please him in every one of us: Meekness, submission, a full condition of surrender.

When he, the King of kings, the Lord of lords, submitted to water baptism by John, that perfect yieldedness brought him to a place where God said, "This is my beloved Son." If you follow Jesus, you will see that from that time he claims his eternal destiny, his authority. From that time on, he lives and proves himself to be the Son of God. You will find there is the same position in destiny for us; our destiny is always pre-position.

We must see that God begins with us by the word and finishes us by perfecting us as sons. **"Unto as many as received him, to them gave he the power to become the sons of God." [Jn 1.12]** They were not sons, but they have the power to become sons. And every person in this place has a perfect right to rise up to perfect son ship, where God indwells, flows, works through him, and manifests him in the world as a son. It is a big subject and seems to get bigger as we talk about it. It is one of those things to which there is no end because God has no end.

Let us turn to this line of faith, the difference between our faith and the faith which the Holy Ghost gives. I might go into the epistles, but I think if we keep on the lines where Paul was at first brought into these things, that will help us more. Let us come to the Acts of the Apostles and see the difference of that growth in the Spirit. Paul had a revelation just as he entered into the new life with Jesus.

If you read the 26th chapter, you will see that his revelation had to be increased on conditions. The increase of the revelation was this that Jesus was showing himself unto him and said he would yet show further things unto him just as he was developed. [Ac 26.16] If you want to know the great climax and finish of that condition, read the 15th chapter of Romans, and see there how he never preached on another man's ground [Ro 15.20] and yet signs and wonders followed.

Just as Joshua closed up his ministry saying, **"That, not one thing that God hath promised hath failed," [Js 23.14]** so this man of God in the latter times came to us like a refined fire out of the mint of God's order. When Paul was speaking to Agrippa, he said, **"I was not disobedient unto the heavenly vision." [Ac 26.19]** Every touch of that vision was made more real every day till God could take him through. The baptism of the Spirit took him into the place that was impossible to be shaken.

There are many things that describe this double faith. One night I got home about 11 o'clock from an open-air meeting. And when I got home I wanted to see my wife; I loved her so much; she was everything to me. **Men, love your wives as Christ loved the church. [Ep 5.25]** There is something in a wife that is brought to you by the gift of God that you will never know her equal.

I stand on this platform because of a holy woman, a woman who lived righteousness, poured her righteousness into my life, so transforming my life from wayward indifferences of all kinds, and so shaping my life that she was practically the means of purging me through and through. A holy wife is worth more than gold. [Pr 31.10] And I say, wives, love your husbands. Let nothing come between. It is the stimulus of your lives; it is the hope of your home; it is the destined eternity which is fixed in the homes.

"Where is she?" I asked. And straightway I was told that she was down at Mitchell's. Mr. Mitchell was very ill. I had seen him that day and knew without a tremendous change he would not last the day out. He and I had been brought up together, and I loved him very much. When I was nearing his house, I heard a great cry, so I felt that something had happened. I passed his wife on the staircase and asked, "What is up?"

"Mitchell has gone," she said.

My wife was inside, and I went in. As soon as I saw Mitchell, I saw he had passed away. I couldn't understand it and began praying. "Oh," my wife exclaimed, "Don't, Dad! Don't, Dad!" But the faith I had, seemed to be a faith God helped me with, and I find that this faith God gives us in a place where God can undertake. I continued praying, and my wife laid hold of me saying, "Don't, Dad. Don't you see he is dead?"

My wife was always afraid that I should have a dead person on my hands some day and there I should be, but I was never afraid of that. When I got as far as I could with my faith, then God laid hold of me. Oh, it was such a laying hold, I could believe for anything! I came down from that place shouting the victory. But my wife said, "Don't, Dad. You see he is dead."

"He is alive," I replied. "Glory to God!"
My wife laid hold of me, weeping, "Oh Dad, don't."
"He is alive!" I said. And he is living today.

Ah yes, our faith and God's faith! We must see that God has a plan for us, and the plan is that the end of you is the beginning with God. But we must go in to possess all the glories of the attitude of the Spirit till we live and move in God. And nothing, by any means, shall ever discourage us. We shall always have a face like a flint. [Is 50.7] We shall not be afraid of their faces, neither in any way shall we be dismayed. [Js 1.9] And as God was with Joshua and Moses, he is with us today.

Smith - "By the GRACE of God, I want to impart the Word and bring you to a place where you will dare to act on it!"

The Glories of God's GRACE

The Lord of hosts camps round about us this morning, with songs of deliverance that we may see face to face the glories of His **GRACE** in a new way, for God hath not brought us into cunningly devised fables, but in these days He is rolling away the mists and clouds, and every difficulty that we may understand the mind and will of God.

If we are going to catch the best of God, there must be in this meeting a spiritual desire, the open ear, the understanding heart. The vail must be lifted. We must see the Lord in that perfectness of being glorified in the midst of us. As we enter into these things of the Spirit, we must see that we are not going to be able to understand these mysteries that God is unfolding to us, only on the lines of being filled with the Spirit.

Even when these special meetings close, the pastor and everybody else will find that we must all the time grow in **GRACE**. We must see that God has nothing for us on the old lines. The new plan, the new revelation, the new victories are before us. The ground must be gained; supernatural things must be attained. All carnal things, and evil powers, and spiritual wickedness in high places must be dethroned. We must come into the line of the Spirit by the will of God in these days.

Let us just turn to the Word which is so beautiful and so expressive in so many ways.

Do we begin again to commend ourselves? Or need we, as some others, epistles of commendation to you, or letters of commendation from you? Ye are our epistle written in our hearts, known and read of all men: Forasmuch as ye are manifestly declared to be the epistle of Christ ministered by us, written not with ink, but with the Spirit of the living God; not in tables of stone, but fleshy tables of the heart. And such trust have we through Christ to God-ward. 2 Corinthians 3:1-4

I want this morning to dwell upon these words for a short time: **"Forasmuch as ye are manifestly declared to be the epistle of Christ."**

What an ideal position that now the sons of God are being manifested; now the glory is being seen; now the Word of God is becoming an expressed purpose in life till the life has ceased and the Word has begun to live in them.

How truly this position was in the life of Paul when he came to a climax when he said:

"I am crucified with Christ: nevertheless I live; yet not I, but Christ liveth in me: and the life which I now live in the flesh I live by the faith of the Son of God, who loved me and gave himself for me" (Galatians 2:20).

How can Christ live in you? There is no way for Christ to live in you but only by the manifested Word in you, through you, manifested and declared every day that you are a living epistle of the Word of God. Beloved, God would have us to see that no man is perfected or equipped in any degree but only to the extent as the living Word abides in Him.

It is the living Christ, it is the divine likeness to God, it is the express image of Him, and the Word is the only factor that works out in you and brings forth these glories of identification between you and Christ. It is the Word dwelling in your hearts, richly by faith.

We may begin at Genesis, go right through the Pentateuch, and the other Scriptures, and be able to rehearse them, but without they are a living factor within us, they will be a dead letter. Everything that comes to us must be quickened by the Spirit. **"The letter killeth, but the Spirit giveth life."**

We must have life in everything. Who knows how to pray but as the Spirit prayeth? What kind of prayer does the Spirit pray? The Spirit always brings to your remembrance the mind of the Scriptures and brings forth all your cry and your need better than your words. The Spirit always takes the Word of God and brings your heart, and mind, and soul, and cry, and need into the presence of God.

So we are not able to pray only as the Spirit prays, and the Spirit only prays according to the will of God, and the will of God is all in the Word of God. No man can speak according to the mind of God and bring forth the deep things of God out of his mind. The following Scripture rightly divides the Word of truth:

Forasmuch as ye are manifestly declared to be the epistle of Christ ministered by us, written not with ink, but with the Spirit of the living God; not in tables of stone, but in fleshly tables of the heart. 2 Corinthians 3:3

God help us to understand this, for it is out of the heart that all things proceed. When we have entered in with God into the mind of the Spirit, we will find God ravishes our hearts.

When I speak about the "fleshly tables of the heart," I mean the inward love. Nothing is so sweet to me as to know that the heart yearns with compassion. Eyes may see, ears may hear, but you may be immovable on those two lines without you have an inward cry where "deep calleth unto deep."

When God gets into the depths of our hearts, He purifies every intention of the thoughts and the joys. We are told in the Word it is joy unspeakable and full of glory.

Beloved, it is the truth that the commandments were written on tables of stone. Moses, like a great big, loving father over Israel, had a heart full of joy because God had shown him a plan where Israel could be made to partake of great things through these commandments.

But God says, "Not in tables of stone," which made the face of Moses to shine with great joy. Deeper than that, more wonderful than that: the commandments in our hearts; the deep love of God in our hearts, the deep movings of eternity rolling in and bringing God in. Hallelujah!

Oh, beloved, let God the Holy Ghost have His way today in so unfolding to us all the grandeurs of His glory.

TONGUES AND INTERPRETATION: "The Spirit, He, it is He, that waketh thee morning by morning and unfolds unto thee in thy heart, tenderness, compassion, and love towards thy Maker till thou dost weep before Him and say to Him, in the spirit, 'Thou art mine! Thou art mine!'"

Yes, He is mine! Beloved, He is mine!

"And such trust has we through Christ to God-ward:

"Not that we are sufficient of ourselves to think any thing as of ourselves; but our sufficiency is of God." (vv. 4, 5).

Ah, it is lovely! Those verses are to keep to pass over. Beloved that is a climax of divine exaltation that is so much different from human exaltation.

The end is not yet, praise the Lord!
The end is not yet, praise the Lord!
Your blessings He is bestowing,
And my cup is overflowing,
And the end is not yet, praise the Lord!

We want to get to a place where we are beyond trusting in ourselves. Beloved, there is so much failure in self-assurances. It is not bad to have good things on the lines of satisfaction, but we must never have anything on the human that we rest upon. There is only one sure place to rest upon, and our trust is in God.

In Thy name we go. In Thee we trust. And God brings us off in victory. When we have no confidence in ourselves to trust in ourselves but when our whole trust rests upon the authority of the mighty God, He has promised to be with us at all times, and to make the path straight, and to make all the mountains a way. Then we understand how it is that David could say, "Thy gentleness hath made me great."

Ah, thou lover of souls! We have no confidence in the flesh. Our confidence can only be stayed and relied in the One who never fails, in the One who knows the end from the beginning, in the One who is able to come in at the midnight hour as easy as in the noonday, and make the night and the day alike to the man who rests completely in the will of God, knowing that "all things work together tor good to them that love Him," and trust in Him. And such trust has we in Him.

This is the worthy position where God would have all souls to be. We should find that we would not run His errands and make mistakes; we would not be dropping down in the wrong place. We would find our life was as surely in the canon of thought with God as the leading of the children of Israel through the wilderness. And we should be able to say, Not one good thing hath the Lord withheld from me (Psalm 84: 11), and "… **all the promises of God in him are yea, and in him Amen, unto the glory of God by us" (2 Corinthians 1: 20).**

The Lord has helped me to have no confidence in myself, but to wholly trust in Him, bless His name!

Who also hath made us able ministers of the New Testament; not of the letter, but the spirit: for the letter killeth, but the spirit giveth life. But if the ministration of death, written and engraved in stones, was glorious, so that the children of Israel could not steadfastly behold the face of Moses for the glory of his countenance; which glory was to be done away: How shall not the ministration of the spirit be rather glorious?

For if the ministration of condemnation is glory, much more doth the ministration of righteousness exceed in glory. 2 Corinthians 3:6-9

Let us enter into these great words on the line of holy thoughtfulness. If I go on with God, He wants me to understand all His deep things. He doesn't want anybody in the Pentecostal church to be novices, or to deal with the Word of God on natural grounds. We can understand the Word of God only by the Spirit of God.

We cannot define, or separate, or deeply investigate and unfold this holy plan of God without we have the life of God, the thought of God, the Spirit of God, and the revelation of God. The Word of Truth is pure, spiritual, and divine. If you try to divide it on natural grounds, you will only finish up on natural lines for natural man, but you will never satisfy a Pentecostal Assembly.

The spiritual people can only be fed on spiritual material. So if you are expecting your messages to catch fire, you will have to have them on fire. You won't have to light the message up in the meeting. You will have to bring the message red-hot, burning, and living.

The message must be direct from heaven. It must be as truly, "Thus saith the Lord," as the Scriptures which are, "Thus saith the Lord," because you will only speak as the Spirit gives utterance, and you will always be giving fresh revelation. You will never be stale on any line, whatever you will be fruitful, elevating the mind, lifting the people, and all the people will want more.

To come into this, we must see that we not only need the baptism of the Spirit, but we need to come to a place where there is only the baptism of the Spirit left. Look at the first verse of the fourth chapter of Luke, and you will catch this beautiful truth:

And Jesus being full of the Holy Ghost returned from Jordan and was led by the Spirit into the wilderness.

But look at Mark 1: 12 and you will find He was driven of the Spirit into the wilderness:

And immediately the Spirit driveth him into the wilderness.

In John's gospel Jesus says He does not speak or act of Himself:

...the words that I speak unto you I speak not of myself: but tbe Father that dwelleth in me, he doeth the works. John 14:10

We must know that the baptism of the Spirit immerses us into an intensity of zeal, into a likeness to Jesus, to make us into pure, running metal so hot for God that it travels like oil from vessel to vessel. This divine line of the Spirit will let us see that we have ceased and we have begun. We are at the end for a beginning. We are down and out, and God is in and out.

There isn't a thing in the world that can help us in this meeting. There isn't a natural thought that can be of any use here. There isn't a thing that is carnal, earthly, and natural, that can ever live in these meetings. It must only have one pronouncement; it has to die eternally because there is no other plan for a baptized soul, only dead indeed.

God, help us to see then that we may be filled with the letter without being filled with the Spirit. We may be filled with knowledge without having divine knowledge. And we may be filled with wonderful things on natural lines and remain a natural man. But you cannot do it in this truth that I am dealing with this morning.

No man can walk this way without He is in the Spirit. He must live in the Spirit, and he must realize all the time that he is growing in that same ideal of his Master, in season and out of season, always beholding the face of the Master, Jesus. David says, "I foresaw the Lord for He was on my right hand that I should not be moved. Then my tongue was glad." Praise the Lord!

For even that which was made glorious had no glory in this respect, because of the glory that excelleth. For if that which is done away was glorious, much more that which remaineth is glorious. 2 Corinthians 3:10,11

I notice here that the one has to be done away, and the other has to increase. One day I was having a good time on this chapter. I had a lot of people before me who were living on the 39 Articles and Infant Baptism, and all kinds of things. The Lord showed me that all these things had to be done away. I find there is no place into all the further plan with God without you putting them to one side. "Done away."

Is it possible to do away with the commandments? Yes and no. If they are not so done away with you that you have no consciousness of keeping commandments, then they are not done away. If you know you are living holy, you don't know what holiness is. If you know you are keeping commandments, you don't know what keeping commandments are.

These things are done away. God has brought us in to be holy without knowing it, and keeping the whole truth without knowing it, living in it, moving in it, acting in it, a new creation in the Spirit. The old things are done away. If there is any trouble with you at all, it shows you have not come to the place where you are at rest.

"Done away." God, help us to see it. If the teaching is a bit too high for you, ask the Lord to open your eyes to come into it. For there is no man here has power in prayer or has power in life with God if he is trying to keep the commandments.

They are done away, brother. And thank God, the very doing away with them is fixing them deeper in our hearts than ever before. For out of the depths we cry unto God, and in the depths has He turned righteousness in, and uncleanness out. It is unto the depths we cry unto God in these things. May God lead us all every step of the way in His divine leading.

Two Kinds of GRACE

I must speak about liberty. There are two kinds of liberty, two kinds of **GRACE**. We must never use liberty, but we must be in the place where liberty can use us. If we use liberty we shall be as dead as possible, and it will all end up in a fizzle.

But if we are in the Spirit, the Lord of life is the same Spirit. I believe it is right to jump for joy but don't jump till the joy makes you jump because if you do you will jump flat. If you jump as the joy makes you jump you will bounce up again.

In the Spirit I know there is any amount of divine plan. If the Pentecostal people had only come into it in meekness and in the true knowledge of God, it would all be so manifest that every heart in the meeting would be moved by that Spirit.

Now the Lord is that Spirit: and where the Spirit of the Lord is, there is liberty. 2 Corinthians 3: 17

Liberty has a thousand sides to it, but there is no liberty which is going to help the people so much as testimony. I find people who don't know how to testify right. We must testify only as the Spirit gives utterance. We find in Revelation that the testimony of Jesus is the spirit of prophecy.

When your flesh is keeping you down, but your heart is so full it is lifting you up - have you ever been like that? The flesh has been fastening you to the seat, but your heart has been bubbling over. At last, the heart has had more power and you have risen up.

And then in that heart affection for Jesus in the Spirit of love and the knowledge of the truth, you begin to testify, and when you have done, you sit down. Liberty used wrongly goes on when you finished and spoils the meeting. You are not to use your liberty except for the glory of God.

Many churches are ruined by long prayers and long testimonies. The speaker can tell if he keeps in the Spirit when he should sit down. When you begin to rehearse yourself, the people get wearied and tired, and they wish you would sit down. The unction ceases, they sit down worse than when they rose up.

It is nice for a man to begin cold, and warm up as he goes on. When he catches fire and sits down in the midst of it, he will keep the fire afterwards. Look! It is lovely to pray, and it is a joy to hear you pray, but when you go on after you are done, all the people are tired of it.

So God wants us to know that we are not to use liberty because we have it to use, but we are to let the liberty use us, and we should know when to end.

This excellent glory should go on to liberality to everybody, and this would prove that all the Church is in liberty. The Church ought to be free so that the people always go away feeling, "Oh, I wish the meeting bad gone on for another hour." Or, "What a glorious time we had at that prayer meeting!" Or, "Wasn't that testimony meeting a revelation!" That is the way to finish up. Never finish up with something too long, finish up with something too short.

ABOUT THE AUTHOR

Dr. Michael and Kathleen Yeager have served as pastors/apostles, missionaries, evangelists, broadcasters and authors for overt four decades. They flow in the gifts of the Holy Spirit, teaching the Word of God with wonderful signs and miracles following in confirmation of God's Word. In 1983, they began Jesus is Lord Ministries International, Biglerville, PA 17307.

Websites Connected to Doc Yeager

www.docyeager.com

www.jilmi.org

www.wbntv.org

Books Written by Doc Yeager:

"Living in the Realm of the Miraculous #1."
"I need God Cause I'm Stupid."
"The Miracles of Smith Wigglesworth"
"How Faith Comes 28 WAYS"
"Horrors of Hell, Splendors of Heaven"
"The Coming Great Awakening"
"Sinners in The Hands of an Angry GOD,"
"Brain Parasite Epidemic"
"My JOURNEY to HELL" - illustrated for teenagers
"Divine Revelation of Jesus Christ"
"My Daily Meditations"
"Holy Bible of JESUS CHRIST"
"War In The Heavenlies - (Chronicles of Micah)"
"Living in the Realm of the Miraculous #2."
"My Legal Rights to Witness"
"Why We (MUST) Gather! - 30 Biblical Reasons"
"My Incredible, Supernatural, Divine Experiences"
"Living in the Realm of the Miraculous #3."
"How GOD Leads & Guides! - 20 Ways"
"Weapons of Our Warfare"
"How You Can Be Healed"
"Hell Is For Real"
"Heaven Is For Real"
"God Still Heals"
"God Still Provides"
"God Still Protects"
"God Still Gives Dreams & Visions."
"God Still Does Miracles"
"God Still Gives Prophetic Words"

"God Still Confirms His Word With Power"
"Life Changing Quotes of Smith Wigglesworth"

Made in the USA
Monee, IL
21 August 2022